Feminist Mysticism and IMAGES of GOD

Feminist Mysticism and IMAGES *of* GOD

A PRACTICAL THEOLOGY

JENNIE S. KNIGHT

CHALICE® PRESS

ST. LOUIS, MISSOURI

Bible quotations, unless otherwise noted, are from the *New Revised Standard Version Bible,* copyright 1989, Division of Christian Education of the National Council of the Churches of Christ in the United States of America. Used by permission. All rights reserved.

The opinions expressed in this work are those of the authors, and do not necessarily represent the opinions of the editors, the publisher, Chalice Press, Christian Board of Publication, or any associated persons or entities.

Cover image: iStockPhoto
Cover and interior design: Elizabeth Wright

Visit Chalice Press on the World Wide Web at
www.chalicepress.com

10   9   8   7   6   5   4   3   2   1   11   12   13   14   15

EPUB: 978-08272-10516 • EPDF: 978-08272-10523
Paperback: 978-08272-10509

Library of Congress Cataloging–in–Publication Data

Knight, Jennie S.
Feminist mysticism and images of God : a practical theology / by Jennie S. Knight.
    p. cm.
Includes index.
  ISBN 978-0-8272-1050-9
  1. Feminist theology. 2. Feminist spirituality. 3. Christian women–Religious life–Georgia–Atlanta. I. Mary and Martha's Place. II. Title.

BT83.55.K66 2011
  231–dc22   2011005124

Printed in the United States of America

Contents

for Sela,
joy of my heart

Acknowledgments

This book could not have been written without the guidance, support, and inspiration of many along the way. I am grateful for the myriad ways that my work has been shaped and informed by those who have mentored me at Emory University both during my doctoral work and then as my senior colleagues at the Candler School of Theology. I particularly want to thank Mary Elizabeth Moore, Brian Mahan, Kimberly Wallace-Sanders, Bobbi Patterson, Joyce Flueckiger, Rodney Hunter, Thee Smith, James Fowler, Elizabeth Bounds, Gail O'Day, Mark Jordan, Ted Brelsford, and Carol Lakey Hess for guiding me to important insights, questions, sources, and clarifications during the process of forming this work. Mary Elizabeth Moore has shaped me as a scholar, teacher, and minister since the beginning of my seminary days at the Claremont School of Theology more than fifteen years ago. Her influence can be seen throughout these pages and continues to push me in all of my work.

I am grateful to the women of Mary and Martha's Place for sharing their lives with me and for allowing me to share their wisdom with others through this work. Thank you to the women of the Christian feminist spirituality movement whom I have not yet met and to those who have gone before. This book aims to represent a piece of the wisdom that you have discovered through years of struggle and laughter. May it be a source of affirmation and a resource for continuing the journey. I am grateful to the many feminist, womanist, and *mujerista* scholars who have influenced my work and life and the lives of countless others. Many are quoted and some are challenged in the pages that follow. However, without your immense contributions, this work would not be possible. I am also grateful to the wise women of the Divine Feminine Sunday School Class and the Mothers of Young Ones Sunday School Class at Oakhurst Baptist Church in Decatur, Georgia.

Amy Benson Browne of the Author Development Program at Emory University and Pablo Jiménez at Chalice Press provided invaluable editorial guidance for this project. Thank you. Students in my classes at the Candler School of Theology have taught me more than they could ever know. Thank you, especially to the students in my "Images of God" classes in 2009 and 2010, for wrestling through these ideas with me and with each other. I am particularly grateful for the diligence, insight, and kindness of Kyndra Frazier and Jenna Strizak, who worked as research assistants with me while editing the manuscript.

I am overjoyed to have a group of women friends who can laugh with me about absolutely anything. Meryl Franco, Stacy Mattingly, Ilise Cohen, Cyndi Cass, Andrea White, Maggie Banda Compton, and Renee Harrison: you keep me sane and inspire me with your kindness, courage, grace, and wisdom every day. Thank you to Marjorie Blum and Kimberly Bonde, my wise mother teachers, for helping me find my way home.

To my parents, Jane Hall Harmon Knight and William Donald Knight, Jr.: I am so grateful for your unfailing love and support in all the seasons of my life. And finally, thank you to my family, Rouslan Elistratov and Sela Rouslanovna Knight. You keep me dancing and surround me with grace. Love.

Introduction

As a feminist theologian, I had read a great deal of writings about God as mother, and I was committed to speaking this way on principle. It had not been clear to me, however, why such language had not helped my prayer, but rather, had filled me with a sense of grief and loss. Now I understood the reason for my grief. To know myself as a woman in the image of God, to know God as Mother, and to know my own mother as a window into God: these three are inseparable. If one is implausible, to the heart, the other two are, as well.

— ROBERTA C. BONDI, *MEMORIES OF GOD:*
THEOLOGICAL REFLECTIONS OF A LIFE[1]

In the late 1990s, Patricia Lynn Reilly danced across the floor before a packed audience, telling the story of creation by a Mother Goddess. Afterward, she shared the story of her journey of spiritual awakening as she had embraced feminine imagery for the divine. When the applause subsided, a Christian feminist theology professor turned to me and said, "Didn't we do this already?" We had not. If we had "done it already," we would not have seminary students graduating every year who have knowledge of feminist thea/ologies that emphasize the importance of female terms for the divine yet who submit, within months of beginning their ministries, to the pressure from their congregations to maintain exclusively male language for God.[2] Clearly, the discussion of the importance of reimaging the divine has not reached seminary students with the depth, force, nuance, and complexity necessary to motivate them to raise the issue with their congregations and to assist them in the difficult process of examining and playing with images for the divine.

Passion for images of the divine as feminine has grown dramatically in recent years. This is evidenced by the increasing number of references to the divine feminine in popular fiction, music, and films, as well as by the significant growth of feminist spirituality movements, both Christian and neopagan. However, in the context of religious practices in Christian churches, little has changed.

Feminist theologians have argued for decades about the importance of gender-inclusive and/or female-gendered language for God. However, few seminary-trained pastors translate this commitment into action when they serve local churches. Little has changed in the context of worship, even in seemingly progressive churches and denominations. Why do pastors

1

encounter such intense resistance when they try to introduce new language and imagery for the divine? Why do they feel unprepared to address that resistance constructively? We have failed as theologians to address the profound emotional connections that each person carries in relation to the image of God that she or he develops in early life. Gender is only one important piece of this image.

We live out of the images that inform us. Images of the divine, other people, and one's self are profoundly interrelated within each person's imagination. They affect every relationship, including with the divine. For this reason it is crucial that we examine the images that shape our lives. In the Christian mystical tradition, the divine is described as a mystery greater than any image or name can contain. At the same time, human minds use images to relate to the divine.

Paradoxically, we can perceive the divine in multiple forms because it is present in all of creation, even while the mystery of the divine is larger than any particular form can convey.[3] Similarly, I would add, every human being is a mystery larger than can be contained by any representation.[4] Nevertheless, we develop images and representations in order to engage in relationships and to live in a complex, relational world. In addition, our images are shaped by cultural representations and social constructions such as gender, race, and class, which are mediated in particular ways through our families and communities. Critical examination of all of these factors helps to create space for alternative images–and thus alternative living–to emerge.

Our understandings and experiences of the divine, of self, and of others are encoded in our memories and emotions through images and can be accessed and changed primarily through the use of images. For this reason, it is inadequate to explore our understanding of the divine simply on a conceptual level. Critical and emotionally honest reflection about images for the divine must be combined with experiences of alternative images of the divine in religious practice. Similarly, alternative understandings of self and others must be lived out in relationship in order to embody holistic transformation. At stake are a more profound spirituality and faith, a more holistic self-image, and patterns of relating with others that empower agency and enable life-giving intimacy.

Each person's imagination draws from the raw materials of external sights, sounds, and smells, as well as from experiences of self, other people, and the divine, in order to create images that help the person to form her unique sense of the world. Therefore, I use the term "image" to include both external and internal representations: not only visual representations (such as icons, statues, stained glass windows, and mental pictures) but also verbal representations and representations that the imagination constructs out of emotional and sensual experiences and memories.[5]

For example, a child growing up in a Baptist church that has no stained glass windows, paintings, sculptures, or other visual representations of the divine might repeatedly hear language about God as "Father" and as "He." The child might then create an image of this male Father God out of her sensual and emotional associations with her human father as well as with other men who are significant in her life. This God image might not only *look* like her father or other men in her life, but her personal, internal image of God might also *feel* like them—meaning that similar emotions would possibly be elicited when relating to that image. For example, there might be associations with the sound of her father's voice, the smell of his aftershave, a big hug, or an experience of rejection or absence. All of these might go into creating an internalized image of the divine in spite of the lack of "pictures" provided to help in that imaging process. On the other hand, she might create an image of a Father God who is opposite from her father in order to compensate for things she finds lacking in her human father.[6]

The process by which images for the divine are created and revisited throughout life is unique for each person, depending on familial context, cultural context, religious environment, and personality. Each person is continually forming and re-forming her internal imagery as she interacts with representations of, and as she experiences relationships with, the divine and other people. Therefore, while a shared cultural and religious background can cause significant similarities to the imaginations of others, a particular person's internal configuration of significant representations and relationships is unique at any particular time. In this work, I explore this uniqueness through life history interviews with four women. In my research with this group of women, we explored the ways that each woman's images and experiences are unique. We also examined their stories together as a group and found common themes in the dynamics of their imaging the divine.

Gender, "Race," and Images

I am passionate about issues of race[7] and gender because of my own experiences of transformation when I shifted from an image of God as male (and, more unconsciously, white) to multiple images of the divine as female and of various skin colors (including the Black Madonna of Catholicism and the Green Tara of Tibetan Buddhism). I found myself, a European American Protestant woman, able to worship and relate to these female images in a much more intimate and empowering way than I had been able to relate to the old images I had internalized. My faith and spirituality became stronger and more central in my life.

As a minister and a seminary graduate, I had been trained to use "inclusive language" when referring to God. I even referred to God as "God/dess" in academic papers. However, years of this practice had not produced the same emotional and spiritual effects as encountering alternative, explicitly female images in the context of worship.

I began to wonder about this disconnect. Why were my emotions and my spirituality so seemingly separate from my intellectual development? Was this the reason that so many seminary graduates stopped using gender-inclusive language when they became pastors in local churches? Were they unable to make the necessary emotional and spiritual connections with their academic and political principles in order to help themselves and their parishioners transform their images at multiple levels? How could we, as practical thea/ologians, enable seminarians and ministers to engage these difficult, emotionally charged images in ways that could lead to significant transformation and greater mutual understanding for all involved? How can communities of faith raise to awareness and transform individuals' emotionally held images through religious practices? Why is it imperative that they do so?

These are the central questions that motivated this work. It is my contention that personal and critical reflection in the context of a supportive learning community, combined with experiences of diverse images for the divine in worship, can lead to profound changes in self-image, relationship with the divine, and agency in the world. This book aims to demonstrate why and how this transformation is both possible and necessary.

A growing movement of women in the United States is passionately claiming the spiritual and psychological importance of shifting toward images of the divine as feminine. Christian feminist theologians have argued for decades for the importance of using gender-neutral and feminine language and imagery for the divine within religious communities. However, because few traditional faith communities have embraced this passion or commitment, a movement of formal and informal Christian feminist spirituality centers and groups has emerged in the United States. While many women leave the Christian tradition altogether,[8] a growing number choose to stay within the Christian tradition but turn to women's spirituality groups and centers in order to fulfill their longing for worship of the divine as feminine. I call this phenomenon the Christian feminist spirituality movement.

Evidence of the pervasiveness of the feminist spirituality movement (both Christian and non-Christian) can be found in the increasing presence of imagery for the divine feminine in U.S. popular culture in recent years. The immense popularity of novels such as *The Secret Life of Bees, The Da Vinci Code,* and *The Shack*; of scholarly writing such as Elaine Pagels' *The Gnostic Gospels*; and of songs about the divine feminine by popular artists such as Shania Twain and the Indigo Girls demonstrates that a large audience of women (and men) hungers to imagine the divine differently.

Similarly, many individuals and communities have shifted to imaging Christ and Mary as black. Through conversations with African American colleagues as well as through research in black theology, womanist theology, and worship of the Black Madonna in several cultures, I have become aware of the power of shifting to an image of the divine that is explicitly black. As with a shift in gender, the shift to an image of the divine as black, rather than the dominant white image, can enable significant spiritual and emotional healing and empowerment. This healing and empowerment often leads to greater political and social empowerment as well.

For many, this healing and empowerment is partially a result of people's being able to see themselves as created in the image of the divine. However, the dynamics involved in this process are unique for each individual. Each person's imagination of the divine is shaped by particular experiences, understandings, and representations within unique family, relational, and sociocultural contexts. Race and gender are significant in every person's imagination, yet they carry nuanced, particular meanings that are dependent on these factors.

The Black Madonna

While changes in the imagery for the divine can be healing and empowering, they can also reinforce problematic racial and gendered stereotypes if they are not examined critically. I have found in researching the worship of the Black Madonna that in a cultural context of white supremacy, as it is expressed in the United States or Western Europe, worship of the Black Madonna by European Americans or Western Europeans can carry complex, sometimes contradictory meanings and effects. For example, research into the origins of images of the Black Madonna in Western Europe has revealed that many of the Black Madonnas are "Christian borrowings from earlier pagan art forms that depicted Demeter, Melaina, Diana, Isis, Cybele, Artemis, or Rhea as black, the color characteristic of goddesses of the earth's fertility."[9] The Black Madonna is worshipped for her power whereas the "white" images of the Virgin Mary are adored for her tenderness and grace.[10] The power of the Black Madonna grows from her association with fertility,[11] directly relating to her ancient origins as the Goddess of the Earth.

This association of a Black Mary to the earth and fertility could serve to reinforce European stereotypes of black women rather than to challenge the social inequalities between whites and blacks in Europe and Africa. Stereotypes of black women as being highly sexualized, and of blacks and Africans as being closer to nature and to natural instincts,[12] could influence Western Europeans' worship of the Black Madonna. It is conceivable that the association of blackness in Africa with primitive instincts and fertile landscapes has served over the centuries to enliven the European imagination about the powers of fertility that the Black Madonna possesses. Therefore, the image of the Black Madonna as having power in relation to fertility and miracles was and still is in a relationship of mutual reinforcement with European stereotypes of black women as being primitive, highly sexual, and closer to the earth.[13]

Interest in the Black Madonna has also been growing in the feminist spirituality movement (both Christian and non-Christian) in the United States. This rapidly growing movement finds in her the ancient goddesses that she came to represent in Europe.[14] In her representation of the Goddess, she is a source of empowerment for practitioners of feminist spirituality who recognize themselves being mirrored in the image of the Goddess.[15] While this is a positive development in relation to the Black Madonna, the cultural heritage of white supremacy among European American women also leads me to question what cultural space the Black Madonna might occupy in their minds. The veneration of a black woman as the primal or original mother of humanity by European American spiritual feminists is problematic. In the context of the United States, the danger is that the image of the black mother (or Black Madonna) could reinscribe the "Black Mammy" image within the imaginations of European Americans. As in Europe, the association of the Black Madonna with a primary stereotype for black women could actually decrease the ability for the worship of the Black Madonna to challenge structures of racism. Similarly, images of God as a black woman, such as that found in the popular novel *The Shack*, can also serve to reinforce stereotypes rather than to challenge racism. I discuss the dynamics at work in the worship of the Black Madonna in chapter 7.

Ethnographic Research

As these examples in relation to the worship of the Black Madonna demonstrate, a particular image for the divine can carry a complex configuration of meanings determined by the cultural and familial context of the person who engages with that image. Because of the complexity and uniqueness of the dynamics involved in imaging the divine, I conducted life history interviews and in-depth analyses of the dynamics in each story. In the analysis for this book, I place the particular stories and the dynamics they reveal in conversation with the larger context of movements toward imaging the divine as feminine and as black. This interweaving guards against the danger of seeing individual stories as somehow separate from larger cultural patterns and movements. In addition, the interplay between personal and cultural analysis allows for a critical examination of the functions of race and gender in particular cultural contexts and the ways that stereotypes of race and gender can be reinscribed when imagining the divine. The particularity of life stories demonstrates the necessity of holding the individual and her larger cultural context in dynamic tension when considering issues of religion and culture.

I conducted the ethnographic research for this book at an extrachurch nonprofit center devoted to women's spirituality and feminist theological study in Atlanta, Georgia, called Mary and Martha's Place. It is a rapidly growing community of over two hundred women in the Atlanta area and is part of a larger national network of similar centers devoted to Christian feminist spirituality. An Episcopal priest and a group of laywomen who had been meeting together to study feminist theology for several years established the center in 1994.

The name Mary and Martha's Place (MMP) was chosen because the "tension between being and doing" that the New Testament story of Mary and Martha represents is a tension that the women felt strongly in their own lives. The women who are involved with MMP are largely in their forties, fifties, and sixties. The majority are European American professionals. The director explained that she originally "wanted to target well-educated women who had been feminist in the workplace but hear only patriarchy in church." She described the women who participate as "women on a spiritual quest," many of whom are "not nurtured by the traditional parish setting" and some of whom "can't go to church without feeling like they will gag." Programming includes several weekly book-study groups, liturgies for the winter and the summer solstices, annual conferences, and a monthly meeting for young women.

I conducted life history interviews with seven women who were actively involved in MMP. These interviews served as exploratory research. I returned to interview four women in-depth and to engage them in a process of reciprocal ethnography in which we worked together as a learning community to analyze their interviews. I interviewed women at MMP because I wanted to talk to people who had been exploring their images of the divine for a significant period of time. By choosing to work with people who are already engaged in this process, I hoped to reveal the dynamics involved with imagination and the divine as they are being actively engaged. Rather than starting with a group who had never considered the issues I raise, or who had never encountered alternative imagery for the divine, I wanted to find out what the experience looked like, while in process, for particular people.

My exploratory research about MMP and the feminist spirituality movement revealed that Christianity is in a state of crisis in relation to the needs of a growing number of women (and, I would add, men). It is a crisis within Christian churches in the United States, in which the theology and praxis of religious communities have been unresponsive to massive shifts in consciousness in large segments of the culture, particularly related to feminist critiques of Christianity. The stories of the women in the Christian feminist spirituality movement demonstrate an urgent need for opportunities for honest intellectual inquiry and for alternative imagery for the divine within religious communities, rather than avoidance or active discouragement of questioning and change.

MMP and other similar centers are meeting a growing need in our society. Many women, particularly those who have questioning minds and spirits and a passion for justice, are looking for a way to reconcile feminism with spirituality. Often, people in our culture leave institutional religions precisely because of the injustices and hypocrisies that the women of MMP are fighting. Many also study religion, spirituality, and feminism on their own or with post-Christian or neopagan religious communities. The majority of women who leave the Christian or Jewish tradition to identify as neopagan first discovered feminist spirituality through reading and research. They eventually found their traditions to be incompatible with their feminism.[16]

In order to avoid losing other passionate spiritual people, the churches should pay attention to the movement of which MMP is a part, listening carefully to what the women there have to say. As I often hear concern in discussions among theological educators that the church is "dying," I hope that church leaders and scholars alike will pay attention to communities such as MMP as being examples of a passion and need for spiritual growth in our culture rather than as aberrant extrachurch organizations. While people will continue in their quest for spiritual growth with or without the church, churches have an opportunity to learn from organizations on the margins of church life such as MMP, which can bring about great life-giving changes within those institutions.

My findings from the preliminary study include the following major themes:

- *A safe place.* MMP is a safe place for women to express themselves honestly and openly, without fear, about their questions and about their lives and beliefs. Several women expressed that their Christian churches are places where they experience a fear of rejection and judgment. They were afraid to voice their questions and beliefs at church.
- *Spiritual questing.* The women at MMP saw themselves as engaged in a spiritual quest. They were actively searching, both in their individual lives and in community with the other women at MMP.
- *The value of questions.* They valued questions highly, understanding that answers lead to more questions. This process was seen as one of healthy growth toward wisdom.
- *Changing images of the divine.* As part of the blend of feminism and spirituality, many of the women were comforted and empowered by images of the Goddess and/or by sacred symbols that represent femininity. They were actively trying to shake out of their minds the male image of God that they had internalized during childhood, a task which they found difficult.
- *Rootedness in tradition.* While some of the women I interviewed were very critical of the Christian church and tradition, all of them wanted to stay within their tradition. They were often in tension with the beliefs of their traditions, however, pushing the boundaries by including images of the divine feminine and other elements from pagan and

Celtic traditions. Yet they wanted to remain within the tradition of their families and culture.

• *The value of women and the empowerment of women.* The women placed emphasis on the value of women and the importance of their finding their own beliefs, voices, and power. They expressed hope that women would be empowered to take leadership roles in society.

The stories of two of the women at MMP (to whom I have given the pseudonyms of Lorraine and Susan) clearly demonstrate the themes listed above. At the same time, each woman's story is unique. The insights that I gained from the analysis of their stories were a driving force behind my passion for this research—both in terms of the significance of transforming imagery for the divine and the need for Christian leaders to hear the stories of women like Lorraine and Susan.

Susan had experienced great pain in her life through associating God the Father with her unloving, chauvinist human father. She had also experienced significant healing and transformation through reclaiming a thea/ology of the Goddess. She exemplified the need for religious communities to provide people with alternative images to those that have caused them pain and that have shaped their faith and spirituality as grounds for intense personal struggle and conflict. Susan was part of a larger cultural movement of women "pushing" toward images of the divine feminine as they discovered their own value as women through feminist awareness.[17] Susan's story, and the stories of many women like her, pushes the church to take seriously the need for providing multiple images of the divine, including female images.

In addition, both Lorraine and Susan demonstrated a strong attachment and commitment to their "tradition." Christian practices and communities have provided both of them with life-affirming experiences, values, and beliefs. Unfortunately, they both felt that they were in a constant state of struggle, tension, and even "war" with their tradition. This demonstrates that many Christian churches have not transformed in a way that responds to their parishioners' needs and praxis. Instead, they have caused women like Lorraine and Susan to feel that they are in danger of harm if they choose to fight for what they believe should be changed.

Lorraine and Susan provide insight into significant religious and cultural contemporary trends. Their stories speak of individual lives transformed in community as they are given the space to question and to "play" with traditional theological and religious beliefs from a feminist perspective.[18] At the time of the interviews, Lorraine was "tired of fighting" and Susan did not want to openly fight with the church and with people who believed differently from her. My hope, however, is that their stories can serve as "fighting words" to churches as these women continue to struggle and long for justice, transformation, and spiritual growth in community.

As a practical thea/ologian who adheres to David Tracy's assertions that "theological truth is ultimately grounded in the authentic and transformative praxis of an intellectually, morally, and religiously transformed human subject,"[19] and that norms for theological reflection are "ultimately grounded not in the self-evident axioms of further theories but in the concrete intellectual, moral and religious praxis of concrete human beings in distinct societal historical situations,"[20] I believe that the narratives of Lorraine and Susan are the creations of transformed subjects who are engaged in authentic praxis. They are, therefore, sources for practical theological reflection. Both Lorraine and Susan have been and continue to be "intellectually, morally, and religiously transformed" as they travel their spiritual journeys. Norms for further theological reflection can be found in their stories of praxis that reflect their distinct social and historical situations. Stories of women in relation to their changing imagery for the divine are important sources for practical theological reflection and for changes in religious practices.

Feminist Mysticism

While their stories are unique, the interviewed women revealed similar dynamics in the process of engaging alternative images for the divine. As they described their processes of moving from the particular God-images of their childhoods, I began to see a parallel process at work. I am calling this process, and the spirituality that it fosters, "feminist mysticism."[21] The process is uniquely feminist because it began for these women with a questioning of their religious tradition's patriarchal language and theology. As they began to explore female language and imagery for the divine in the context of liturgy as well as in reflective discussion groups, they found that the process of reimagining the divine is a long and difficult one. As Julie recounts, even when she tried actively not to imagine God as an "old, white man in the sky," when she goes to pray, "there he is!" She realized that feminist theological study was inadequate to transform her image of, and therefore her relationship with, the divine. Instead, she recognized that transformation involves an ongoing process of encountering alternative images in the context of worship where she can relate differently with the divine in her "heart." She explained, "But it still feels very intellectual to me, and not in my heart. I think it will probably take years of doing that, and years of those kinds of rituals, to create in me like a real sense of the divine that's feminine or without this very paternalistic side."

As their stories and discussions in the following chapters reveal, the other women in the group also felt that the process of exploring their images for the divine was an ongoing process of spiritual growth and personal development. Ultimately, through challenging the traditional white male image for God; through engaging alternative images for the divine, particularly feminine images and images from nature; and through honoring their own experiences of the divine, they moved through a journey of reimagining to an awareness of the divine as "presence." They experienced this presence as dwelling within themselves and all of creation. At the same time, they continued to engage with images, moving in a spiral motion between images and an awareness of divine presence. The mystical spirituality that they described is one of paradox—an awareness that the divine both is and is not adequately represented by a particular image. Instead, images came to function as part of an active process, a moving through, so that they could come to rest in the presence of the divine.

Gaps in the Current Literature

Current theological literature about reimaging the divine—and the social, psychological, and political reasons for that reimaging—is remarkably devoid of examples from particular lives. Feminist, womanist, and black theologians have addressed the importance of reimaging the divine. These discussions of the connections between gender, race, and imagery for the divine have given little attention, however, to the lived experience of individuals as they interact with particular images in their cultural contexts. The discussion of reimaging has thus failed to convey the powerful emotional connections that people have with particular images, the ways in which those connections have been created and sustained during their lives, and the processes needed for them to transform their images and to experience a more empowering and intimate spirituality. In particular, feminist theologians have failed to recognize the paradoxical relationship that practitioners have with images for the divine, as they move through images in a mystical journey of affirmation, negation, and then transcendent affirmation,[22] moving finally to an awareness of divine presence.

In my research, I provide an in-depth analysis that explores the intersections among individual imagination, cultural influence (particularly as manifested in constructions of race and gender), and divine agency. I recognize that no author can do everything and that theological studies are selective in purpose and method. However, a study of divine imagery and its influence on human lives requires attention to the particularities of individuals in relation to their cultural and communal contexts.

While academic writing has paid insufficient attention to the dynamics involved in particular individuals' imaging of the divine, a growing genre of literature—the feminist spiritual autobiography—addresses those dynamics directly. Several books recount powerful personal narratives of psychological and spiritual transformation.[23] These authors describe when they encountered female images of the divine for the first time in their lives. As discussed earlier, Cynthia Eller explains that most women she interviewed had first encountered feminist spirituality through reading books about the topic.[24] Almost all of them had moved from reading to action, leaving their traditional religious affiliations of Christianity or Judaism to become practitioners in neopagan goddess-based religious groups. The genre of literature about awakening to the divine feminine is therefore having a direct impact on the spiritual life of a growing number of women as well as on the landscape of religious life in the United States.

Despite the empowering and enlivening effects that this literature has had on many women (including myself), I have some concerns about its content. First, while several European American writers analyze sexism in religion, family, and culture, they provide no analysis of the cultural construction of race and how race influences their experiences and images of the divine. It is crucial that an exploration of self-image, formative relationships, and images of the divine include an exploration of the formation of racial identity and the "images" that have supported that formation.

Second, while the stories are evocative, a more critical analysis is needed to uncover the complexity of various issues. The authors often use sweeping generalizations about gender, culture, and goddess religions that, while emotionally persuasive, do not explicate the complex dynamics involved in the interplay of gender, culture, and images of the divine. Third, women who turn toward images of the divine feminine often feel that they must leave traditional worship settings because their powerful transformation in relation to these images has not been taken seriously by their religious leaders. My hope is that this work will convince traditional religious leaders of the urgent need to address this issue.

Dance of Transformation

While my research is focused primarily on the spirituality of women, the insights gained are equally relevant for men. For example, psychologist and religion scholar James Jones described the process by which his patient, whom he calls Phil, was able to transform his image of the divine and thereby to connect spiritually in a more intimate, sustaining way with the divine. Jones described how Phil began to realize during counseling that his image of the divine was drawn directly from his image of his domineering and critical father. The judging, exacting male Father God worshipped at his nondenominational Protestant church was very similar to his experience of his human father. As Phil began to express his rage toward his father, he began also to express anger toward the judgmental and controlling God that he had worshipped from a distance for most of his life and with whom he had never been able to experience an intimate connection.

During this time, he saw an image of the Virgin Mary on a televised mass and was deeply moved by this nurturing, female image for divinity. He began to attend a Catholic church, where he found himself able to pray spontaneously and intimately to Mary in a way never possible when relating to his distant Father God.[25] The case study of Phil demonstrates that reflection in the presence of a compassionate, accepting listener about images of the divine and their connections with significant relationships and religious practices, combined with worship that involves an alternative image for the divine, can be powerful in transforming a person's spirituality, faith, self-image, and ability to relate intimately with other people.

Just as Phil's story is uniquely related to his family dynamics and religious heritage, the stories of the women in this book demonstrate the complexity and uniqueness of the web of relationships, experiences, and cultural influences in the individual's psyche within which imagery for the divine is woven. By illuminating the unique and powerful ways in which divine imagery functions in individuals' lives, I aim to help readers recognize the inadequacy and danger of imposing and assuming only one image for the divine in a particular community.

Second, I hope that this illumination will inspire religious leaders and practitioners to encourage "play" and the exploration of multiple images for the divine in ritual and worship as well as in reflection—both in educational and counseling settings. The stories in this book demonstrate the need for people to explore their current or previously held images for the divine and the emotional connections that these images carry—particularly in relation to race, gender, and formative relationships. I hope that religious leaders and educators will respond to that need by engaging congregants in reflection, education, and worship practices that assist congregants to transform their relational patterns with the divine, with other people, and with themselves. Through my research methodology, I develop, demonstrate, and evaluate effective practices of communal reflection, worship, and transformation. These practices of religious education, pastoral care, and worship are discussed in chapter 9. While the practices may not be exactly replicable in every congregation, they serve as an easily modifiable example of an effective process for addressing these issues.

The process of transformation is an extensive one over time. The process of opening up divine imagery is a dance, a spiral movement among self-reflection, individual religious practice, reflection in community, and communal religious practices. This transformative dance requires people to reflect emotionally and critically about the relational resonances and, perhaps, the relational stereotypes that their imagery carries. The context of a safe community in which to share these reflections allows people to feel supported in challenging previously held images and relational patterns. In conjunction with communal reflection, communal worship that incorporates alternative images for the divine allows transformation to occur at the emotional and spiritual levels. Through this holistic engagement, people can be freed to move along a mystical path toward greater intimacy with the divine presence in their lives. Through naming and negating incomplete or false images of themselves, of other people, and of the divine, they can move toward the transcendent affirmation and experience of divine presence within themselves, other people, and all of creation.

A Map for the Journey

This work is an effort to bring together diverse theoretical resources as conversation partners with the stories of actual women involved in the Christian feminist spirituality movement. A rich, multilayered discourse results from taking the lives of particular people seriously and engaging the complex dynamics at work in each life. Every strand of the discussion—whether theological, psychological, historical, or ethnographic—is interrelated with the others so that no one aspect can adequately be considered alone. I draw together several disparate areas of theory and theology in order to retrieve and create theoretical constructs and religious practices in relation to imaging the divine. In addition, the reciprocal ethnographic[26] research method takes the interpretations of the research subjects seriously, both by including their interpretations in the research findings and by co-creating religious practices that are consonant with our findings.

I explore the subjects of gender and race in a unique way. Rather than discussing "sexism" and "racism" in generalized terms, this work provides a window into the particular ways that gender and race function in the psyches of individuals, intersecting in unexpected ways in specific cultural contexts. Finally, I provide a unique forum for voices of women involved in the Christian feminist spirituality movement as they struggle to find a place within traditional Christian institutions where they can freely embrace alternative images for the divine and create new religious practices. This interdisciplinary, ethnographic approach to understanding divine imagery will provide the insights, the tools, and the impetus for readers to engage these issues in their lives and in their religious communities.

While these areas of discussion are interwoven throughout the book, the chapters are divided as follows:

Chapter 1 provides an overview of the psychological dynamics involved in imaging the divine, the self, and others.

Chapter 3 describes the context of the Christian feminist spirituality movement as well as the research process.

Chapter 5 is an analysis of the theological implications of previous chapters, particularly in relation to mystical theology, feminist theologies, and womanist theology.

Chapter 7 is a cross-cultural case study of the worship of the Black Madonna.

Chapter 9 provides practical recommendations for engaging these issues in religious education, pastoral care and counseling, and liturgical settings.

The stories of the four women are interspersed beginning with the second chapter. The stories can be read in any order. Each story intersects with each chapter in a particular way.

1

Psychology and Imaging the Divine

Images of the divine are not static pictures. They are an essential aspect of every person's spirituality and faith. They function in complicated, unique ways in each person's psyche. Psychological theorists have argued that each person's image for and corresponding relationship with the divine are shaped profoundly by her formative childhood relationships. Therefore, theological discussions about images of God are not merely theoretical exercises. They engage the core psychological formation of each person. In addition, formative relationships take place within a larger culture. The values placed on gender roles, ethnicity, sexual orientation, and economic status in turn affect and interact with family dynamics in particular ways depending on cultural location and factors unique to each family.

Thus, the exploration of the psychological dynamics involved in imaging the divine must include attention to these cultural factors and their implications. Recognition of the psychological formation of images is a crucial step in helping people move beyond the limitations that those images place on their self-images, relationships with others, and relationship with the divine. Even if images are essentially positive, they are limited nevertheless. An integral part of the process of moving through images involves recognizing these limitations and then affirming those images that paradoxically both do and do not represent a larger, mysterious whole.

Images for the divine, self-images, and images of other people are profoundly interrelated. Psychological theorists have developed diverse schemas to explain this interrelatedness, and while each theory provides helpful insights, questions remain unanswered. No answer is complete. Each is a helpful tool to explore the mystery of the human experience. Therefore, in this chapter I weave psychological theories into a tapestry of diverse but mostly complementary understandings of selfhood, human relationships, and relationship with the divine. From this base, I add to this tapestry by exploring the impact of race and gender on the formation of the self, relationships, and images of the divine. Thus far, the psychological theorists who have explored images of the divine have largely neglected these significant aspects of psychological, relational, and spiritual formation.

Interrelated Representations

The God-image of each person is unique. It is influenced by the theology and images of the divine offered by religious institutions, but it is not determined by them exclusively. Rather, it interacts with them in complex ways, depending on the individual. Psychoanalyst Ana-Maria Rizzuto analyzes the case studies of four inpatient psychiatric patients in order to explore the development of their images of the divine and how those images function in their lives. Her case studies demonstrate that a person's God-representation can become an obstacle to the positive development of her self-representation, her faith, and her relationships with others.

For her analysis of God-images, Rizzuto draws on Freud's theory of the parental imagoes. Freud argued that children create internal objects (called "imagoes") to represent their parents in their psyches. Rizzuto disagrees with Freud on many of his uses of this theory in interpreting religion and God-representations. For example, she criticizes Freud for his assertion that the paternal imago alone formed the God-representation. However, she uses the concept of imagoes as her starting point for discussing the way that a child develops internal representations of her parents, herself, and the divine. She argues that her patients' God-images were formed out of various relationships, usually with one more prevalent than the others. Significantly, she found that her patients formed their God-images not only out of the "parent in real life" but equally out of the "wished-for parent and the feared parent of the imagination." Thus, imaging the divine involves creativity as well as memory.[1]

This final point is crucial. Each person is constantly involved in a process of balancing experiences and representations within the psyche. It is an ongoing process of transforming representations so that people can establish a psychic balance that will make them "psychologically viable people in the real world."[2] Representations can change at different moments in a person's life. A variety of factors influence the changes, including psychologically defensive maneuvers, need for the idealization or devaluation of a particular person, changes of the representation due to a continued relationship with that person, and changes in the representation caused by changes in a person's self-representation. Changes in self-representation lead to a reevaluation of representations from the past and a modified understanding of those primary people in present life.[3] The dynamic reworking of object-representations is central to mental life because of the interrelationship between the self-representation and object-representations.

Because of this interrelatedness between self-representation and object-representations, a person would "go crazy" if he or she tried to destroy a representation. Once a representation has been coded in a person's memory, it can only be transformed and reworked in the light of changes in a person's life and self-representation.[4] It is for this reason that a God-representation cannot be destroyed. If a representation is associated with negative, distressing emotions, it can be defended against through repression or other defensive maneuvers. If it is repressed, it can be worked through during the processes of free association and transference in psychoanalysis. If this does not occur, however, one may experience personal loss.

Rizzuto explains the consequences this way: "If massive repression of objects and the corresponding self-representations takes place, the individual may experience loneliness, emptiness, a fear of losing oneself, a fear of being abandoned, or when it is expressed in bodily metaphors, of having a hole where the objects supposedly belong."[5] If a person's God-representation has been formed out of a matrix of painful relationships with parents and other caregivers and in relation to a negative, painful self-representation, it may remain unavailable even during analysis. A person can then experience a sense of emptiness, a hole, where God should be, yet she may continue to repress the God-image because it is experienced as a negative, painful presence when it does come into conscious experience.

The most mature level of object-representation occurs when a person is capable of "playing" with her or his representations. This capability is called "maturity of memory." When a person reaches this capacity, she has integrated a healthy distance between her "present sense of self" and her internal objects. She then has the freedom to play with her internal images.[6] The ability to "play" with an object representation creates freedom in the relationship with the actual object. Even though in real life a person may not actually do everything enacted in playful fantasy, the freedom of her internal "play" with her self-representation and her representations of others can enable her to explore new ways of being in the world. Theistic religion is experienced precisely in the psychic space where "play" occurs. It is the transitional space between internal psychic experience and external objects.

This discussion of the God-representation as an object-representation that can be played with could easily attract the criticism that the reality and existence of God is not being taken seriously—that these claims are irreverent, even blasphemous. However, theology cannot afford to avoid the issue of individual representations of the divine. If we are to place the claims of psychoanalysis in serious dialogue with theology, we must recognize that each individual relates to the divine from within his or her particular self-representation and representations of other important people in their lives. The representation of the divine that she creates will reflect both positive and negative aspects of those representations combined with cultural or traditional, institutional representations of God.

Conflict

A child's adaptation to her cultural and religious context can be achieved partly through the creation of a God-representation that is in harmony with the "official" cultural representation of God. However, if a child's (or adult's) God-representation does not coincide with that official representation, "the private and the official God provide endless potential for maladaptation and for raising family tragedies to a cosmic level."[7] In addition, suffering can be caused when the two representations coincide too closely. For example, a patient named Daniel Miller created his God-image almost exclusively from the representation of his domineering father. The God that was offered to him through his Jewish faith was "unfortunately too similar" to his father. The religious education that he received did not help him to lessen his fear of this Father God.

Rizzuto recognized the tension and wariness this created for Daniel: "Under such circumstances, it was impossible for him to have any wish to be involved with a God who offered nothing to alleviate his longing for a protecting and loving adult who would listen to him and appreciate him."[8] While Daniel longed for a different image of God, one that was compassionate and loving, he could not permit himself any emotional contact with that new understanding of God. He was too afraid of encountering his old God-image, particularly the painful feelings associated with his father. He could not tolerate being disappointed by God in the same way that he had been damaged by his relationship with his father.

People do not always create their God-representations exclusively from their father images. However, the official representation of God as a dominant father can have negative consequences, both for those like Daniel, whose images coincide with their religious education, and for those whose images do not coincide with their official religious or cultural contexts.

Even when one's official religious context teaches that God is loving rather than domineering, a person's familial context can cause her to create an internal representation of God that conflicts with religious teachings. For example, a woman named Bernadine experienced God as her enemy because she was unable to believe that God loved her. She had experienced herself as unlovable in relation to her parents. Rather than accepting the painful reality that her parents had been woefully inadequate in their care for her, she preferred to maintain that she was unlovable. Her religious heritage had taught her that God is loving; however, she could not accept that God loved her. She held in tension a belief that God loved other people yet could not love her. Therefore, while she longed for God to love her, she was unable to accept any grace from God because it would jeopardize her self-understanding as unlovable.[9] This would force her to face the unbearable realization that her parents were incapable of loving her. Bernadine's example demonstrates that a God-image can be altered to support an untenable self-image and false images of others if it is experienced as psychologically necessary for survival.

Patterns of Relationship

As these case studies show, images of God and a person's self-representation are part of a complex web of relationships. For this reason, James Jones argues that Rizzuto's theories focused too much on the individual psyche and too little on relationships. For Jones, the self is composed of relationships. A person's relationship with the divine is central in the formation of the self. Rather than focusing on "pathological individuals," he chose instead to look at neurotic patterns of relationship.[10] An inherently relational self is made up of particular patterns of relationship. It is these patterns of relationship—with the divine and other people—that must be examined and transformed, rather than the representations.

The approaches of Jones and Rizzuto are both necessary and complementary. His emphasis on affective patterns of relationship is indeed a helpful and necessary complement to Rizzuto's sometimes obscure and confounding theories of internalized objects. The most fruitful discussions about imaging and relating to the divine can take place in this intersection between intrapsychic images and interpersonal relationships.

Jones argues that patterns of transference, as enacted with a therapist, reflect the essential patterns of relationship that a person has learned in primary familial relationships. The person enacts the same affective, relational patterns with the divine. One's image of the divine is thus shaped by one's emotional God-relationship.[11] Rather than simply focusing on an image of the divine, Jones argues that a person's "affective bond with the sacred" serves as a person's "transferential ground of self."[12] For example, he says that a child who experiences herself as guilty and unworthy because of her relational patterns with her parents will ground that sense of herself in an image of God as judgmental and wrathful. On the other hand, a person who feels loved and secure will ground that sense of security in an image of God as loving and forgiving.

In order to understand a person's image(s) of the divine, one must start by understanding his internalized relationships and then investigate how that person's relationship with the divine is resonant with those relationships. In looking at these patterns, one must ask, "What has been projected? Is God critical, mirroring, unresolved meaning, or symbiotic?" To understand the relational patterns with the divine and how a person's image of the divine functions in that relationship, one must look to religious practices as well as abstract beliefs, asking, "What inner relational patterns go into our devotional exercises, meditational disciplines, and philosophical theologies?"[13]

Because God is the "repository of what is most valuable" to the person and because transference is a person's "most fundamental pattern of interaction and meaning-making," her relationship with the divine will disclose her primary patterns of relationship ånd transference. In other words, one can use her relationship with God to understand her "larger relational world."[14] Jones argues,

> An experiential image of sacred reality grounds our sense of who we are: the child who feels secure grounds that security in a caring God; the child who feels guilty and terrible grounds that sense of self by reference to a wrathful God; the child who feels estranged envisions a distant deity or dreams of a compensatory, warm and tender selfobject God.[15]

Through focusing on a person's patterns of relationship with the divine, Jones seeks to discover the ways in which that relationship "resonates" with other internalized human relationships that "constitute the sense of self."[16]

Significantly, these patterns of relationship can be altered. Transformation and healing are possible. Jones asks, "What is the connection between the coming of a new sense of self and the development of a new image of God?" He argues that answering this question involves "tracing a person's sense of self and transferential patterns and seeing how these changes are mirrored in relation to God."[17] He provides several case studies that described clients' changing patterns of relationship with the therapist, with themselves, and with the divine. For example, a woman named Sylvia said, "I always thought of God as loving; I always knew God was guarding me; yet didn't really feel it or experience it." Through the course of therapy, Sylvia gradually accepted empathy from the therapist and was then able to have empathy for herself and to "feel and experience God's empathy."[18] Sylvia explained, "Only after I accepted myself could I accept that God and others cared."[19]

This question of the connections between changes in self-image and the development of a new image of the divine is the central focus of this book. The research process demonstrated that the work of transforming images and relational patterns is not limited to a counseling relationship. A supportive, communal, educational environment can also illuminate the complex, unique process involved in transforming images of self, images for the divine, and relationships. The interviews, group discussions, and creation of worship experiences during the research process allowed us to explore the relational patterns that were being enacted in the women's current religious practices and experiences as well as in their past and current relationships.

The Self-in-Relation

The writings of Heinz Kohut also shed light on the complex interactions between representations of self, significant people in a person's life, and the divine. Kohut emphasized that while the self's primary function throughout life is to develop and maintain "a cohesive sense of itself," it does so only through relationships. The self cannot exist outside of relationship.[20] Selfobjects (what he called the significant people in a person's life, such as parents, spouse, etc.) serve two primary functions. First, in order for a child to develop a cohesive self, she needs a selfobject to mirror her feelings and accomplishments back to her empathically, affirming her sense of herself as valuable. Second, she needs a selfobject that empathically allows itself to be idealized.

This theory was developed primarily within the framework of a two-parent heterosexual family. There is room within Kohut's theories to postulate alternative gender roles and family structures. However, he placed the main burden for the empathic mirroring of the infant's "grandiose, narcissistic self" on the mother. The father, considered to be the secondary caretaker, was understood to be the parent who took on the role of empathically allowing himself to be idealized by the child. The mirroring of the mother and the idealization of the father (called the "idealized imago") were internalized gradually into the psyche of the child through a process of "transmuting internalization." Therefore, experiences of the parents actually formed essential parts of the child's cohesive self. Experienced as distinct from the parents, the cohesive self arose out of the "matrix of mirroring and idealized self-objects"[21] through the process of internalizing the parents' empathy and responsiveness as well as through gradual experiences of tolerable disappointments with both parents.

Kohut recognized that many of his patients in psychoanalysis suffered from narcissistic wounds that were caused by inadequate mirroring or by traumatic failures of the idealized imago. In psychoanalysis, he found that patients could heal only if they were allowed to act out the transference of those wounds onto the analyst. The analyst, in turn, should respond empathically, through mirroring and through allowing himself or herself to be idealized. While Kohut found these techniques to be effective in treating narcissistically wounded patients, he also believed that all people struggle throughout their lives to maintain a healthy, cohesive sense of self. They do so through relationships with others—including through their relationship with God.

The "independent self" is actually one that is strategically interdependent throughout life. A "selfobject support system" provides support for the cohesive self but also demands that the person give support to the selves of others. Kohut argues,

> Values of independence are phony, really. There is no such thing. There can be no pride in living without oxygen. We're not made that way . . . An independent self is one who is clever enough to find a good selfobject support system and to stay in tune with its

needs and the changing of the generations. To that system one must be willing to give a great deal.[22]

The relationship with the divine is one aspect of a good "selfobject support system."

For Kohut, the primary function of a God-representation is to meet the need for idealization. We cannot do away with the concept of God because "there must be something idealizable, something that nears perfection or that is perfect, something that wants to lift one up, something that lifts one up."[23] In addition, religion meets additional human needs. The experience of God helps to soothe narcissistic blows by evoking "our earliest encounter with the maternal selfobject matrix," when we were comforted during times of distress. In addition, religion meets mirroring needs through "grace." Strozier explains, "The psychological point is that God's grace is available for us to heal our wounds and to mirror our needs simply for the asking, in the same way the protective secure mother, especially the gleam in her eye, provided cohesion for ourselves through all the vagaries of development."[24]

However, those who never experienced a secure relationship with a caregiver and did not witness that "gleam" in their eyes will not be able to experience the grace of God in that way. Those who had painful relationships with their caregivers will create their image of the divine out of those relationships and will relate to the divine in the same patterns established by those relationships. As Jones indicates, only a process of transforming all relationships and images can heal this tragic situation.

Gender, Self, and Imaging the Divine

The theorists discussed thus far pay little attention to the dynamics of gender in the formation of the relational self. However, gender plays a prominent role in the formation of self-images, images of others, and divine images because gender is central to all of our relationships. While gender roles and expectations vary among cultures and between particular families, whatever those constructed roles and expectations are have a profound role in shaping our experiences.

The traditional male God of some religious communities is presented as unmovable, autonomous, and all-powerful. This image is perhaps "idealizable" but it is not always presented as empathic and capable of symbiosis. This can lead to detrimental results in a person's relationship with the divine. My research revealed this dynamic at work. One of the women I interviewed, Theresa, said that she experienced God as "remote," modeled on her father as "remote, and nothing else," yet unshakably male and powerful. Because of this correlation, she was unable to have any intimate relationship with the divine.

Gender and Divine Images: Case Studies

In addition to my interviews, several case studies from the psychological literature help to flesh out the complicated issues surrounding gender roles in culture, family, and religion and how they can impact the God-representation. In Rizzuto's case study, Daniel was unable to relate to his God-representation because it had been formed exclusively from his image of his domineering, abusive father and was reinforced by the religious education at his synagogue. Equally significant, however, is that Daniel was unable to incorporate aspects of his mother's personality and relationship with him into his God-representation. Rizzuto explains,

> The mother was, in her way, a caring person, but she had no power over the father. On the contrary, she submitted to him completely and feared him. She herself was frightened and ineffectual, and in any emergency she needed him to function for her and her children as a protective mother would do . . . The picture emerges clearly of a childish mother who submits totally to her husband and who is incapable of offering any protection to the children against a tyrannical father . . . I propose that such a mother could not be used to elaborate an image of God because of her submission to an existing superior person.[25]

Rizzuto demonstrates that Daniel used his image of his mother to create an alternative to his God-representation: a benevolent, sad, yet powerless witness to suffering on earth. Intellectually, he wanted to believe that God could be benevolent and that God cared about his suffering. However, his experiences of his mother's inability to stop his father's tyranny, the source of his own suffering, made him unable to experience God as actively loving. His only weak hope lay in his belief that at least he had a compassionate witness to his pain.[26] In Kohut's terms, due to a lack of ability to idealize either his mother or father and because of a lack of empathy from both parents, Daniel was unable to have any affective relationship with his God-image other than one of repressed anger, fear, and longing.

Another case study discussed by Jones provides insight into the ways that this painful dilemma of being unable to relate to a dominant, frightening conception of God could be alleviated. Jones describes Phil in ways that are remarkably similar to Daniel:

> He never felt he could become close to his father or that his father had any time for him or was there for him. The only relationship he had with his father was laden with criticism. He felt that he had to prove himself to his father by being a financial success and that he had to prove himself to God through his church activities . . . The only feelings Phil associated with God were shame and guilt for falling short and not doing enough or being good enough–the

same feelings he associated with his father . . . The church's image of God matched the one he brought to the door, as Rizzuto puts it.[27]

Like Daniel, Phil was unable to include aspects of his mother in his God-representation. In relation to his dominant father, his mother's influence in the family was experienced as minimal. Jones explains,

> His mother played little role in his life. Father was dominant in the family, and she was even more peripheral at family gatherings than his siblings . . . As she was not there to buffer him from his father's harshness, so there are no nurturant qualities in his God representation to mitigate the divine harshness. And to relate to these maternal qualities was to cut oneself off from the world of men.[28]

For Phil, like Daniel, the gender roles in his family and in the society that surrounded him, including his church and the theology it espoused, served to cut him off from the possibility of a nurturing, maternal image of the divine.[29]

However, Phil had a remarkable spiritual transformation while undergoing psychotherapy with Jones. During a time when he became able to express anger at his father and at his God, he began to realize that his God-representation had been created in his father's image. He saw a televised mass that was focused on the Virgin Mary and found it "strangely moving." He decided to attend noonday mass at a nearby Catholic church. Jones recounts,

> What he found most compelling, he told me as we explored his experiences there, were the statues of the Virgin that filled the sanctuary. Images of the mother and child and Marian devotions centered on maternal nurturance and forgiveness were psychologically irresistible to him . . . Images of the wrathful Father God faded and were replaced by feminine images of Mary. He said he could spontaneously pray to Mary, in contrast to the dutiful formality of his prayers to God the Father. Gradually he experienced her as a "presence"(his word) in the church, again in contrast to his lack of positive, felt connection to God. . . . In this instance, his religious practice was a positive, causal factor in his psychological development.[30]

For Phil, simultaneous processes of questioning his former image of the divine and encountering new, more positive and nurturing images allowed him to move into a positive, nurturing, and sustaining relationship with the divine.

Selfhood, Divine Images, and Gender

Like Phil, many contemporary women have been questioning the image of God as a dominant Father and the impact it has on their spirituality, their self-understandings as women, and their relationships with the divine. My research with women in the Christian feminist spirituality movement revealed a complex of tensions they experienced when they challenged the "official" male God of their childhoods, trying to image the divine as feminine. For example, they realized that they did not consider women worthy to be representative of the divine because they did not experience women as powerful. Even though they had all been trying to change their image of the divine to a feminine image for a number of years, they still struggled to do so because they did not feel themselves, their mothers, or other women to be powerful or worthy enough to represent the divine. In addition, all four of the women interviewed described in different terms the ways that their image of God had been largely created out of personality aspects of their fathers or of other men because they had difficulty seeing their mothers or other women as representative of the divine.

Their long process of embracing feminine images of the divine thus involved a process of claiming their own power and self-worth and of questioning the images and expectations of gender (both of people and of the divine) that they had created out of their experiences as women in a patriarchal society and a patriarchal religion.

Through the research process, they recognized that their mothers' patterns of relationship and their own were valuable in their own right, even though they were not valued in a society that valorizes a male ideal of independence. At the same time, they recognized the need to embrace their own power and selfhood while maintaining their ways of relating in the world.

Gender, Selfhood, and Classical Theology

The cultural valuation of the male ideal of independence and power-over is modeled clearly on the classical image of the male God. As the women I interviewed demonstrated, this image has profound implications for self-image, human relationships, and a relationship with the divine. Conceptual theological images of the divine, as provided in classical theology, are deeply connected with the emotionally laden images that determine how we live our lives as gendered people.

Selfhood in Western society has been modeled according to a traditional image of a male God (and that God-image was created out of an ideal for masculinity), such that men are conditioned to be in that image, and women are expected to support men in their Godlike selfhood while sacrificing themselves in the process.[31] The traditional concept of God as self-contained, isolated, and authoritarian was modeled on—and serves as a model for–a frontier-type male understanding of self. Catherine Keller explains,

> The traditional perfections of God read like a catalog of the heroic ego's ideals for himself . . . Classical theology decries self-enclosure as sin; let me suggest, however, that self-enclosure–with its accompanying arrogance, isolation, and dominance–is precisely what the *imago dei* came to convey! Things are all turned around here . . . The association in this epoch between separatism and masculinity is so tight that as long as God is imagined in mainly masculine metaphors, there is simply no chance for conversion to a fundamentally relational spirituality. And the reverse holds equally true: as long as divinity is externalized by the traditional perfections of self-sufficiency, omnipotence, impassionability, and immutability, "God"–even were she made in name and image a woman, an androgyne, or a neuter–will support the oppression of women.[32]

The gender dynamics described in the stories of Phil and Daniel are deified through classical conceptions of the divine. This deification contributes to the oppression of women, raising up traditional male ideals such as self-sufficiency, isolation, and dominance to be worshiped as characteristics of ultimate value.

At the same time, women are denied access to the divine and are kept in a subjugated position through this theological anthropology. The male "separative self," modeled on the male God-image, can only exist if supported by a female "soluble self" who continually feeds "the pretense of the male ego." Keller quotes Virginia Woolf, who said, "Women have served all these centuries as looking-glasses possessing the magic and delicious power of reflecting the figure of man at twice its natural size." In other words, a woman's support of a man's ego serves to maintain the sense that the man is "god-like" and to project that image onto God.[33] In order for women to engage in this building up of male dominance, they have been formed through millennia of patriarchal culture to have narcissistically selfless selves and to devalue themselves as female, as outside of the realm of the divine.

Keller's contribution to the discussion of the impact of gendered images of the divine in the formation of selfhood is crucial. She advocates for new models of self and of the divine that reflected the relational nature of reality. She calls her new model of self "the connective self"–a self that has a cohesive core yet is profoundly and essentially relational. This model mirrors the reality that object relations theories of the self have demonstrated.

In order for new models of selfhood to be possible, it is necessary for society to be transformed on the level of its myths and images of the divine. Keller explains,

To find images empowering of a selfhood beyond that of the separative ego and its selfless complement, we inevitably journey through the deep past, through a mythic memory heavy with dream and charged with desire . . . Re-membering means nothing if not re-connecting. And reconnection, as will gradually become apparent, requires a complex cohesiveness of relation and of self . . . An entire way of life seems to have been dismembered along with the Goddesses.[34]

Keller recognizes that images of the Goddess are powerful metaphors for the divine because they invert the patriarchal view that women cannot embody the divine. However, a new image of the divine should not simply be a new, reified image of a Goddess. The Goddess-image that she envisions is one that embodies the active relationality for which she advocates. She describes it through the metaphor of a spider spinning a web. However, she also states "Our way of reconnection, as religious action, must retain a pluralistic, metaphorical consciousness."[35] Precisely this type of "pluralistic, metaphorical consciousness" predominates in the Christian feminist spirituality movement.

Keller's work was based in Western mythologies, and her models of female and male selfhood were models of European and, particularly, European American male and female selfhood. It is therefore helpful in terms of providing challenges to the models of selfhood in a European American-dominated society. The myths that serve to form the selves of men and women from other cultures would inform different models of selfhood for maleness and femaleness. However, the ideal of the connective self, one that balances relationality with autonomy, and Keller's view of reality as a relational web, might be helpful for and consonant with ideals from various cultures.

Keller's sole reliance on Western culture makes her work problematic and potentially alienating for readers from non-Western backgrounds. On the other hand, in a postcolonial world, readers who have experienced colonial Christianity through the legacies of European and European American colonization or slavery would likely recognize the European masculinist ideal in the theologies and images of a white, male God and Jesus in their churches.[36]

Race and Divine Images

None of the authors discussed thus far addresses the issue of race as a significant aspect of imaging the divine. However, the construction of race and the representations that are used to enforce those constructions are deeply implicated in the creation of images of the divine, self, and other people. Just as the gender of an image of the divine has a profound influence on the ways that people relate to that image, race significantly affects the way that people relate to an image depending on their own racial identity and socialization into the constructed racial system of the society.

While this chapter focuses primarily on the psychological dynamics at work in imaging the divine, it is important to emphasize that the psychological and emotional dynamics of individuals are deeply impacted and constructed by political, social, and cultural factors. While each person experiences his racial identity as an intimate part of himself, racial (and gender) identities are constructions that serve political purposes as well. For this reason, I turn in this section to exploring the historical trajectory of the construction of race, particularly "whiteness," in American society. This discussion demonstrates that the psychology of individuals is far from apolitical. Rather, a person's formation of self-image and divine image is profoundly affected by political and historical dynamics as they are mediated through a particular context.

The image of God as European (white), when used in a white supremacist context such as the United States or Western Europe, could reinforce a sense of white superiority in European Americans and Europeans, precipitating marginalization of people of non-European descent. A white child growing up with images and experiences of white men and women as being more powerful and more valuable in society would correlate the power and value of that whiteness with her own and with the whiteness of the images of Jesus, Mary, and God that she encounters in her church and religious teachings. The combination of religious images of the divine as being white and social teachings and experiences of whiteness as superior would deeply impact the child's internalization of racism.

When I entered the Episcopal church of my childhood, I was surrounded by images of a white Jesus, white angels, white disciples, and white saints. While few images were female, their whiteness was familiar to me, comfortable, as a European American child. There was no reason for me to question that the holy was equivalent with whiteness. Even as an adult, when surrounded by those same images I am comforted on some level. My white supremacy is not challenged. I may criticize the images as racist and historically inaccurate and I might experience feelings of remorse and anger, but I am still allowed, through these images, to "bask in privilege"[37] and the comfort of the familiar as a part of my religious experience. The same issue arose in my research. In her interview, Julie acknowledged that even though she was raised to be antiracist, and even though she actively tried to avoid internalizing the image of God as a white man, she nevertheless took in the messages of her church and of the larger culture. She recognizes now that she learned to value blonde hair and whiteness over darkness and that she internalized the dominant images of God and Jesus as white.

On the other hand, many white, European Americans have experienced more unconditional love from an African American woman employed by their parents to take care of them as children than from their own parents.

They have developed an image of God as an African American woman in connection with the teachings of their religious tradition that God is unconditionally loving. This image has emerged recently in U.S. popular culture in the novel *The Shack,* resonating with millions of readers.[38] This raises the question, however, of whether this God-image enables them to challenge their inevitable internalized images of white people as superior in a white supremacist context. Perhaps the image of the less powerful, more loving African American woman coincides with an image of Christ as long-suffering and therefore does not challenge assumptions and inspire action to alleviate the suffering of African American people. Perhaps this image reinforces stereotypes of black women as a mammy or an earth mother, able to give endlessly, with superhuman strength, without challenging the racism of white people. These complicated issues will be explored in greater detail in chapters 5 and 7.

On the other hand, African American children growing up in a context of white supremacy—in which God, Jesus, Mary, and the angels in their Bibles, stained glass windows, Sunday School textbooks, and so on are all portrayed as white—would probably experience profound inner conflict. While they would internalize experiences of African American parents, family members, and other significant people into their God-representations and self-representations, the images of the divine as white would encourage them to see the oppressive white society as more closely identified with the divine. In Rizzuto's terms, women and men who challenge that culture by confronting white supremacy and imaging the divine as black become "maladaptive" to the culture at-large.

In Jones' terms, an image of God as a white male can reinforce transferential patterns of racism and sexism, in the sense that people would relate to that image as they relate to white men. While this would be significantly complicated by each individual's experiences of relationship to white men in their lives, in general those who have been harmed by racism and/or sexism in a white supremacist, patriarchal culture might be inhibited in their ability to create an intimate, trusting relationship with the divine if they are continually told by their religious institution and culture that God looks like a white man. Their fear and mistrust of powerful white men and their anger at having been mistreated and seen as less than fully human might lead them to be estranged from the divine as they transfer relational patterns of fear, mistrust, and anger onto the image of the divine.

On the other hand, an image of the divine as a black woman might empower an African American woman to see her self-image reflected in the divine and might encourage patterns of relationship that are similar to her patterns of relating with her mother or grandmother, rather than her patterns of relating with white men in a racist, sexist social system. Therefore, the dynamics of race and gender are as nuanced and complex as are family relationships and cultural-religious contexts in shaping a person's images and patterns of relationship.

Selfhood and "Race": The Formation of "White" Selves

Just as the white, male image for God supports particular ideals for gender, it also shapes ideals for raced selfhood. While these ideals differ depending on ethnicity, I focus in this section on the ideal images for white womanhood and manhood in the context of the United States. These ideals are upheld through our cultural images of God. Every person is racialized in a highly racialized society such as the United States. As long as whiteness is considered normative and unnamed, racism will remain intact. Those considered "nonwhite" remain as "other" (read inferior; somehow less than human) to the norm.[39] Scholars and activists have argued for decades that white supremacy will not change until "white" people consider themselves to be "raced," just as people of color are "raced." For this reason, I have chosen to focus on the construction of white maleness and femaleness in the United States in exploring the impact of ethnic and cultural identity on the imaging of the divine.

Theologian Thandeka argues that American white supremacy and a God-image that supports it result from the formation of "white" selves among European Americans. She analyzed interviews with European Americans about their experiences of being socialized into whiteness and argues that the process of becoming "white" is devastating to the selfhood of European American children. One of the stories that she tells is that of "Sarah." She writes,

> At age sixteen, Sarah brought her best friend home with her from high school. After the friend left, Sarah's mother told her not to invite her friend home again. "Why?" Sarah asked, astonished and confused. "Because she's colored," her mother responded . . . Sarah persisted, insisting that her mother tell her the real reason for her action. None was forthcoming. The indignant look in her mother's face, however, made Sarah realize that if she persisted, she would jeopardize her mother's affection toward her . . . Nothing—Sarah had always believed until that moment—could jeopardize their closeness. But now, she had glimpsed the unimaginable, the unspeakable—the unthinkable. Her relationship with her mother was not absolutely secure. It could crumble . . . Her mother's affection was conditional. It could be lost.[40]

Sarah's experience illustrates that socialization into a white identity involves the traumatic recognition that one must choose between the love of one's own family and community (who are already socialized as "white") and feelings of affection and affinity for people of a different racial or ethnic background. For many, this experience occurs at a much younger age than sixteen, during the childhood years when their primary sense of selfhood and identity is being formed.

Thandeka argues that the trauma of being forced to deny one's own humanity in order to maintain the security of being loved and accepted is a form of child abuse, a "white racial attack" against the child. Drawing on the psychological theories of Kohut, she explains how this abuse leads to a child's loss of her core sense of self and thus of her sense of wholeness.

By the age of two or three months, an infant has a sense of itself as "a separate, physical, coherent being with its own feelings and physical history."[41] Daniel Stern calls this the "core sense of self."[42] This feeling of having a separate core self, however, is dependent on the experience of having a relationship with another person who has a core sense of self. Thandeka explains, "It is a sense of being both distinct from and also related to but not fused with someone with a different core sense of self." The infant gains his core sense of self through the recognition of the difference between his feelings and actions and those of his caretaker. [43]

In order for this relational core self to be affirmed in the infant, caretakers must recognize, affirm, and be able to tolerate the distinctiveness of the infant's core self. They must love the child's distinct core self unconditionally. In order to do this, caretakers must already have a core sense of self, established in their childhood, so that they can tolerate and appreciate differences between themselves and the infant. When parents fail to provide this unconditional love, and instead retaliate when the child acts differently from their expectations, the effects are devastating.[44]

Many parents are incapable of providing this unconditional love of the child's uniqueness because they themselves have damaged core selves due to a lack of unconditional love in their own childhoods. Because of this damage, the parents often look to their infant children for the affirmation of their own feelings. The infant is vulnerable to the need of his parent because he is completely dependent on the parent for his survival. The child becomes the mirror of the parent's emotions and self rather than vice versa. The result is damage to the child's core sense of self. One of these moments of denying difference occurs when a child is required to conform to the caretaker's feelings about people of a different "race."

Thandeka theorizes that throughout life, when a "white" person encounters a person of the race that her caretaker forced her to reject by the implicit threat of abandonment, the feelings that accompanied that trauma are brought back into awareness. Because the trauma itself is usually too painful to remain in the person's conscious mind, she finds herself with extreme negative emotional reactions when she encounters a person of that particular ethnic background.

When a person is forced to raise feelings to consciousness that were not allowed to remain part of her core sense of self, she feels shame. Shame is felt when emotions arise that call on parts of the self that have been "split off" in order to please one's caretakers. Thandeka explains,

> The parts of the self that have not been consistently, lovingly, and empathically affirmed because they are different from what the caretaker expected are "split off" from the child's operative, conscious activities of engagement with others or separated from it through repression. We call these split-off feelings of one's self an abridgement of one's ability to relate wholly and coherently to the world in which we must live.[45]

When the shame and pain of the lost core self are raised to awareness, a person can react with rage, which is often projected outward toward those of a different race whose presence elicited the unbearable emotions.[46]

Racial formation is intimately tied to one's sense of self. If a child has been raised to lose her core sense of self and to define herself in relation to pleasing her parents and taking care of their emotional needs, she will experience the need to please them by acting according to what they consider appropriate as "white" as one more attack on her core self and one more instance in which she must sacrifice her true feelings. Her shame around race will be combined with a larger sense of shame (and suppressed grief and rage) about the loss of her core sense of self. Thus, a person who has been raised without the unconditional love of her parents in general would experience the threat of the loss of the parent's love in relation to racial identity differently than Sarah did, who had always felt that the love of her mother was unconditional before the moment described by Thandeka.

Racialized Projections

A white person's shame about aspects of herself that have been rejected by her parents can also lead her to project those characteristics onto people who are different from herself and to despise them. This dynamic helps to explain the intense, irrational hostility and hatred in racism. It begins through childrearing practices within "white" families and is carried outward into society.

A parent's shame about certain aspects of himself causes the parent to project those aspects onto his child and then to try to eradicate them in the child. Alice Miller explains, "Child-rearing is used in a great many cases to prevent those qualities that were once scorned and eradicated in oneself from coming to life in one's children."[47] She demonstrates that the popular "pedagogies" for childrearing in Germany from the eighteenth century through the early twentieth century advocated just such a dynamic by urging parents to "suppress everything in the child" that did not fit with the image of what the parents wanted him to be. This method of childrearing is passed down from generation to generation because of its internal dynamics. It is supported by the psychological needs of parents who have been raised in the same way. Miller argues,

> The pedagogical conviction that one must bring a child into line from the outset has its origin in the need to split off the disquieting parts of the inner self and project them onto an available object. The child's great plasticity, flexibility, defenselessness, and availability make it the ideal object for this projection. The enemy within can at last be hunted down on the outside.[48]

This mechanism can play itself out in the context of white racial identity in several ways. One of the internal characteristics that may be "hunted down" within the child is his natural feelings of attraction and affection for people of all racial and ethnic backgrounds. Miller quotes from an interview with a former member of the Nazi Youth organization. This young woman had never known a Jewish person, yet had been raised with much shame and suppressed rage. She described her experience with Nazi Youth by saying, "It was just so good to have someone to hate."[49] Societal permission to hate or to dehumanize allows for the expression of rage caused by the shaming of young children.

In addition, a "white" person learns to project onto people of color those characteristics that are considered unacceptable for herself—for example, laziness, stupidity, sexual expressiveness and promiscuity, or squalor.[50] These characteristics have been used as negative stereotypes of African Americans and Native Americans in order to justify violence and discrimination. As part of a white identity, a person learns to project these unwanted characteristics onto people different from herself and to then "hunt them down" in those people. Shame about a lost core self then leads directly to violence against others.

The Beginnings of "Race"

What, then, are the ideals for "white" manhood and womanhood? What parts of the core self must be sacrificed in the process of the socialization of a child into one of these roles? From where did the ideals come? How does formation into white male and female selves affect imaging of the divine and relationships with others?

While the dynamics of splitting off and projection are perhaps a universal human phenomenon, the particularity of the process within the context of racism in the United States deserves particular attention. An examination of the historical development of the ideals for white manhood and womanhood within the United States will reveal the ways that these psychological dynamics have been intertwined with the historical develop-ment of racism and the formation of a "white" racial identity. The ideals for masculinity and femininity described by Keller (the autonomous self and the soluble self) are ideals for white masculinity and white femininity.

The male God-image that supports those gender identities is definitively a white, male God-image. The European and European American image of a white, male God has developed out of the ideal for white masculinity, as defined over and against people of other ethnicities.

Theories of race and racial difference have, from their inception, been devices used by those in power (a small group of European and European American males) in order to maintain their power and to justify the exploitation of people of different "races." Not until the late eighteenth century was "race" the most commonly used concept to separate and differentiate people. In reality, there are more biological differences within a particular "race" than there are between people of different "races."[51]

In the late eighteenth century, however, during the time of the African slave trade and the expansion of European colonialism, scientists began to attempt to classify people and their differences just as they had done with animals. They were influenced by Darwin's theory of evolution and therefore arranged people according to a hierarchy, with Europeans, not surprisingly, designated as the superior race. They associated physical traits and cultural characteristics, so that they claimed to determine much about the value of a person based on her or his biology.[52] The term "Caucasian" did not exist to describe "white" people as a "race" until 1775, when scientist Johann Blumenbach created his own schema of racial classification, with five human races: Caucasian, Mongolian, Ethiopian, American, and Malay. He chose the term "Caucasian" to designate whiteness because he "believed that the Caucasus region in Russia produced the world's most beautiful women."[53]

Legislating Whiteness

Defining who was "white" was originally a political tool for a small group of powerful European American men who wanted to divide the interests of those who worked for them. Because of the great costs to themselves, working- and servant-class European Americans were reluctant to take on a white identity in opposition to their nonwhite coworkers. However, different immigrant groups gradually came to associate themselves as "white" in American society because of the power available through identification as "white."

Thandeka reveals that the legislature of the colony of Virginia, made up of its most powerful men, gradually enacted "race laws" in order to separate white from black and Indian. They passed legislation forbidding free blacks and Indians from owning white servants. On the other hand, in 1680 they gave any white Christian the legal right to give "thirty lashes on the back" to "any negroe or other slave" who "dared to lift his hand in opposition to a Christian," with "Christian" being synonymous with "white." In 1705, they passed legislation confiscating all property owned by slaves and then sold it to benefit poor whites. In addition, that same year they required masters to provide white indentured servants with "corn, money, a gun, and clothing" at the end of their indentureship. They thereby systematically raised the status of white indentured servants (who constituted the majority of the white population in the colony) while simultaneously lowering the position of nonwhite slaves, servants, and freed men and women.[54]

The policing of interracial sexuality was also part of this legislative creation of the raised status of whiteness. Abby Ferber explains, "To discourage white women who continued to cohabit with black men, laws were passed in 1681 forcing white women who gave birth to mulatto children into five years of servitude, and forcing mulatto children into indentured servitude until age thirty. Additionally, white women who engaged in miscegenation faced banishment from the colony."[55] The legislature thus had the power to literally legislate and punish the sexual activity of white women and black men, while laws at the same time encouraged interracial sexual activity between white men and black women so that the resulting children would become the property of white slaveowners. White women who dared to deny their white identity risked extreme punishments while white male servants were lured toward solidarity with whiteness by gaining benefits at the expense of their nonwhite coworkers.

Fears of miscegenation, or "race-mixing," became most strong in the European American psyche after emancipation. The fear of interracial sex, specifically between African American men and European American women, continues to be the most prevalent issue in white supremacist discourse and propaganda today. It arises, however, from the historical legacy of mainstream America. In this framework of needing to keep the white race "pure," white women came to be symbolized as the border between the races that needed to be protected by white men. Whiteness is associated with masculinity while femininity is associated with being nonwhite,[56] with white masculinity seen as superior. "White" identity was therefore defined primarily in terms of a white masculine identity. However, European American women were socialized as white in a different way.

White American Femininity

In this symbolic, cultural, and political system, for women to be "white"—to fit the ideal of white womanhood—they must be protected, that is, controlled by white men in order to ensure that they were the sole property of white men and breeders of white children. For European American women, the children of an interracial relationship remain with the mother and thus represent a breakdown in the purity of the white community and a threat to white male power and white supremacy. After emancipation, the lynching of black men and the raping of black women by white men were used as tools of maintaining and enforcing white male control and power over black men and women and over white women.

In this context, while African American women and men, as well as European American women, have been victims of violence by white men, with their suffering left unacknowledged or validated by the larger society, white women have been constructed as constantly in danger of being victimized by African American men. An essential part of the trauma inflicted on the core selves of European American women has thus been the shaming of their agency, assertiveness, and sexuality. They are socialized into a victim mentality in which they feel that they are in constant need of protection by European American men—who thus have control over their lives.[57]

The rhetoric about white women as victims has been used to justify countless acts of violence against African Americans. The possibility of interracial sex has persistently been the greatest fear among European Americans throughout U.S. history—greater than fears of legal equality, political participation, or economic empowerment for African Americans. Whenever African Americans have achieved some of these legal, political, and economic goals, the fear that interracial sexual relationships would result from greater interactions has led to increased violence against African Americans. Ferber explains,

> Historically, whenever any change occurred in the four latter areas of discrimination, the white community responded with fear and accusations that black males were a threat to white womanhood. For example, emancipation, voting rights, and black competition with whites for jobs have all led to white violence aimed at blacks in the name of protecting white womanhood, and warding off the threat of interracial sexuality.[58]

Clearly, the construction of "white womanhood" as being in constant danger served—and continues to serve—the purpose of policing African Americans.

This identity for white women was thus a political tool for white men in power yet it also became a psychological legacy passed down through the generations. In terms of the theories of Miller and Thandeka, for European American girls to become "white" women, their sexuality, righteous anger and assertiveness, agency to determine their lives and to defend themselves, and affinity for people of different ethnicities are "hunted down" by their caretakers in order to socialize them into proper white women and to relieve their mothers' and grandmothers' pain over their own losses of self.

In addition, while they are socialized to see themselves as victims, they have also been socialized to objectify and oppress people who are not "white." The socialization as victims perhaps contributes to the inability of "white" women to recognize their guilt and responsibility in the victimization of others. Their feelings of affinity toward people different from themselves have been policed with particular vigilance due to the perceived danger of interracial sexual activity. However, these feelings have also been split off in order to perpetuate the overall system of racial classification and hierarchy.

Generalizations can be dangerous and each person's socialization is unique. However, it is important to consider general characteristics of socialization into "white womanhood" in order to explore the ways that constructions of race and gender intersect to create the false images out of which we image ourselves and the divine. It is only through naming the false images by which we have identified ourselves, others, and the divine that we can move toward more authentic selfhood, more just relationships, and a more intimate spirituality.

White American Masculinity

The socialization into white manhood has taken a different form. The ideal for white American masculinity is remarkably similar to the classical image of God described by Keller—autonomous, dominant, and unmoved by the feelings of others. This ideal for white men grew out of a combination of the classical European ideals for masculinity and particularly out of the American dynamics of the freedom of the frontier and racial difference as defined by the complete lack of freedom of African slaves.[59]

Toni Morrison analyzed works of fiction by several European American authors in order to explore the constructions of whiteness that appear in the texts. She discovered typical characteristics of the European American man, arguing that European American men were eager to determine an identity that was distinct from Europeans. In order to do so, they defined themselves in opposition to the enslaved populations in the United States. She explains,

> Black slavery enriched the country's creative possibilities. For in that construction of blackness *and* enslavement could be found not only the not-free but also, with the dramatic polarity created by skin-color, the projection of the not-me. The result was a playground for the imagination . . . Cultural identities are formed and informed by a nation's literature, and . . . what seemed to be on the "mind" of the literature of the United States was the self-conscious but highly problematic construction of the American as a new white man.[60]

This "new white man" was thus defined in opposition to the black population. His whiteness came to signify characteristics such as "autonomy, authority, newness and difference, absolute power."[61]

These characterizations and concerns about European American male identity in literature translated from and into very real social dynamics in U.S. culture. Morrison argues,

Autonomy is freedom and translates into the much championed and revered "individualism"; newness translates into "innocence"; distinctiveness becomes difference and the erection of strategies for maintaining it; authority and absolute power become a romantic, conquering "heroism," virility, and the problematic of wielding absolute power over the lives of others. All the rest are made possible by this last, it would seem—absolute power called forth and played against and within a natural and mental landscape conceived in a "raw, half-savage world."[62]

The values of American society were therefore established as characteristics of white men who were considered "civilized" and free in spite of their construction as violent in their absolute power over those who were deemed "savage."

The American, white male identity also came to be constructed as "solitary, alienated, and malcontent," like a lone cowboy. These characteristics arose out of the emphasis on individualism and autonomy. Morrison ponders, "What, one wants to ask, are Americans alienated from? What are Americans so insistently innocent of? Different from? As for absolute power, over whom is this power held, from whom withheld, to whom distributed?"[63] These questions resonate with the psychological perspectives of Miller and Thandeka. While white men were originally defined in opposition to slave populations, the construction of white masculinity in the United States has continued to be defined as autonomous, authoritative, and alienated after the abolition of slavery. White male identity has continued to be defined in terms of difference and power over others. It has also been constituted through alienation from the core relational self. For a child to be socialized into a white American male identity, his core self must be assaulted.

Recalling that "autonomy is impossible," in the sense that the core self is defined in terms of its relationality with others, it is clear that white American men have to deny this inherent relationality within themselves in order to fit their social role. Their feelings of relatedness to others, their compassion for others, and their feelings of vulnerability all must be hunted down by their caretakers in order for them to be socialized into the ideal of the "new white man." While few men actually live up to this ideal in its extreme, like white women they must negotiate the social consequences and internalized false images and shame that motivate conformity. Fear, shame, and rage result from failure or when split-off feelings of vulnerability surface. Their false sense of self is determined by a false sense of autonomy and separateness from others. They are required to be alienated not only from people who are different from themselves but also from themselves. It is no wonder, then, that many are also "malcontent."

In addition, this ideal is both heterosexual and heterosexist. Challenging the norms in this ideal challenges the entire system of gender, race, and sexuality.[64] For this reason, homosexuality and "gender-bending"[65] are particularly threatening in this social order. For a white American man to lose his power (and/or perceived superiority) over others would mean a loss of the identity that was established for him in childhood, with great cost to himself. This is why the policing of the boundaries of difference remains a defining concern for many European American men. Their identities are at stake and the pain of the loss of their core selves is "unspeakable."

This helps to explain why the image of the white male God is so intractable in our culture. Many white men may be unable to "play" with images of the divine because they are unable to face the pain of what they have lost in themselves. Only unconditional love can help to heal this shame and pain. Alternative images, explored in a loving community, may help many men to challenge their self-images and relationships with others. As one white man told Patricia Lynn Reilly, after hearing her present about the divine feminine, "Thank you! I was so tired of having to be in charge!"[66]

More is at stake than a simple shifting of images. Truly at stake is the sharing of power, the recognition that all people are equally representative of the divine image, and at the same time, that difference is to be celebrated rather than policed. This goes against centuries of racialized and gendered social policies and socialization, enacted in order to ensure the power of elite white men in American society. To challenge the whiteness and maleness of God is to challenge the very power structure of our society, particularly when the image of God is of one who is invulnerable and all-powerful.

The question remains whether alternative images can challenge structures of social inequality, whether changes in social life can lead to changes in imaging, or whether both need to happen simultaneously. I contend that an ongoing process of transformation is needed, involving changes at the personal, political, social, and religious levels simultaneously, with each influencing the others.

Conclusion

The human self is in an active state of change and psychic balancing through the use of internalized representations of self, others, and the divine. This psychoanalytic understanding of theology challenges theologians and religious leaders to take into account the reality that each individual interacts with the "official" theology of the church, or with conceptual theologies, in a particular way based on her object-representations, self-image, and cultural locations. If we take seriously the variety of "experiential"[67] images of sacred reality and the ways that those images reinforce self-representations, we will provide opportunities for people to play with their images and to find new, more life-giving images.

The challenge is to help people who have not internalized caring, secure relationships, and therefore who do not have positive self-representations or a nourishing affective relationship with a God-representation. They must be enabled to engage in the difficult process of examining and transforming those relationships and representations so that they might find a new psychic balance, a new sense of self, and a new way of being in the world. As Rizzuto explains, this involves a process that engages the person on the conceptual, affective, interpersonal, and intrapsychic levels. In Keller's terms, through this process they might reconnect and re-member.

In addition, people need a supportive environment in which to examine critically their self-image and divine-image as gendered and raced in relation to the historical context of racism, sexism, and heterosexism. Religious institutions, with their multiple functions of religious education, pastoral counseling, worship, and fellowship, have a unique potential to engage people on all of these levels. However, they can only realize this potential if they are willing to move beyond reified, oppressive images of the divine and to allow people the freedom to play and to explore in a supportive, empathic matrix of care. Just this kind of freedom is embodied in the Christian feminist spirituality movement. Women have come together to create these supportive environments for one another. In the following chapter we turn to this movement and toward the mystical spiritual process that has emerged from these gatherings of women.

2

First Story

Theresa

Theresa is in her early seventies. She is originally from Colombia, South America. She moved to the United States in the late 1950s when she was twenty-one years old and had recently married her husband, who is from Venezuela. She was passionate about women's rights from an early age and has devoted much of her life to helping women. She was raised Roman Catholic and then renounced the Catholic Church and became Baptist during her twenties. She worked as a lawyer in South America for a number of years. She is now a marriage and family counselor. She is married and has two married adult daughters and one young granddaughter. She left her Baptist church when she became active in Mary and Martha's Place (MMP) because of the church's patriarchal teachings. At the time of this research, she was still searching for a church community where she could feel comfortable.

Imaging and Relationships

Theresa has considered herself to be a spiritual and religious person throughout her life. She named "the church" as one of the most influential relationships in her life. However, she has never had a personal image of God and finds herself unable to pray. She said that she does not "feel" the divine and describes herself as "empty." She explained that when she spends time at the beach or in the mountains, when she looks at beautiful flowers or an old tree, she thinks, "There must be a God." However, in spite of feeling happiness and peace in these places of nature, she said that she does not "feel the divine." She experiences transcendence while listening to music in church or during times of silence in rituals such as the winter solstice ritual at MMP and she described those experiences as "spiritual." However, she said that she feels a "spiritual vacuum."

41

In her interview, she explained, "I feel this desire to speak about the divine, to feel it . . . I cannot feel it. I want the spiritual aspects, but I don't know how to integrate it, to feel it . . . It wouldn't be honest to say I know the divine. I cannot feel it." She explained that while she learned how to pray according to the church's teachings, these prayers do not satisfy her longing. She said, "I learned how to pray according to the Baptist church. But I didn't pray much. I began to realize: 'No. That is not what I want to do. I want to come out from within myself.' I'm still empty."

Theresa exemplifies Rizzuto's observation that "even someone who believes intellectually that there must be a God may feel no inclination to accept him [sic] unless images of previous interpersonal experience have fleshed out the concept with multiple images that can now coalesce in a representation that he [sic] can accept emotionally."[1] Theresa longs for an image of the divine that she can accept and relate to emotionally. Even as a child she never had an image of the divine. She said, "I never pictured. That never worked for me . . . I did not form an idea about God. God was very remote and nothing else." She said that she felt "nothing" about God while growing up. She explained that "He was just there."

While she said that she did not have a sense that God was "a father, or a punitive father, or nothing," her experience of God as being "just there, . . . remote and nothing else" corresponds directly with her experiences and descriptions of her own father. When asked to describe the most influential relationships in her life, Theresa did not mention her father. However, in describing her family during her childhood, she said, "It was dysfunctional. My dad controlled everything. My mom was a very submissive person . . . she could argue, but at the end, my dad was always the one in control. And that, I didn't care for at all." During our first group discussion, she described her father as "a nonexistent father." She explained that while he was authoritarian and controlling with her mother, he was distant from the lives of his children. She described him in the same way that she described God: "remote." She explained, "I could not count on my dad. He was not controlling, but he was not there. He was an army man, so he was always busy with his job . . . In the way that I see it, a more remote person. We knew that this is dad, but that was it. He did not participate in our personal lives."

The parallel between Theresa's relationship with and image of her father and her relationship with and image of the divine is striking. Her experience of God as "remote and nothing else" corresponds with her experience of her father as "nonexistent" and "remote." As James Jones would argue, Theresa's pattern of relationship with God is a direct reflection of her pattern of relationship with her father—there is no relationship except one of distance and control (via control of her mother).

Growing up in the Catholic Church, Theresa related directly to Mary rather than to this remote God. She experienced Mary as a mediator between God and herself. In Jones' terms, Theresa's pattern of relationship with her mother is mirrored in her pattern of relationship with Mary. Just as her relationship with her father was mediated through her mother, Mary mediated her relationship to God. However, just like her mother, Mary was experienced as powerless to make decisions or to solve problems on her own. She was under the control of the Father. When she left the Catholic Church and became a Baptist, Theresa stopped praying to Mary and began praying directly to Jesus instead. To her, both Mary and Jesus served as mediators, more immediate than God. When she left the Baptist Church and began to question the divinity of Jesus, she was left without either of her mediators. Now she finds herself unable to pray, largely because she is left with a God who, to her, is "remote and nothing else."

In discussing Mary, Theresa revealed the connection between her image of Mary, her experience of her own mother, and her deep anger at the oppression of women in the Catholic Church. She explained,

> I stopped praying to Mary when I left the Catholic Church. I still have difficulty even with the mystics. Knowing what they have accomplished, I still believed that they submitted totally to the Catholic Church. It is still my belief that you, as a woman in the Catholic Church, or even in the Baptist, that you allow men to control you. So I would put Mary like a good mom, but with no power . . . Controlled by men. When I left the church, I thought, "Good-bye, Mary." Just like that.

For Theresa, Mary was like her own mother—"a good mom, but with no power."

During our second group discussion, she explained the role of Mary as mediator during her youth in Colombia. She revealed that even though Jesus was also a mediator between humans and the remote God, Mary was a lower-level mediator with less power and access to God than Jesus had. She was believed to mediate between people (particularly women) and Jesus, not God. She was experienced as a woman who understood the pain of women but did not have much power of her own. Theresa explained,

> In South America, there are black and white images of God-women, but they are not considered powerful. You pray to them. You consider them mediators—that a woman will go to speak to the Virgin Mary because she's going to understand your pain, and perhaps will go and speak to Jesus and will help you, to help with your pain. But not because she's going to be able to make any decision and solve your problem.

During our first group discussion, Theresa had revealed that through reading the transcript of her interview, she realized her reason for leaving the Catholic Church (and Mary with it). It was directly connected with her powerlessness as a woman in the church and in her church-based culture in Colombia. Her leaving was connected with what she calls "the theme all of my life: that women are abused as long as they are not allowed to understand that they have control of their bodies."

She recounted that when she and her husband moved to the United States soon after being married, she did not want to get pregnant. She planned to continue her education. She was thrilled to move to the United States, expecting to find "heaven" because of women's rights. She explained that at that time, she was "submerged" in her culture, in which you went to the priest with any problem. She was afraid that she would be denied communion if she practiced birth control—the policy of the Catholic Church at that time.

In spite of her experiences of sexism in the church throughout her upbringing, she still held out hope that a priest in the United States would be different. She went to speak with a priest in New York, hoping that he would allow her to continue receiving communion even while using birth control. Instead, she found that the Catholic Church in New York was as patriarchal as in Colombia. The priest was furious with her and told her that it was her "duty" to have children and to take care of her husband. He told her that she "was going to be corrupted forever." Theresa responded by saying, "Good-bye. I don't need you." She never returned to the Catholic Church. After leaving the church and attempting unsuccessfully to find birth control while speaking no English, Theresa found herself pregnant three months into her marriage.

Theresa's "good-bye, Mary" reflected her anger at the church and her frustration that the Catholic Church in the United States failed to support her dreams of freedom as a woman. She did not need a weak woman like Mary, who could only sympathize with her oppression as a woman. She needed someone who could make a real, decisive difference in the concrete reality of her life as a woman. To her, Mary became an image of another submissive woman with no power, "completely controlled by men" and by the male-dominated church. Her frustration with Mary's lack of power (and her anger about the powerlessness of her mother, herself, and other women in her culture and the Catholic Church) caused her to leave Mary behind.

To this day, her distaste for the Catholic Church is revealed in her spirituality. She says, "I never cared for altars, or to make things and candles for them, because I always identify that with the Catholic Church." This is significant because making altars with multiple images for the divine on them, as well as other personal, spiritual objects, has became a common expression of spirituality in the feminist spirituality movement. Theresa did not resonate positively with these practices because she was still deeply angry at the Catholic Church for its rejection of her and of all women as powerful.

Self-Image, Gender, and Spirituality

After leaving Mary and Jesus behind, Theresa was left with only her remote God as an image for the divine. While her image of God as "remote and nothing else" was directly related to her experience of her father's remoteness, her experience of "emptiness," of feeling a "spiritual vacuum," may have resulted from more than just a simple identification of God with her father's remoteness. The feeling of emptiness might have resulted not only from her father's distance but also from the pain and anger that Theresa has repressed—about her father's control of her mother and of the family, directed at the remote Father God, and about her experiences of growing up female in a heavily patriarchal church and larger culture. The repression of these intense feelings can lead to a "hole" or "emptiness" where an image would be otherwise. As Rizzuto explains, a God-image that is associated with a painful relationship and with a corresponding painful self-representation can be repressed and defended against. She argues that "if massive repression of objects and the corresponding self-representations takes place, the individual may experience loneliness, emptiness, a fear of losing oneself, a fear of being abandoned, or when it is expressed in bodily metaphors, of having a hole where the objects supposedly belong."[2] Theresa's conflicted self-image, as well as her feeling of emptiness in relation to the divine, indicates that she has defended against feelings connected with her self-image, her father, and God.

Theresa's conflicted self-image became apparent when she began to describe herself in terms that did not match the stories that she told about herself. Theresa has experienced strong anger against sexism throughout her life. She has expressed that anger through leaving both the Catholic and Baptist churches, her clandestine membership in the National Organization for Women, her resistance against the nuns in her Catholic elementary school, her rebellion against her law professor (causing her to jeopardize her graduation from law school), and her assertion of herself in her marriage. However, while she has taken these dramatic actions of resistance, she has been conflicted in her self-image, seeing herself primarily as "the good girl," "passive," and "quiet."

She explained that growing up in a patriarchal family and culture in which she witnessed her mother's powerlessness, she did not like the dominance of men and the inequality between the sexes. When I asked how she felt about being a girl and about becoming a woman when she was growing up, she said, "I think that I hated it. But I was not aware of it . . . What I did not like was the inequality, that men had to be in control of my life. I didn't care for it." At the same time that she was angry and frustrated, however, she said that she was unable to articulate her frustration or to name her anger. She was "not aware" of hating it, even while she hated it.

The expectations of her culture—that she should be good, passive, and obedient—caused her to split off her awareness from her actual feelings, to repress and deny aspects of herself. Theresa developed a false self to comply with the ideology of her family, church, and culture. Theresa explained,

> Looking back, I lost my voice. Probably like so many feminists say, by twelve years old I was molded to say "Yes" and to say "No," regardless of my choice, and that is very sad. Because it took me my life, and the search of understanding why there was that contradiction between some feelings that I had and the reality of life.

While the other women in our discussion group saw Theresa as having enormous personal strength and as a person who has spoken out repeatedly against injustice throughout her life, without a community of support, Theresa did not see herself in that way. She said,

> But because I was so passive and because I accepted, I was kind of the good girl . . . I admire women that do have that strength to fight even since they were very small, because I don't know that I belong in that group. Even today, working as hard as I do, it is tough. My tendency is to be quiet, and I don't like it. It is one of those contradictions.

Ironically, in our second group discussion, Rosalyn said that she admired Theresa precisely for her strength to fight from an early age. Similarly, I told her that I was surprised by her self-characterization because when I had interviewed her three years earlier about her life story, I had seen her as "such a fighter."

She explained that although she has not seen herself as rebellious throughout her life, when she looks back on her life now she can recognize "small pockets" where she was rebellious. She recognized that leaving the Catholic Church to become Baptist was "total rebellion." She also now saw that "I was a total fighter, definitely, when it came to women's rights." Both in her professional and personal life, she experienced "tremendous struggle." She also saw that she has raised two adult daughters who are "completely independent and professional" and "speak their minds." She said, "So I wonder: Did I contribute a little bit in there. I don't know." She is now beginning to claim her power and to recognize the ways that she has been strong and resistant throughout her life.

By seeing herself as quiet, passive, and "the good girl," perhaps Theresa had been protecting herself from the full awareness of how strong, active, and disobedient she actually has been throughout her life. Because she has seen women as powerless and rebellion as risky, perhaps it has been too threatening for her to recognize her considerable strength and power. Perhaps her experience of losing herself and her voice at such a young age caused her to disassociate from her awareness of her self–to try to portray an image of a passive, quiet woman, both to herself and to others–while at the same time engaging in acts of significant resistance throughout her life.

The emptiness that she experienced in relation to her image of God as remote is probably connected both with the repression of her self-image as strong and powerful, and the repression of the pain and anger at being controlled by her father within a male-dominated culture. As she reclaims and affirms her power, and as she fully acknowledges and embraces her anger and pain in relation to her father and the larger male-dominated church and culture, she can perhaps begin to fill that emptiness with a sense of the divine love and power within herself.

Imaging the Divine Feminine

Imaging the divine in female form is extremely difficult for Theresa, however, because of her experiences of women as powerless. She struggles to imagine and relate to a female image for the divine. She explained in our second group discussion that after several years of "imagining God as a woman," it was still "almost impossible." She said, "I can see God in the ocean or mountains, but equating it with female is still very difficult . . . In my thinking, no woman could possibly be God . . . I always saw women as so powerless, including myself, so how could I qualify God with being a woman?" Thus, even though she had been trying to imagine the divine as feminine for several years, she could not "feel" it. She said that when she first imagined the divine in feminine terms, "it was so liberating. It was like 'Wow. This really gives value, the value that I've been looking for in God's eyes.'" However, her struggle, even years later, to maintain her sense of the value of women as created in the image of the feminine divine demonstrates the deeply rooted emotional level at which images are formed and at which they function.

When Rosalyn and Marie discussed their experiences of giving birth and of mothering as profoundly spiritual experiences of cocreating with God and of identifying themselves with the divine, Theresa interjected,

> I don't have those images, because, for me . . . birthing a child was depending more on the relationship you had with your husband, on the fact that you were married. And it could be a blessing or a punishment, because you didn't know exactly what was going to happen to the child or to the mother. So I never had any image of God in that respect . . . perhaps I was robbed from that experience.

Because of the Catholic Church's refusal to allow women to use birth control, she explained, "I felt that it was like a punishment for women to have children, because they would be more at the hands of men to be victims. In South America it is perceived that way."

Fear of Questioning the Church

Theresa explained that rather than seeing God in a female image, she grew up asking "'Where is God? Who creates such an imbalance between men and women?' Women and men were God's creation. Certainly, I felt that there was not equality. And I felt that it was God's problem." However, at the same time that she admitted having this frustration with God, she "always had that fear that was enormous." She felt terrified to challenge religious teachings. Yet she recognizes now that she resisted them consistently. Contradicting herself about whether she questioned religious teachings or God demonstrated the intense conflict and fear she still felt about it.

Theresa directed her questions largely toward herself. She blamed herself for having questions, thinking that she was "crazy" and so different from everyone else. Like many of the women in the Christian feminist spirituality movement, she felt totally alone with her questions and anger. She explained, "There were many times I questioned myself and said: 'Everybody's this way, and they go and they do. Why? Why am I so different?'" These feelings of frustration with herself were so difficult to face that she "didn't want to verbalize" them. She is able to verbalize them now because she has found so many other people like her at MMP. She has realized that she is similar to many women. Through finding this community of like-minded women, she has been able to free herself from her "fear, which was enormous."

Standing Alone

While Theresa has recently found this supportive community where she no longer feels crazy and alone, she looked back over her life and said that the theme of her life has been to stand alone when she has to. For example, when she left her Baptist church to become active in MMP she lost all of her friends from church. She recognized, however, that she had found "the answer to all of [her] problems" at MMP and could not go back to her church. She explained, "I thought, I will stay here, even if I don't have any friends for the rest of my life." Theresa draws strength and inspiration from a poem about Jesus titled "Solitary Man," which she has carried with her for years. She has kept it with her, she explained, because "I felt on many occasions, in spite of being surrounded by people, that I was totally alone. And that poem talks about that, being totally alone, but kind of Jesus supporting you somehow spiritually."

Theresa's sense of spiritual strength sustaining her when she stands alone causes her to identify spiritually with old, strong trees. Rather than a personal image for the divine, she recognizes a spiritual connection with trees, in which she sees herself. In our first group discussion, she recounted,

I have a tremendous attraction for old trees, those very big, old trees, that sometimes have weathered storms, and they are cracked up and down. Somehow I can identify with them. And I say, "That seems like . . . this is my life." That I have been so much up and down and this poor tree is all broken down, but it's still standing. That's how, perhaps, I feel "God is in this." I don't know how, but it's like the strength. That's the way that I can identify with an image of God, if that's the case.

For Theresa, the gender-neutral image of a tree was easier to see in terms of divine strength than a female, personal image. However, the tree allowed her to connect with God's presence in the strength within herself.

Spiritual Experience and Relationship with the Divine

When I asked Theresa about any significant spiritual or religious experiences, she told me that she has had only one in her life and that she had never told anyone about it until that moment. Her experience and her understanding of its significance paralleled her discussion of the tree image. She had the experience at a time of great conflict with her husband, when she was around thirty years old. She said, "It was a moment when I had to make the decision to get out from the marriage or not." She rushed home alone from a party with her husband's colleagues because of an argument and began to take a bath. She recounted,

I was at the end of my wits. I remember that I was absolutely ready to divorce. I said, "What am I going to do?" And I went in the bathtub and I opened the faucet and began to fill it up, and I got inside, and I was with my hands like this [gesture], crying desperately. Just saying, "I need some help." And I began to feel like someone, even now I feel this, like "Be at peace. Be with yourself."

At that moment, her husband came into the room and the experience was over. She decided to stay in her marriage.

When I asked her whether she felt a "sense of presence" or a "peace from within," she said that it was "absolutely a presence, no presence of anybody, but peace within myself." This peace spoke words of comfort to her, telling her to be calm and to stay where she was. In our second group discussion, she said that she experienced the "hand of God giving me some comfort." She experienced peace within herself as being the hand of God. Rather than sensing a presence external to herself, she experienced connection with divine peace and strength.

In spite of the power of this experience, however, she devalued her description, saying, "Kind of empty, right?" Even though she experienced divine peace within herself and recognized divine strength internally at that moment, and even though she experiences joyful transcendence in the arts, at the beach, and among trees, she still feels that she doesn't yet know God and that there is an emptiness, a vacuum, where God should be in her life.

For Theresa, there is a disconnect between spiritual experiences within herself—feelings of strength, comfort, peace, awe, joy—and a recognition of intimacy with the divine in those moments. For this reason, she could describe the most significant spiritual experience of her life as "kind of empty," even after saying that she could still feel the peace of that moment after more than thirty years. This emptiness seems to be an absence of relationship.

She desires the ability to "feel" and to "know" the divine so that she can pray and can speak about the divine in the glowing, loving terms that she hears other women use at MMP. While she feels that God is somehow within her in her strength to stand alone many times in her life, ultimately she has felt aloneness.

While her experiences of God within herself and within nature allow for a thea/ology that is imminent, implying a mystical sense of the divine throughout creation and within each person, Theresa does not feel the emotional, intimate connection with the divine implied by her thea/ology. Her image of God as remote, powerful, and masculine is so deeply rooted that she has not yet been able to embrace fully and to relate to the divine in herself and in nature. Perhaps she resists a feeling of mystical connection with the divine because she sees her experiences as void of what she thinks God is supposed to be, contradicting her deeply engrained image of a controlling, remote male God.

Prayer and Play

When I asked Theresa if she would be willing to write a prayer of invocation for the liturgy, she hesitated to do so alone. I offered to help her. She told me the feelings and concepts that she wanted to express and I turned them into prayer form. She gave me the following words to work with: "ocean, sand, sun, silence, peace . . . happiest and most peaceful at the beach and can image God at the beach, not in human form, but in majesty that I see and peacefulness of the moment . . . crave to carry that feeling with me all the time." In order to make her words into a prayer of invocation, I changed them very little. I simply addressed them to God, saying,

God of the ocean
God of the sand
God of the sun
God of the silence
God of peace,
we feel your peace
where the ocean, sun, and sand meet.
In our happiness,
we meet you,
not in human form,

but in the majestic beauty
and peace of the moment.
We pray that your peace and joy,
so palpable by the ocean,
might be with us this evening and always.
Amen.

Theresa said that the prayer conveyed well what she wanted to say in the invocation.

She explained in her interview that she wanted to pray in a way that "comes out from within" herself, yet she did not know how. However, this simple exercise demonstrated her ability to express her feelings about the divine, drawing them out from within. Where she struggled, however, was to allow herself to play with those words and to address God in an intimate way.

James Jones argues that many people in Western society have lost the ability to "play." They have lost the ability to engage their imaginations, to enter into space that is created in relationship—in-between the self and others—and that is experienced as a reenactment and imagination of interpersonal relationships. For some, this is because of painful interpersonal experiences in childhood, such that the child never experiences a safe place to play in relation to others, a place to imagine. For others, the reductionist mentality of Western culture that divides the world into "truth and falsity, reality and delusion"[3] becomes internalized to the point that they are no longer able to engage their imaginations, to enter an experience that transcends those rigid dichotomies.

Theresa seemed to be experiencing both aspects of difficulty playing. Because of her painful emotional associations with her parents, causing her to develop a false sense of herself, she was still in the process of trying to gain "a certain emotional distance between [her] present sense of self and the objects that have contributed to the texture of [her] psychic experience"[4] that would allow her to play with her image of the divine, with her sense of self, and with her representations of her parents.

At the same time, Theresa recognizes now that she has spent the majority of her life trying to achieve power as a woman in male terms. In discussing her decisions to pursue numerous degrees, she explained that she probably did so to make herself feel more powerful. She said,

> I've spent my life just studying and reading and thinking that I needed to have degrees and degrees to cover, to cover I don't know what, because, at the end, I realized that it was not important. I could be very contented with myself and my inner peace. So, but again, I needed to mature and grow to understand that.

Through her efforts to "cover" her sense of inadequacy and powerlessness as a woman, she also denied herself access to her imagination and her emotions, causing her to feel "frozen" for many years. She offered,

> I think that for many years I was frozen. That's a word I used to use for myself. Even thinking—Why did I go into law? And why did I want to become a judge? It was just very linear. I still think in those terms. Why perhaps for me imagining is so difficult. Because I did not allow myself to be *in there* at all.

She then shifted to saying directly that the group discussions had been "very therapeutic" for her. She had never spoken with anyone about most of the topics raised through this research, even though she is a professional counselor and has been active at MMP for years. She told me that she thought "no one would understand" and that her experiences were "too private." Significantly, she named the therapeutic nature of our work together after acknowledging that for most of her life she did not allow herself to be in her imagination at all. In this state of feeling frozen, she was unable to experience relationship with the divine. This process of exploring her images, her spirituality, and her relationships, within a supportive group of women, allowed her to move into the process of thawing out her imagination.

Transformation

The research process thus allowed Theresa to begin to access her imagination, to begin to unfreeze her feeling of disconnection with the divine and to honor the feelings of spiritual connection and personal power that she has experienced in her life. Theresa has been engaged in a long process of claiming her true self, her beliefs, and her feelings. However, this process—of engaging her imagination of the divine in light of her formative relationships, self-image, experiences as a woman in a male-dominated religion and society, and spiritual experiences—allowed her to recognize and to share aspects of herself that she had never shared before. James Jones asks, "What is the connection between the coming of a new sense of self and the development of a new image of God?"[5] Theresa was deeply engaged in working out the answer to that question for herself.

As she became more aware of her own strength and power, and as she affirmed that aspect of herself throughout her life, she was moving toward being able to embrace a feminine image for the divine. After I told her my theories about the connections between her imaging of the divine and her images of her parents, Theresa reflected,

> I feel in a way a little bit sorry that I couldn't identify with my mom, because the more I think about her, the more I realize that, yes, she was strong in many ways. And a great supporter of me,

and perhaps I needed to go fully through to understand that I also was strong in many ways and I never saw myself as being strong.

As her sense of herself and of her mother became more congruent with reality, she was more able to celebrate the strength of women and to recognize that the divine could be experienced in feminine form. Her imagination was becoming freer to embrace new images as her emotional associations connected with herself, her mother, and with women in general began to shift.

As Roberta Bondi said in the epigraph that begins this book: "To know myself as a woman in the image of God, to know God as Mother, and to know my own mother as a window into God: these three are inseparable. If one is implausible, to the heart, the other two are, as well."[6] For Theresa, it was becoming more plausible to her heart that women can represent the divine. Through embracing this reality, she can break down the separation in her mind between her image of a remote masculine God and her experiences of the divine within herself and within nature.

3

Christian Feminist Spirituality

The heart of this book is the reciprocal ethnography with a group of four women from Mary and Martha's Place (MMP), a nonprofit center for feminist theological study and spirituality. I chose to focus on the lives of a particular small group of women within the context of a larger community and a national movement for several reasons. First, imagination of the divine is unique for each individual. It is therefore crucial to focus in depth on the stories and experiences of particular people rather than to generalize. As Abu-Lughod argues, researchers need to be "wary" of generalization for two reasons. First, "as part of a professional discourse of objectivity and expertise, it is inevitably a language of power. It is the language of those who seem to stand apart from and outside of what they are describing." Second, "by producing the effects of homogeneity, coherence, and timelessness, it contributes to the creation of 'cultures.'" General ethnographic descriptions of people's beliefs or actions risk obscuring "contradictions, conflicts of interest, doubts, and arguments, not to mention changing motivations and historical circumstances."[1]

When speaking about Christian religious communities, the language used by church hierarchies and academic theologians often "contributes to the creation of 'cultures'" through generalizations about accepted beliefs and actions. The effect of this generalizing language is much like what Abu-Lughod describes.

To be fair, religious professionals and academic theologians often discuss issues of conflict and change within their communities. However, even systematic theologians who yearn to challenge sexism and racism in religious communities and society frequently rely on generalizations when writing about "experience." My hope is that by taking the voices and stories of particular women seriously I can help to demonstrate the complexity and uniqueness of individual's experiences, relationships, and imagination of the divine. These particular stories can challenge sexism and racism in a way that generalizing language cannot.

Alongside this emphasis on individual uniqueness, I worked with a group of individuals who are part of a shared community. This allowed me to explore the dynamic interplay between individuals and their community—the ways that individuals both shape and are shaped by community. In addition, the women already had developed a certain level of trust with one another because of their shared investment and experiences in the community. Establishing trust was crucial for our discussions.

My second reason for choosing to work with a group of women actively involved in MMP was to interview people who had been exploring their images of the divine and working to transform them for a significant period of time. I was interested to find out what difference this had made for them and why. I also wanted to explore what that process had been like for them: easy? hard? painful? exhilarating? all of the above? By choosing to work with people who are already engaged in this process, I hoped to reveal the dynamics involved with imagination and the divine as they are being actively engaged.

I asked the individual women to be part of the interview group because they represented diversity within the membership of MMP. They varied in age—from late twenties, to middle thirties, to fifties and sixties. One was ordained and the rest were laywomen. Two were Episcopalian, one was United Methodist, and one had been both Roman Catholic and Baptist. Two held graduate degrees and all had college degrees. One was Latina, born and raised in South America, while the other three were European American from the southern United States.

The lack of African American and Asian American women in the study is a weakness. Like most of the feminist spirituality movement, the membership of MMP is predominantly European American, middle-class, educated women.[2] A few African American women and Asian American women occasionally attend the annual large conferences sponsored by MMP, but they are only connected tangentially through that attendance. One African American woman, who had been more significantly involved with the programs and whom I had hoped to interview, moved out of the state before the research began. Theresa was one of few Hispanic women involved with the center.

While perspectives from women of African and Asian descent would have added greatly to this study, I hope that this study will serve as an impetus for further work on these issues in the African American, Asian American, and Hispanic communities, as well as in those rare diverse communities that have a substantial representation of people from a variety of backgrounds. Theresa, one of the interviewees, opined that the gender dynamics of her family and of her relationship to the Catholic Church were very common among the Hispanic women whom she sees in counseling and that many Hispanic women might benefit from engaging in a similar process. I hope that the practical guide in the final chapter will help small groups in a variety of settings explore their images of the divine and the ways that they are shaped by their life experiences, relationships, and culture. I have provided guidelines that are flexible so that the program can be adjusted depending on the cultural and social context in which it is being used.

I also chose to work with three European American women and one Hispanic woman in this study because issues of "race" are usually assumed to relate to people of color but not to "white" European Americans. By interrogating the meaning of whiteness for the three European American women, I was able to explore some of the complex and unique ways that a white racial identity can be experienced. The women's stories of their experiences of race challenged my generalizations about the socialization of white Southern women while also demonstrating the pervasiveness of white supremacy in the larger culture. Their stories revealed the depth to which issues of racial injustice have shaped their families and themselves. Our discussions pushed them to consider the ways that their racial identities and their internalized racial and gender stereotypes have shaped their imaging of the divine. Theresa's experiences of being a person of the dominant, majority ethnicity in her home country of Colombia and then of experiencing racial discrimination as a woman of color in the United States demonstrate that the experience of ethnic or racial identity is fluid depending on cultural context.

In the following sections, I provide an overview of the MMP community as the context for this research, placing it in the larger national contexts of both the Christian and non-Christian (post-Christian, post-Jewish) feminist spirituality movements. I then describe the methods used in the research process.

Context: Mary and Martha's Place

Mary and Martha's Place is an extrachurch nonprofit center devoted to women's spirituality and feminist theological study. An Episcopal priest and a group of laywomen who had been meeting together to study feminist theology for several years established the center in 1994. Since its inception, Mary and Martha's Place (referred to as MMP) has affected the lives of over seven hundred women in the Atlanta area. Approximately two hundred are involved regularly, while hundreds more participate in large events or read the newsletters. Programming includes several weekly book-study groups, liturgies for both the winter and the summer solstices, annual conferences, and a monthly meeting for young women.

For some of the women involved, MMP is a continuation of a lifetime of seeking and activism. For others, MMP is a place to voice questions that they have been afraid to ask anywhere else. MMP seems to attract women who are searching intensely for spiritual growth. For many of them, the focus on spirituality has become more urgent during midlife.

The opportunity to combine feminism with spirituality is one of the great appeals of MMP and one of the strong emphases of the spiritual journeys of many of the women at this point in their lives. This trend also reflects a larger cultural interest in the intersection between feminism and spirituality.

Participation in MMP is empowering for many of the women because of its primary belief in "a woman's worth." This is symbolized in the honoring of the divine feminine and of women's experiences and in the symbols of women's lives seen as sacred. It is expressed in the creativity of the participants being honored and encouraged. It is also shown through the mission of MMP to support women in their efforts to be empowered as leaders in the larger culture.

MMP provides a place where many of the women can honor their own traditions while looking at them critically. This rootedness in tradition and the respect for its positive aspects allow participants to engage in critique without fear of losing everything they have held dear. The director encourages the members to hold on to the valuable aspects of their Christian tradition, and many of the women feel that they could not lose the Christian part of their identity even if they tried. Paradoxically, the ecumenical nature of MMP allows many of the women to feel more rooted in their own denominations as they learn from the women around them and come to understand their own heritage more clearly.

Feminist Spirituality Movements in Context

MMP is representative of a national Christian feminist spirituality movement as well as a larger feminist spirituality movement that includes a variety of religious perspectives. Ethnographic studies of both movements reveal that the major themes I found at MMP resonate loudly with thousands of women throughout the United States.

In a comprehensive ethnographic study of the contemporary feminist spirituality movement in the United States, Cynthia Eller focused on women who located themselves firmly outside of traditional religions. In defining feminist spirituality, Eller observes, "Feminist spirituality is unique in its determination to remain true to the concerns of women, both politically and spiritually. And it is religiously innovative, always pushing beyond tradition, and often leaving it altogether in it search for spiritual resources that will prove powerful and transforming for women."[3] While MMP is firmly rooted in the Christian tradition, its programming draws extensively on the philosophy and practices of feminist spirituality. It is solidly in the center of the Christian feminist spirituality movement, where the two traditions are brought together to create a synthesis of beliefs, patterns of interaction, and religious practices.

Sociological Profiles of the Feminist Spirituality Movement

Most of the participants at MMP also fit with the majority of women in Eller's "sociological profile of the feminist spirituality movement." She says that the profile "can be summed up like this: white, of middle-class origins, fairly well-educated (beyond high school), of Jewish or Christian background (usually, though not always, having had a significant amount of religious training), in their thirties and forties,"[4] although there are also a "healthy number of older women" as well. Interestingly, the women at MMP are largely above the average age of the feminist spirituality movement in general.

Many of the women in midlife are being introduced to feminism for the first time and experience it as a time of great crisis. Perhaps the relative age difference between the majority of the women of MMP, who mainly remain connected to Christianity, and the majority of spiritual feminists, who mostly leave traditional religion, helps to explain the greater tendency for MMP to emphasize remaining connected to tradition. The quick growth of MMP demonstrates that a large pool of women in U.S. society who are within Christian churches are longing for feminist engagement with their traditions.

Feminist Spirituality and the Divine Feminine

Imaging the divine as feminine is a central aspect of the feminist spirituality movement. The image of Goddess helps women to claim their own power and to revalue aspects of their lives that have been devalued in a sexist society—their bodies, their sexuality, nurturance, and connection with the earth and with beauty. While the four women I interviewed did not use the term "Goddess" often, their struggles with imaging the divine as female revolved around some of the themes raised by Eller, particularly around reclaiming women's sexuality, childbirth, childrearing, and homemaking as positive, strong values rather than as signs of women's lesser value. Our discussions illuminated the difficult, long process for these women of being able to see women (including themselves and their mothers) as powerful and worthy representatives of the divine image in the face of a lifetime of the devaluation of women's traditional roles in and contributions to society.

Context: The Christian Feminist Spirituality Movement

While MMP is representative of some of the central aspects of the larger feminist spirituality movement, the women of MMP revealed significant differences as well. MMP is representative of a particularly Christian feminist spirituality movement that has grown significantly over the past few decades.

Christian spiritual feminists live in a state of tension between the Christian tradition and their feminist commitments, both of which they love passionately. The strong attachment that women from MMP have for their "tradition" demonstrates that Christian practices and communities have provided them with many life-affirming experiences, values, and beliefs. However, the fact that a number of the women felt they were in a constant state of struggle, tension, and even "war" with their tradition indicates that many Christian churches have not transformed in a way that responds to their needs and praxis and that they have, instead, caused some women to feel they are in danger of harm if they choose to fight for what they believe should be changed. The urgency of their desire to remain part of their tradition and the difficulty that they experience in doing so also demonstrate that churches have been negligent in responding to the needs of people who are educated about theology and religion and deeply committed to Christianity yet who need community support for questioning and education.

Ultimately, the stories of the women interviewed at MMP call attention to a growing cultural shift that, if not attended to thoughtfully and with care, will lead toward greater alienation between institutional Christianity and the larger culture. Large numbers of people are demonstrating a hunger for spirituality and religion through a growing trend of reading numerous books on those subjects. The women interviewed had been profoundly shaped by their immersion in Christianity and in a Christian-based culture. However, active involvement with the Christianity that shaped them was proving to carry a high price to their well-being.

While Christian leaders often criticize American culture for being too individualistic, the stories of the women I interviewed indicate a longing for community and a willingness to struggle for it. However, they also demonstrate that church communities are often responsible for alienating many people who long for a religious community in which they can speak back to generalizations, doctrines, and assumptions. People experience authentic vulnerability, relationship, and spiritual experience within the context of community when they are allowed to question honestly with one another. Christian feminist spirituality groups throughout the country are providing a context of "safe" religious community for thousands of women like those at MMP who long for a just Christian community that embraces and empowers women and allows for honest, critical questioning. These groups bridge the gap between traditional Christianity and post-Christian feminist spirituality but not without struggle and a great emotional cost for the women involved.

The findings from a national study of such Christian feminist spirituality groups, conducted in the early 1990s and published under the name *Defecting in Place,* revealed that at that time, thousands of women throughout the United States were struggling with similar tensions and found hope and empowerment in community with other women. Winter, Lummis, and Stokes sent a questionnaire to approximately 8,000 women, in all fifty U.S. states, who were or had been involved in women's spirituality groups with a feminist orientation. The majority of the 3,746 women who responded to the questionnaire were still actively involved with their traditional Christian congregations and denominations.[5] They approached the project with several major questions: "Why do feminist women remain within congregations? Just how alienated are they from the institutional church? How does their involvement in feminist spirituality groups made up of like-minded women affect their relationship to their denomination and their congregation?"[6] Their findings reveal patterns similar to those of the women of MMP. The researchers explain,

> Our report concludes that a growing number of women today are taking responsibility for their own spiritual lives. Many of these women are still affiliated with the church. Many belong to a parish or congregation. Many are active participants in their local church. Many hold significant leadership roles as clergy, lay ministers, educators, administrators. With regard to institutional religion, these women are "defecting in place."[7]

Many of the women who responded were involved in small feminist spirituality groups. The authors discovered well over one hundred such groups throughout the country. They varied in size and emphasis but they generally attracted women between ages thirty-five and sixty-five in order to provide mutual support and deepen feminist awareness and to share leadership. Most of these groups, like MMP, were outside denominational structures.[8] However, the authors found that participation in a feminist spirituality group supported and enabled participation in a Christian denomination and congregation for most of the women surveyed.[9]

The authors provide a list of common characteristics of the majority of the feminist spirituality groups:

> For most groups in this study, the group arose out of a felt need, is fairly small and relatively stable, meets regularly, ordinarily in homes, compensates for what is lacking in institutional religion, contributes to the raising of feminist awareness, liberates individual women, deepens spiritual connections, results in group loyalty and bondedness, is feminist with or without the label, [and] continues only as long as it is meaningful.[10]

This description fits precisely the small group of women who gathered to study feminist theology around a kitchen table in the early 1990s and eventually went on to establish MMP.

The national context that Lummis, Winter, and Stokes describe reveals that MMP is solidly representative of a larger religious movement. In discussing these findings, I place them in conversation with my research at MMP to demonstrate the resonance between the two studies and the place of MMP within a larger national context.

Feeling alone in congregations. Many of the women felt alone in their congregations. The authors theorize that many may simply not know about other women in their congregations who were struggling with similar issues. They explain,

> One of the assumptions underlying this project is that feminists in parishes and congregations have not "come out" because the climate has not been conducive and support has not been visible. We hope that this study will help other feminist women find their voice so that they might find one another.[11]

This assumption was confirmed by my interviews with women from MMP. Several women expressed fear about making their beliefs known in their congregations. Julie explained that she was stunned to see a woman from the choir of her church at an MMP conference. She assumed that the people at her church were not interested in feminist theology. Theresa expressed her "tremendous fear" about questioning the teachings of the church. She felt alone and wondered if she was "crazy" for having so many questions. Rosalyn explained that she felt alone with her discomfort in churches.

Longing for spirituality and taking responsibility for their own spiritual lives. Many of the women surveyed for *Defecting in Place* expressed that they were on a spiritual search, looking for spiritual growth and fulfillment that they did not find in their congregations. The authors explain,

> Many women feel let down by their churches. They feel deprived, discounted, and stifled in areas of significance to them. One such area of concern to women is their own spiritual life. Women in eleven different [Protestant] denominations living in twenty states located all across the country wrote that they are not being spiritually fed by their churches. Both clergywomen and laywomen spoke of being spiritually starved or spiritually confined in congregations that are "largely irrelevant to my spiritual growth" and sometimes even a source of psychic injury."[12]

Many of these women were finding spiritual sustenance in feminist spirituality groups. The women at MMP expressed similar feelings about their longing for spiritual growth and their frustration with a lack of opportunities for growth in their churches.

For many of the women quoted in *Defecting in Place*, their congregations felt spiritually stifling because of their exclusivity and failure to address social justice issues. The authors explain,

> It is difficult for many women to entrust their spiritual development to a church that makes little effort to reach out to and welcome those who are poor, those who are ethnic minorities, and others who are

in need. They say their congregations avoid addressing issues that affect us all, issues women consider vital to spiritual integrity . . . Some women are strongly critical of the church's response to single women, lesbian women, and women of color, and challenge its attitudes regarding marital status, sexual orientation and race.[13]

Similar themes emerged in my research. Frustration with their churches about social justice issues, particularly about the exclusion of gay and lesbian people, the refusal of ordination to women in the Catholic Church, and discrimination against women within both Protestant and Catholic churches was strongly felt among a number of the interviewees at MMP.

Being involved in social justice work. Involvement in a feminist spirituality group corresponded with a greater likelihood of being involved in action for social justice. While feminist spirituality is often criticized as being apolitical, the involvement in a group that is both spiritually nourishing and encouraging of one's work for justice leads to greater involvement in social justice action. Women who "most want inclusive language in all church services and women who are in feminist spirituality groups that use female imagery and names for God, or who themselves image God to some extent as 'Goddess' give *more* time, not less time, to social justice causes."[14]

This is congruent with what I found in interviewing women at MMP. Most of the women with whom I spoke had been activists or were involved in social service. They were all passionate about justice and social issues. The authors of *Defecting in Place* conclude, "This study demonstrates that feminist spirituality, especially when reinforced by group participation, helps women to be more involved in social justice actions and leads to political actions . . . Women who image God as female are advocates of social justice and support political actions for systemic transformation."[15]

Having multiple images and names for the divine. The majority of the women who responded to the survey preferred to use multiple images and names to refer to the divine. They chose names and images that arose out of their experiences of the divine. Women were naming and imaging the divine and themselves out of their own experiences.

Many of the women quoted in *Defecting in Place,* like the women of MMP, demonstrated imaginative exploration of *experiences* of divine presence in themselves, in people and animals they loved, and in the whole of the natural world. The women experienced the divine presence as real, yet at the same time, mediated through imagination.

These examples from *Defecting in Place* demonstrate a journey through divine images similar to the process revealed by the women I interviewed. Images are a means through which divine presence can be experienced. Lummis, Winter, and Stokes report that a Catholic Sister in her fifties from the Northeast stated briefly, "I experience God as a presence in my life, more as a spirit, with images and symbols being important to that experience."[16]

A UCC woman in her forties from the American West demonstrated the cyclical, progressive nature of the spiritual journey in relation to images and divine presence, saying, "I must admit that as I get older, I pray and sing less in images than in presence."[17] A Catholic woman in her forties, from the South Central region of the United States, described her struggle in relation to new images for the divine, explaining that different images were more helpful for her on particular days. She said,

> Growing into and owning feminine images of God seems to require a being present to the expressed pain of women who have suffered discrimination and slavery to the patriarchal powers of the church. I mourn the slowness of the clergy to help us bring to birth this enlarged experience of God which we have been deprived of all these centuries . . . It is a struggle to grow beyond one's secure understanding of the Divine into something unknown, uncon-firmed, untaught, and for which one may become the target of ridicule or criticism. Yet it is a Way, once taken, one cannot return to that old comfortable place. The comfort of knowing a "good Mother God" and all the attending rich symbols and metaphors fills me with joy some days, and confusion other days, when I do not know what to do with that old and familiar Father, and God becomes once again mystery-unity-source-creator-love. It is a struggle worth taking, but gives me pause before initiating another to join me on the Way.[18]

She turned to genderless, nonpersonal language for the divine when the struggle of how to relate to her old Father-God image and still experi-ence the joy of knowing God as Mother became too frustrating. Thus, while addressing the issue of gender in her images for the divine was of great importance to her, the turn to nonpersonal names for the divine, drawn from spiritual experience, allowed her relief and a freedom to relate to the holy in a way that did not highlight gender.

Interestingly, the authors found that "images such as 'Encompassing Presence,' 'Wisdom,' 'Liberator,' and 'Help' are considerably more a part of their overall conception of God than images of God as 'Father,' 'Mother,' 'Jesus,' or 'Goddess,' or even 'Father-Mother' or the Trinity (Father, Son, Spirit)."[19] However, most women did not have just one primary image for the divine; they used multiple, changing names and images when relating to or speaking of the divine. The authors explain,

> Our data show that the great majority of women respondents are inclined to have shifting, changing images of God and not one or two clear, definite images. They do see God as Father or Mother at least to *some* extent, but only one-fifth (21%) say they envision God as Father or as Mother to a *great* extent. Half the sample see

Jesus as a major figure in their image of God. But if women were to choose one image that is most important or pivotal in their conception of God, it would be "Encompassing Presence."[20]

Although I did not ask the women from MMP to list and rank their many names or images for the divine, the same patterns revealed in these results were reflected in their stories. Several of the women I interviewed spoke of experiencing God primarily as "presence." Like the women quoted earlier, they alternated between gendered images for the divine, including the struggle to move beyond the limitations of their old Father-God image and their experiences of the divine as a presence that is beyond gender. Both were important aspects of their spirituality. The journey beyond the old, white man image of God from childhood involved affirming both feminine imagery and language for the divine and imagery and language that evoked the mysterious presence of the divine in all of creation. They enjoyed moving between and among different images and varied language. This movement allowed for a more genuine expression of their experiences of the divine than one, solitary image could allow.

Interestingly, while the majority of women had multiple images for the divine, a person's cultural and religious background had a significant effect on the grouping of images that would be most meaningful for that person.[21] For example, African American and Asian women were more comfortable referring to God as Mother. A separate national study done in 1991 found that this was because both of these cultural groups consider the role of mother to be a powerful role.[22] Additionally, African American and Hispanic women were more likely to say that Jesus was a primary personification of the divine for them. In contrast, the majority of European American Catholic and liberal Protestant women were more comfortable imaging "Goddess" rather than a parental image for the divine. For many who imaged the divine as Goddess, Jesus was compatible with Goddess. These women were still distinctly Christian, even as they imaged the divine partly in a strong female image.[23] The authors explained that most of the women who espoused Goddess imagery for the divine did not do so exclusively. In church contexts, language about God tended to be gendered in terms of "Father, Son, or Mother God," even while most women did not name these as their most central images or names for the divine.[24]

Lummis, Winter, and Stokes do not distinguish between images and names that the women preferred to use and supported intellectually and those images that were perhaps more deeply rooted due to their upbringing in the church. This leads to confusion about which images were actually the most influential in the women's lives and which were the images that they believed *should* be most central. So, for example, while many might say that nongendered language is the most important, a number of the quotes provided from the questionnaires demonstrate that they are engaged in a struggle to move beyond the male images that they had learned to relate to for most of their lives.

One woman explained, "While my image of God is definitely expanding to include the feminine, I can't say I'm totally comfortable with it yet. It's difficult to let go of what has been culturally engrained for years."[25] A Presbyterian minister in her thirties from the Southeast offered, "God 'the father' still dominates my image of God, even though I try very much to change that to a more female image. I regret that my gut feeling image of God is male. Intellectually, I reject a completely male image of God, but twenty years of indoctrination is hard to overcome."[26] Thus, the "gut feeling image of God" is often in competition with new images that women wanted to embrace. For many women, perhaps, the "cluster" of images that they endorsed in their answers to the questionnaire included both types of images. The comfort in moving among different images for most women in the study and for the women I interviewed at MMP is probably derived in part from a continual struggle to alternate between old, patriarchal, "gut feeling" images and new feminist images.

The "Network of Women's Centers
for Spirituality and Liberation"

The Christian feminist spirituality movement has grown significantly since the research for *Defecting in Place* was conducted in the early 1990s. Just as MMP grew from a small informal gathering of women around a kitchen table into an incorporated nonprofit organization, centers similar to MMP have grown up around the United States. There is no mention of nonprofit centers like MMP in *Defecting in Place*. However, in 2009 there is a vibrant network of Christian feminist spirituality nonprofit centers throughout the United States. These centers have developed a network of relationships among themselves, helping to strengthen the Christian feminist spirituality movement as a whole. Thus, the Christian feminist spirituality movement has grown more institutionalized over the past two decades. Centers are able to reach out to many more people than the informal groups of the early 1990s were, providing unique resources and opportunities for spiritual growth and empowerment.

Since the early 1990s, nonprofit groups similar to MMP have been established across the United States. They include the Cedar Hill Enrichment Center in Gainesville, Georgia; Holy Ground in Asheville, North Carolina; Greenfire in Tenants Harbor, Maine; The Leaven Center in Lansing, Michigan; Springbank Retreat Center in coastal South Carolina; and the Women's Interfaith Institute in Seneca Falls, New York. While each center differs slightly in terms of emphasis, they all offer programming focused on feminist spirituality, ecology, and social justice. Most of the centers own their own land and offer retreat opportunities and liturgical and educational programs related to the earth. All the centers have boards of directors and extensive donor lists. They are involved in the administrative work of financing and running a nonprofit organization. All the centers were founded and are directed by ordained Protestant women or Catholic Sisters. They consider this work their ministry.

MMP is thus solidly within a national movement. In addition, this national movement is part of a larger global movement of women making connections between spirituality, theology, women's empowerment, and ecology.[27] I focus exclusively on the context of the United States in this book because adequate ethnographic exploration of the varied cultures and sites of these movements proved unwieldy for this research. However, feminist spirituality is on the rise and on the move in varied forms throughout the world.

These centers make connections between spirituality, feminism, ecology, and social justice. They offer women (and, as one of the directors of Cedar Hill Enrichment Center told me, "a few good men") the opportunity to nourish their spirits in supportive contexts that encourage health and wholeness for women, for all of humanity, and for the earth. In their educational programs, they emphasize receptivity to and inclusion of various religious traditions as well as practical guidance for women longing to be effective agents for social change.

The voices of individual women from MMP therefore represent a growing, national movement that will surely continue to grow as it becomes more organized and well-known. While their individual stories are unique, they reflect larger cultural patterns at work. Their interviews demonstrated that their lives not only were shaped by and constitutive of the work of MMP but are also interwoven with the lives of thousands of women and men on similar paths throughout the United States and the world. In the following section, I provide a detailed account of the unique process of interviews, group discussions, and liturgy that we engaged in for this research.

Reciprocal Ethnography

For my research with four women from MMP, we followed a method of reciprocal ethnography.[28] After conducting individual interviews with each woman, I provided them with the transcripts of all four of the interviews. We met for two group discussions in which we explored common themes and questions that emerged from reading all the transcripts. In addition, the women were able to critique, challenge, and confirm my theories about their imaging of the divine. Finally, we created a liturgy together to embody the themes most significant for the group. We invited other women from MMP to participate in the liturgy and a discussion that followed. In this context, the women were colearners and analyzers with me. The discussion groups and liturgy process became an educational experience as part of the research process.

While the process of providing written transcripts for the whole group to analyze and engage in discussion would not work in many contexts (nonliterate contexts or cultures where such personal discussions might be discouraged), it was an ideal process for women from MMP who were accustomed to discussions about texts and about their spirituality, beliefs, and struggles. In addition to the ethical benefits of testing my analyses with them, the discussions served to illumine issues and insights that I never would have understood in the same way when working alone. As Elaine Lawless explains,

> Our goal is understanding, but attaining one level of understanding is only to acknowledge that yet another level of understanding lies just beyond our ken. Through reading, thinking, and dialogue, then, we aspire to that next level of understanding. Understanding is not realized here as a generalized fact or conclusion but rather as a celebration of the multiplicity of experiences and points of view that are present in the group.[29]

Through this reciprocal process, I present a more complex, nuanced portrait of the dynamics involved in imagination of the divine.

The process followed these stages:

1. *Individual interviews.* I engaged each woman in an intensive individual interview so that we might explore the unique dynamics at work in her imagination of the divine. The questions in each interview followed the same general format although follow-up questions varied depending on the initial responses:

    a. *Life story.* Tell me about your life, your life story; how you came to be where you are today.

    b. *Relationships.* What have been the most important and influential relationships in your life? How would you describe these people? How would you describe your relationships with them? How have the relationships (and the people) changed over time?

    c. *Childhood/gender.* How would you describe yourself as a child? When you were growing up, how did you feel about being a girl? What was that experience like for you? How did you feel about becoming a woman? What were your feelings about boys and men?

    d. *Race/ethnicity.* Do you remember when you first understood that you were a part of a particular ethnic or racial group? How did you feel about being part of your group? What feelings or questions did you have about people of different racial or ethnic groups?

e. *Images of the divine.* How did you picture the divine when you were a child? What did you imagine God to be like? How has your image of the divine changed over time?

f. *Spiritual/religious experiences.* Take a moment and remember a significant spiritual experience. Can you describe it for me? How did you feel? How did you experience the divine? What is the significance of the experience for you?

g. *Practices.* What spiritual or religious practices have been important for you? Why?

h. *Mary and Martha's Place.* How has your involvement with MMP influenced your image of the divine? Your self-image? Your relationships with significant people in your life?

2. *Transcription, sharing, and analysis.* I sent all four of the transcripts to every person in the group. In preparation for our group discussions, I asked them to read the transcripts for common themes or differences. I also asked them to notice any insights or questions that were raised for them.

   Before our first group discussion meeting, I read the transcripts for connections between experiences of self, important relationships, and relationship with the divine at particular points in the life stories. I paid special attention to dynamics of race and gender as they impacted these relationships. I was careful not to force patterns but was inevitably influenced by my engagement with the literature. In addition, I looked for commonalities and differences between the women's responses. I identified common themes and dynamics in their stories. I developed the questions for our group discussions out of my analysis.

3. *Group discussions.* In the third stage of the research, we gathered for two meetings at Marie's home. Before sharing my readings and theories with them, I asked them if they had seen any major patterns or themes that emerged in a particular story or in the stories when read together. I asked them if they saw any significant differences between the stories when read together and if any questions were raised for them when reading the transcripts.

   After they shared their responses, I offered my observations about significant themes that they had omitted, asking for their feedback to see if my observations were consistent with their experiences. In addition, I joined in the discussion occasionally, reflecting on their insights or offering my own experience. I shared relevant theories that influence my perspective with them as a way of testing the theories and expanding on them. In these discussions, the women's stories and interpretations became part of the critical imagination process about imaging the divine, in dialogue with the theories that we brought to the discussion. My intention was to create an environment where we could learn together as a community, with all perspectives respected and valued in the learning process.

The first discussion followed this free-flowing format, touching on the themes listed below as well as other topics that arose from the reflection on the themes. I did not intervene often with directed questions. I allowed the discussion to flow naturally in order to gain insight into which topics sparked the most interest and enthusiasm among the group. We did not discuss the themes in the exact order listed here because the participants raised most of them spontaneously at different times. I did not provide them with a list of themes. Instead, I listened for which themes stood out for them. I offered my insights and asked follow-up questions after they had shared their reflections.

In the second discussion, I engaged them in a direct discussion about race and imaging the divine. I asked them, "What would it be like if you imaged the divine as a Black Goddess?" The discussion that followed touched on a variety of issues in relation to imaging the divine as both raced and gendered. I then focused on each individual's story, offering my interpretation of the dynamics involved in their imaging the divine throughout their lives and asking them for feedback on my interpretations. The first discussion allowed us to build a community of trust so that they could feel safe during these more personal and challenging discussions. I transcribed the discussions and sent copies to all the women. I asked the women to read the transcriptions in preparation for our creation of a liturgy together.

4. *Liturgy.* In the fourth stage of the research, we met and created a liturgy together based on the themes raised in the individual interviews and group discussions. We invited other members of the MMP community to join us for the liturgy several weeks later. After the liturgy, we discussed their reactions to the liturgy and the themes it invoked.

I chose to engage the group in the process of creating and leading a liturgy for several reasons. First, the experience of liturgy allowed for imaginative engagement with the issues that we had discussed in ways that our conversations could not. As mentioned in previous chapters, images are experienced in worship or liturgy at emotional and spiritual levels that are pre- or postverbal understandings. Images for the divine can be formed and changed during liturgy in ways that are not reached by rational discourse. As Marjorie Procter-Smith explains, liturgy is largely an exercise of the imagination. Imagination "makes possible a sense of paradox and multivalence which is necessary for authentic liturgical celebration; that is to say, it makes symbols possible."[30]

In the exploration of imaging the divine, it was thus crucial for us to engage the issues we had explored in a liturgical context, and not simply in a discussion format that primarily engaged our rationality. A mentality of "paradox and multivalence" pervades the feminist spirituality movement in relation to images and symbols for the divine. The creation and enactment of the liturgy as a part of this reciprocal ethnography allowed us to experience a mode of relating to the divine that is prevalent in the feminist spirituality movement.

The second reason for creating and leading liturgy together as a part of the research process was that it provided a space for the group to integrate our discussions into a form that we could share with others as well as one another. It served as a culmination of our discussions, allowing the women an opportunity to reflect on the totality of the interview and discussion process and to generate a creative response that addressed the themes that they found most central. It allowed us to embody those themes in liturgical, imaginative form.

Finally, the process of creating and leading the liturgy also had unanticipated benefits for the research. The women decided to choose excerpts from their interviews or the group discussions as readings for liturgy. They also each brought images of the divine that were most important and evocative for them. Their choices of both texts and images allowed me to gain a more profound understanding of the meaning of the process for them. Each woman chose texts and images that demonstrated growth of awareness during the process of the interviews and discussions. The liturgy thereby reflected the growth process of individuals within the group as well as of the group as a whole.

4

Second Story

Julie

Julie is a European American woman in her early thirties. She became involved in Mary and Martha's Place several years ago when she moved to Atlanta after working in China for a year. At the time of the research, she worked in hospital administration and was involved in the discernment process for the priesthood in the Episcopal Church. She has since graduated from seminary and has been called to serve as an Episcopal rector.

Imaging the Divine

Julie grew up actively trying not to picture God. In her activist, intellectual, feminist, and antiracist household, she learned very early that the image of God that she saw in the larger culture—that of an old white man with a beard—was inadequate. She explained that as a child, she liked to picture Jesus. She pictured him as a "very white" man with "flowing, brown locks and the beard and the robe . . . I thought he looked like a really friendly guy." She also liked to picture Jesus as a lion, like the Christ figure of Aslan the Lion in C. S. Lewis's books. She explained that part of the appeal of imaging the divine as Jesus when she was a small child was that she had learned of Jesus' love for little children. She imagined Jesus being present with her, protecting and watching over her as she slept, and experienced his presence as comforting. Relating to Jesus became more difficult for her as she grew older however, because, she said, "there are the Jesus people who were just so into Jesus and believing in Jesus—they were a little bit creepy."

Julie experienced imaging the divine as difficult. She found the image of God as an old, white man deeply engrained in her imagination. She explained,

> I think that imagining God over the years was always so hard because I knew that I didn't believe in a God who was an old man, who seemed cranky a lot . . . I knew that was not what I believed, but it was hard to get that picture out of my mind. You know, like media images, God is this all-powerful, strong man, who is kind of elderly too.

Her mother exposed her to stories of goddesses and gods from other religions and her father instilled in her an intellectual approach to religion. However, she found that the dominant Christian images were deeply rooted in her emotional memory, so that alternative stories or intellectual skepticism could not uproot them. She explained,

> And so I guess I had these core images in my head of God as the old man and Jesus as the white beautiful child. But I knew, again early on, that that's not what I wanted personally, and I didn't know whether you should go to some other culture for that or if it was all a big lie. So I think I spent a lot of time trying not to picture.

Her exposure to many religious traditions and a mythical, metaphorical consciousness about the divine did not help her as a child to find comfort and clarity in her personal image for God. Although she recognized that she didn't have all the answers, she was not able to "hold on to anything in particular." She was left with the dominant image from her Episcopal upbringing and from the larger culture.

Imaging and Relationships

Even though she imaged God as an old, white man, she did not identify God as a Father. She realized during her interview that she did not like to image God as a parent—either as Father God or as Mother Goddess—because to do so would be a betrayal of her actual parents. She explained, "I think the parent images of God, whether it's god or goddess, are difficult for me because I think I have issues with my own parents, and even the task of imagining like a better parent seems like a betrayal." I asked, "Of your parents?" and she responded, "Of my parents. Like, so, it's been somewhere where I didn't really want to go, to think about a father god or a mother god. So those images have been difficult." She explained that she wanted to emphasize her parents' good qualities, not to criticize them.

Julie particularly had a difficult time criticizing her mother and a fear of betraying her. She described her mother as the "most loving person on earth." She said that her mother "just loves people" and is "so good." She described her as "very political" yet without the angry edge that she sees in many activists. She explained, "She is so sweet-natured that she really doesn't come across as threatening at all, and she is so good about knowing people, and she is intuitive and empathetic. She was a great mom."

Immediately after saying that she was a great mom, however, she shifted to saying,

> She was kind of a mess. Our house was always a mess, and she worked too many hours and was stressed out, and had a difficult marriage and then a difficult breakup. And she also, she has a panic disorder. She is on disability now, and just has a hard time dealing with the world. And it feels like such a waste because she has so many gifts.

The tension in her relationship with and image of her mother was reflected in her description of their relationship. She said that she depended on her, could talk to her and tell her anything, and felt completely accepted and supported by her. At the same time, however, she said, "It is hard because I also feel like she needs to be looked after. I felt some resentment about that."

When Julie's sister, who is five years older, left for college, Julie was left at home alone with her mother. She found herself in the role of mothering her mother, alone, for most of her adolescence. In spite of feeling "some resentment," however, she did not express any anger or criticism toward her mother. Her fear of betraying her fragile mother, who she sees as the most loving person on earth, however, had left her without the possibility of a maternal God-image, one that might help to compensate for the nurturing, strength, and comfort that her human mother was not able to give to her.

Julie also expressed fear of betraying her father. She also wanted to emphasize his positive qualities rather than focusing on the negative. He left their family when she was in high school, devastating her mother and his daughters. He has become emotionally distant and has changed his values since his former life of activism. He does not ask questions about her life. He is cynical about the activism that she, her sister, and her mother still value greatly. There is no intimacy in their current relationship. Julie explained that it is "kind of like he was captured by aliens and then got his memory erased."

She described him as trying very hard to be a good father when she was younger and said that their relationship was "the closest" in her family. However, when he left the family, it was a "severe break." It was obviously a traumatic event in her young life. She described having to move directly into worrying about and taking care of her mother, who entered a long depression. She did not have the comfort of her mother or her older sister during that time. Instead, she became the caretaker. Perhaps she did not want to criticize him because it was simply too painful to face the grief over the loss of her father.

Julie's other significant relationship was with her older sister, whom she described as "extremely strong . . . born strong . . . kind of take-over-the-world-type of strong and definitely a leader in my life . . . everywhere she goes, she'd be a really natural leader." She said that her sister "is definitely more of a challenging type, and sees the world more in black and white, and has a real sense of justice." Even though she and her sister "clash" in terms of the way that they approach the world, she admired her sister's strength.

She saw herself and her sister as a study in opposites. She described herself as disorganized and tiring easily and admired her sister as the opposite of those qualities. Being five years younger than her sister, accompanied by her sense of her sister as admirably strong, caused Julie to be reluctant to challenge her sister. Even though she said that they were now friends, she explained, "She definitely has a power over me that is hard to get away from. It is hard to imagine challenging her directly." Thus, even as an adult, she did not feel strong enough to speak up against her sister when they disagreed, and, at the same time, did not think that her mother was strong enough to be challenged.

Vulnerability, Power, and Imaging

Julie's sense of herself as lacking power and strength became clear during our second group discussion. When we were discussing whether it made a difference to imagine a black Goddess, as opposed to a white Goddess, Julie reflected,

> In some ways, it's easier to imagine an older black woman as God. And that just sounds so, that the power, or, like I think about the strong singing voice, and like the power of being able to, the strength in being able to endure and continue to nurture. And then I thought about a young black woman, and I thought, still, it seems like a powerful figure. I have this vision of young black women as . . . even though oppressed in our society, there's just that, I imagine a strength there. And, then, when you were talking about imagining God as yourself, then that was totally new to me. It seems really foreign. It seems like there's *no* power there [Laughter] . . . And then, maybe, no matter what, it's always easier to imagine God as other.

The group laughed at Julie's sense of having "no power." However, that self-judgment was significant to the way she experienced the world and particularly significant to her experiences in her family relationships.

She felt powerless to challenge her strong older sister, powerless to make her mother well and happy, powerless to challenge her or criticize her, and powerless to change her father, who was emotionally absent from her life and from his former life with his family. She did not see herself as a worthy image for the divine because she saw herself as having no power. On the other hand, she recognized strength in black women who endured oppression, nurtured others, and had strong voices. She did not recognize her own strength in being able to take care of her mother, survive her parents' devastating divorce, and raise herself to adulthood. She had endured much hardship but did not recognize this as strength and could not see her own power.

After a discussion about the ways that romanticizing black women as stronger and more powerful than white women can be dangerous, reinforcing stereotypes of black women and denying their full humanity, Julie began to question the ethics of imaging the divine in human form. She asked,

> I was just thinking, is there any way to image God in new ways that isn't false in some way—that distancing or romanticizing of the woman with the hair, or the strong, black woman, is there a way to do that that's not . . . I mean are you always going to be telling some sort of lie or causing some sort of damage with another image?

After asking these questions, however, she immediately went on to ask whether it is possible to have an image of the divine that incorporates human frailty and vulnerability. She thought immediately of Jesus. The following discussion ensued:

> *J:* I mean, what's so great about Jesus, in some ways, is that he's a real person, with real characteristics, and it's not that people don't project different things, of course, but it seems simpler, in a way, than just God, who, I don't know exactly how to express it, but it seems like it's easier not to . . . I'm not exactly sure.
>
> *R:* I was thinking when you were talking about, that's the same thing that I was thinking of: is there a way to do that? It seems like there was a group of people who did that with Jesus and his life. I don't know that he would have necessarily represented an image of God in that time.
>
> *J:* Right, that he's not beautiful . . .
>
> *R:* That he suffered, he died . . .
>
> *M:* He looked like all the other Jewish guys. Why would they think he looked like God?
>
> *J:* I was just thinking, you know, a peasant . . .
>
> *R:* Right, born in a stable, I mean, who knows, at least the stories lend some . . . I guess equating with God came later, but it seems like for the time it meant pretty revolutionary to equate an image . . .
>
> *J:* Yeah—with frailty. I mean he's beaten down. I mean, could you do that in some other way, of taking a black woman, and it's not just strength, it's also, in terms of imagining someone who has your interests and your concerns, could you image God who suffers and who's doubtful? The way Jesus wasn't sure the night before he died? Something more real.

This discussion of recognizing frailty and vulnerability as well as strength and power in any human image representative of the divine, of imaging God as one "who suffers and who's doubtful," allowed Julie to move toward imaging the divine in new ways. She longed to avoid the dangers of stereotyping and romanticizing others by allowing a full expression of humanity in any image.

For the liturgy, she brought a large portrait of her mother's face when she was a young woman. The beautiful image seemed to preside over the other, smaller images on the same table, like a loving mother Goddess. While Julie was not able to challenge or to criticize her mother, she was able to embrace a maternal image for the divine without feeling that she was betraying her mother. By allowing for frailty, suffering, and vulnerability in the divine, she was able to move beyond her impasse of not being able to image the divine as parental, whether male or female. In the collective prayer that she led at the end of the liturgy, she also referred to seeing the divine in a reflection in the mirror, saying, "Gracious God, whether it is in the stained glass window of a church or in a mirror we hold up to our own faces, keep finding us throughout our lives." It seems that this process allowed her to embrace herself as a worthy reflection of the divine image, even in her sense of vulnerability and powerlessness.

Integrating Spirituality and Activism

Julie's story revealed that critical awareness about social issues is not enough to sustain a spiritual life or a life of work for social justice. She was raised to be a critical thinker from an early age. She had learned about the crimes of Christianity. She was encouraged to be a social activist and even felt guilty during high school for being involved in a church that was not involved in activism. She initially decided to go back to church during high school, after a long time away, for her "mom's sake." However, she found there a place where she could feel "like a child again." She said that she "fell in love with the service," especially the music and the liturgy. She felt guilty about her love of church, however. She explained,

> But it was almost kind of a secret thing for me because by that time I had really developed a lot of prejudices against Christianity. And especially against a church that didn't take such an active role in social justice . . . It seemed wrong in some way to be involved in an organization, you know, white-dominated hierarchy, and then knowing the history of Christianity. I was drawn to it, but almost like a guilty pleasure.

During this difficult time in her life, the experience of being in community—of "saying things in unison" and of returning to physical actions that were familiar from her childhood, such as kneeling and rising together—served as a source of great comfort. The music and the liturgy functioned to sustain and nourish her spiritually, giving her a sense of the beauty and abundance in the world and of a divine presence.

In spite of her political misgivings, the emotional and spiritual needs that she felt so strongly at that time were met in her religious community. She has found in MMP a rare community where spirituality and social activism are integrated. She also hoped to find such integration through her vocation as a priest.

Race, Gender, and Imaging

Julie was raised to be aware of issues of racism and sexism, and was encouraged from a young age to counter them, to see all people as the same. At the same time, however, she recognizes now that this emphasis on sameness came with its difficulties. She explained,

> I think one side effect of how politically correct we were is that becoming a woman or becoming a man wasn't really thought about. Becoming a person. And I think, in a way, that's lost. I think that one thing I am exploring is what it might be to become a woman, and it doesn't have to be scary to think about that.
>
> And, in grade school, we grew up again in Chapel Hill talking about race a lot, and about talking black history . . . I don't think that I ever recognized that I thought it was better to be white and have blonde hair.

The emphasis on sameness in her upbringing caused Julie to struggle in developing an identity as a woman, to claim what that might mean for her. At the same time, she has struggled to recognize the ways in which the larger culture has influenced her in terms of racism and sexism. Julie's critical awareness about gender and race and about the multiplicity of images for the divine in other cultures made her hesitate to image. She recognizes now, however, that her critical awareness about gender and race did not prevent her from internalizing the dominant image of God as an old white man that was presented to her over and over again through the liturgy and images of the Episcopal Church that she loved.

Transformation

Julie described eloquently the long, slow process of internalizing new images for the divine. Because of her lifelong intellectual study of religion, she was acutely aware that images for the divine are not transformed through reading books. Even though she had read about goddesses in different contexts during high school and found them appealing, she still could not "think of a woman" when thinking about God. For her, the transformation occured gradually, as she slowly built up experiences during liturgy and worship as well as through stories of God as feminine, which counteracted the years of liturgy in which the male image for the divine was the only image.

From a young age, she knew that she "wanted something amorphous" to represent God, but she also recognized that the old, white, male image was deeply engrained. She explained, "I don't have the years of story to go along with the Goddess. So it's like thinking of a picture of someone you don't know." In other words, she did not have the emotional associations with the female image that she had with the male image. She had related exclusively with the male God during worship for so many years and had heard his story throughout her childhood. Therefore, even though she liked the idea of the female image, she did not know her in the same familiar, intimate, experiential way. She explained,

> So I think that using female language or gender-neutral language with MMP . . . I found really liberating, that I don't have to do this double-talk in my head . . . I grew up, you know, Rite I Episcopal language, and it's very paternalistic. I loved it because it's what was spiritual to me . . . what was holy. But I think that layers and layers of that, year after year, create a lot of difficulty. So I find it really refreshing and just easier on me to have the gender-neutral language, or language that is actually feminine, and looking at ways that God is female. But it feels very intellectual to me still, and not as, and not in my heart. I think it will probably take years of doing that, and years of those kinds of rituals to create in me like a real sense of the divine that's feminine or without this very paternalistic side.

Even though she did not want to internalize the male image for God, it had accumulated inside her to the point that it was a strong association for her. She reasoned that it would take years of experiences with the divine feminine in order to build up a similar familiarity with her. She believed that participation at MMP was important for her because it was a place where she could do that work. She explained,

> Like I said, I think it's kind of slow, slow work . . . But I always find that putting myself in that place is really good for me. Because it is just another layer of a feminine God that is going to build up over time and is going to be a part of my spirituality. But I think again that it's the taking me out of my head and listening to the words and the music and letting go that creates that. It's not, you know, reading a book about it.

I asked her what she meant when she said that it "creates that." She returned to her understanding of liturgy as creating space and engaging her at a nonintellectual level. She described it as "stripping away" the layers of her political correctness so that her true feelings and prejudices could be acknowledged. It was through this process of revealing the truth, she explained, that she could arrive at a deeper truth about the reality of God. She went on to say,

> That creates the space in my mind where you could have a femi-nine image, like a "yeah," deep in my core, as opposed to like all these other hidden things, like racism and hatred of the feminine and a male God. That if you strip away the layers of my political correctness you would find, and I think it is really, you have to, through music, through ritual, through poetry, through work in silence, and work in a community—that is how you really get to the heart of those things.
>
> I think the truth is that God is feminine and masculine and beyond genders, and I don't know exactly what that truth is, but I know that God is not a man. So it is not just that I have to change who I am; it is that I have to find a part of me that is receptive to that. I mean, I don't know exactly how to think about it. It's getting closer to the truth. So I guess in a way it's finding, opening up the pathways that can be receptive to that.
>
> Yeah, I don't know exactly how to describe it. It is going to be more successful. It's going to improve my whole spirituality because it is going to be closer to a real connection to the real and living God, as opposed to this kind of narrow image of God. And so it's not just what is comfortable to me or what is satisfying to my self-image and ego; it is what's closer to the truth of the world and that is my faith. So I think living out my faith in a more real way is what MMP is offering.

She described a mystical process in which she was gradually opening up to a greater awareness of the truth about God and to a "real connection to the real and living God." For her, then, the journey of moving beyond the limited, dominant image of God was a central aspect of her spirituality and her faith.

This process of moving closer to the "truth of the world" and the truth about the nature of God had made Julie "more comfortable and more accepting" in her relationships with other people. She explained that a belief in one image of God as the only correct image leads to division and intolerance, since people who believe differently are all seen as wrong. She felt this division and tension in church and realized that she was "on the outside" for challenging the traditional, white male image of God. She explained that this tension and division within the church could be avoided if the congregation would accept "different metaphors for God." Currently, she said that MMP "allows me to be more of myself" because it allows her to embrace multiple images for the divine. She felt constrained in being fully herself in churches that did not embrace and embody her belief that God is not a man.

As she moved through the process of honoring her connection to various images, she was traveling through the mystical process, as she described it, of coming closer to "a real connection to the real and living God" as well as closer to the truth of herself. While she was still struggling to reconcile her conflicted feelings about her parents, particularly about her mother, this process pushed her to consider those feelings in relation to her image of the divine. At the same time, our discussion about allowing frailty and vulnerability as well as strength and power in our imaging of the divine helped her to embrace her mother as reflecting the image of God, even in her frailty. It was my hope that this would allow her to embrace herself more fully as being worthy of embodying and representing the divine.

The prayers that Julie wrote for our liturgy beautifully reflected her learning in this process and her wisdom about the connections between imaging, spirituality, and a relationship with the divine. She first led the communal prayer, following the time of engaging with images, saying,

> *In our desire to know you and be true to you, we seek your face. Sometimes we get stuck with one name, one image. We find ourselves closed off and resistant to the many ways you might be revealed to us. We ask you now to open us to images of you that will enlighten, renew, and challenge. Instead of diminishing our experience of you, we trust that we will be enriched by finding a face that is a partial reflection of the One who includes us all.*

5

Inclusive Language Is Not Enough

Imagining the Divine, Religious Experience, and Thea/ology

You called him a her . . . Excuse me. I have a question. Is God a boy or a girl?

—MY SIX-YEAR-OLD NIECE, AFTER HEARING
A BLESSING ADDRESSED TO MOTHER GOD

To understand the dynamics involved in reimaging the divine, one must be willing to engage in the paradoxical, the metaphorical, and the mystical aspects of experiencing divine presence. One must be willing and able to "play"–spiritually, psychologically, and thea/ologically. An image can evoke new awareness of aspects of one's self, allow for an experience of divine presence in working for justice and wholeness, or foster a new sense of the simplicity and power of divine love. A new image can help to shatter previously held limiting and oppressive images. A new image can also validate and give a name to an experience of the divine that was considered unimportant because it was incongruent with old images. A female and/or black image of God can serve the political purpose of challenging white, male supremacy and the ways that it has colonized even our imaginations and our spirituality. Ultimately, the movement through images allows for a freedom to create new images out of one's experiences of divine presence. This freedom allows people to experience newfound political and spiritual empowerment as they begin to name and to honor their own experiences and worth.

Paradoxically, the freedom to play with images allows for the freedom to move beyond images to experiences of presence and then to return to images for more play and creation. This journey through images–a continual cycle of returning to the childhood image of the white, male, controlling

God in order to shatter it once more through new images that represent authentic experiences of divine presence and action—is exemplified in the stories of the women in this book.

In her Pulitzer Prize–winning novel *The Color Purple*, Alice Walker provides a powerful and often-quoted dialogue between the main character, Celie, and her friend and lover, Shug, both African American women, about imaging the divine. Shug describes her experiences of unconditional divine love and divine presence within all of creation and explains that she was only able to experience that love and presence freely when she allowed herself to leave behind the image of God as a white man. After Celie admitted that she imagined God as an old white man with a beard and blue eyes, Shug laughs. Celie recounts, "Then she tell me this old white man is the same God she used to see when she prayed. If you wait to find God in church, Celie, she say, that's who is bound to show up, 'cause that's where he live . . . Cause that's the one that's in the white folks' white bible." Shug explains, "Ain't no way to read the Bible and not think God white . . . When I found out I thought God was white, and a man, I lost interest."[1] However, after losing interest in the white, male God of her Bible and church, Shug was able to experience the divine as present within herself and within everything. She describes her process of reimaging the divine in multiple ways that resulted in a mystical experience of union with the divine and with all of creation.[2] Celie is overwhelmed by these new images and ideas about God and began her own journey of trying to reimage. She tries "to chase that old white man" out of her head.[3]

Walker's brilliant fiction portrays beautifully the dynamic process of reimagining the divine. It was only when I began the interviews for this research that I remembered that Walker's description of reimaging the divine in *The Color Purple* had been life-changing for me when I was sixteen years old, allowing me to begin to dislodge my old image and to honor my experiences of the divine that contradicted the theology with which I was being raised. Rather than scripture, I chose to read the excerpts quoted earlier at my first "preaching" experience during a devotional for my entire evangelical Christian, almost exclusively white, Southern high school. I am still amazed that the chaplain allowed me to use this text. However, Walker's powerful narrative had entered our literature classes, and if we allowed her wisdom to challenge us we were forever changed. As an adult, I continue to speak about the urgency of allowing people the opportunity to challenge their old images of the divine and to explore new images—so that they might honor their experiences of divine presence and love and so that they might nurture imagery for the divine that allows them to experience that presence and love more freely.

Feminist and black theologians have argued for decades for the need to move away from a unitary, static image of God as a white, male ruler. Their work is extremely important and has served to open the discussion of imaging the divine. However, their work pays insufficient attention to the complexity of religious experiences and needs in relation to imaging and reimaging the divine. Their writing has stayed at the conceptual level and has not delved sufficiently into the depths of human experience in relation to imagery and language for the divine. My niece's questions about the gender of God, and her already solidifying assumption that God is male, demonstrate that the lack of female imagery and language for the divine in contemporary religious institutions is already impacting the formation of God-images (and thus the formation of self-image and of relational patterns with the divine) for the next generation.

Theologians such as Elizabeth Johnson, Sallie McFague, and James Cone have provided important arguments about the need for changing imagery, but they have not dealt systematically with the ways that theological language and imagery are deeply and complexly interwoven in peoples' lives. Their citings of "women's experience" or "black experience" serve as blanket generalizations but do not adequately address the complexity of lived experience. This alienates readers whose experiences do not fit their descriptions. At the same time, the failure to draw theological conclusions from the actual stories of people who are struggling with the need to reimage the divine can allow unsympathetic readers to dismiss the claims of feminist and black theologians more easily because there is no appeal to compassion for particular people who are struggling with the traditional imagery. My contention is that the theological "texts" of human lives, and the complexity and nuances of peoples' experiences in relation to theological beliefs and imagery for the divine, serve as more powerful arguments for the need to free up the imagining of the divine.

While feminist, womanist, *mujerista,* and black theologians have successfully condemned the idolatry of having only one image of the divine along with the societal oppression upheld by that idolatry, they have failed to demonstrate sufficiently the spiritual, psychological, and social necessity for people to play with multiple images of the divine. Their discussions have not accessed and expressed the depth of religious experience that is necessary in order for substantial social as well as spiritual change to take place. Therefore, the voices of people who have experienced profound growth in their imagery for the divine and in their spirituality and selfhood have not been included adequately in the theological discussion about reimagining the divine.

Thea/ology and Feminist Spiritual Experiences

How can an image or metaphor for the divine be both "real" and imagined? How can an image or metaphor allow for an experience of divine presence even while the person having that experience maintains an awareness of the image or metaphor's constructed nature? How can a person hold these two realities in tension when, according to Schneider, they cause feminist theologians so much confusion? It is this paradoxical and mysterious nature of the relationship between the imagination, religious experience, and the divine that I explore further in this chapter.

The complex relationship between metaphor and image in thea/ological language and religious experiences is discussed to different extents by Laurel C. Schneider, Sallie McFague, and Elizabeth Johnson. However, each of these authors fails to rely sufficiently on the experiences of actual practitioners and thus fails to explore the dynamic, often paradoxical, nature of metaphor and imagery in religious experience. Discussions of metaphor (often used interchangeably with the term "image" in feminist thea/ological writings) become conceptual, static, and separated from experience and the realities and relationships to which they refer.

In contrast, I argue for an experiential understanding of reimaging the divine as a religious practice necessary for spiritual growth and social transformation. In mystical theology and spirituality, images or metaphors for the divine are part of a dynamic, dialectical process through which spiritual growth occurs. In addition, I argue that the "race" and gender of the image and the person imaging must always be addressed when exploring the significance of divine images. Through my research, I have discovered what I am calling a uniquely "feminist mysticism,"[4] in which women move through multiple images to an immanent sense of divine presence within themselves and all of creation.

Schneider has attempted to reconcile the particular spiritual experiences of feminists with the abstract understanding of metaphors provided by McFague. However, in spite of this goal, she has provided very few examples and scant analysis of actual experiences. Her arguments raise interesting questions to pursue for the purposes of this work. She notes a tension in many feminist[5] theological writings between claiming women's experiences as their primary source for theological reflection and relying on what she called the "metaphoric exemption," which, she argues, denies that any metaphor for the divine actually refers to the divine itself.

This skeptical metaphoric exemption has been used primarily to expose and destabilize the oppressive functioning of the white, male, ruler God in social systems.[6] However, the experiences of feminist religious practitioners do not follow this skeptical logic. They are not experienced as "metaphors" in the sense of being somehow less than real. Instead, they are experienced as profoundly real manifestations of divine presence, even when people recognize that their imaginations play an active role in their imaging of and experiences of the divine. Feminist theologians' reliance on the metaphoric exemption is directly challenged by the claims of women who experience the divine as present and real in their lives, mediated through multiple images.

It is crucial for feminist theologians to take account of the religious experiences that many women (and men) have in relation to specific manifestations of the divine as goddess or god. Schneider asks

> What is the place of this kind of lived experience in the work of feminist theologies that seek to guide and inform these various communities and individuals in their spiritual explorations? . . . The question is whether or not there is room for the glimpsed gods and goddesses of complex religious experience in their theologies. Feminist theologies cannot yet account for feminist spiritual experience (which is itself inspired by the work of womanist, mujerista, white feminist, and other feminist theologians).[7]

Here, the disconnect between academic theology and practitioners of feminist spirituality becomes clear. Practitioners are often inspired by academic writings but their inspirations are unruly and cannot be accounted for by reductionist rationality.

Schneider chooses to reconcile the tension between the metaphoric exemption and feminist spiritual experiences by arguing that ultimately, feminist spirituality challenges the "metaphor" of monotheism. She claims,

> The God who is One in a universal sense cannot remain both One and universal when embodied, since concrete embodiment by definition is particularistic and bounded by existence in space and time. Any embodiment that is not particularistic embodiment—a here-and-now kind of thing that is both real and present—is abstract embodiment. [8]

She argues that the "metaphor of monotheism," of God as "One," must be seen as simply another inadequate metaphor for the divine—one that has excluded other images of divinity for millennia.[9] She asserts that instead, the divine must be seen as "unlimited and multiple."[10]

At this point, her argument starts to break down. It is unclear what she means when claiming that practitioners of feminist spirituality are having experiences of the divine as "concrete" rather than "abstract." This approach does not allow adequate room for the possibility of paradox—of both/and—of a divinity that is both One and many, both abstract and embodied, both in creation and beyond creation (as in panentheism).

Several poems and stories in Schneider's book recount experiencing the divine as present in nature, in a beloved cat, in oneself, and in a son. However, the authors depict the divine as present *within* rather than as "concrete" in the sense of being an external and separate deity. Other poems recount experiences of particular goddesses such as Tishku or an unnamed African goddess. However, these poems cannot be interpreted in literalistic ways. Rather, the authors are playing imaginatively with images of the divine with which they relate. In one poem, the author quotes from her conversation with an African Goddess: "Jesus okay, She say. You gotta live. But She don't go away. Dream me, She say. You mine still to the ends of the earth."[11] The poet's inclusion of the Goddess's command to "Dream me" indicates the slippage between "concrete" presence and presence in dream and imagination. Similarly, Schneider's mother says in one of her many poems, "I am learning how to dwell in the tributaries of my dreams. This is the season for which I have yearned."[12]

For the women having these experiences, there is not a clear division between "concrete" and "abstract." Rather, they explore imaginatively their *experiences* of divine presence in themselves, in people and animals they love, and in the whole of the natural world. Like the women of the Christian feminist spirituality movement, these women experience the divine presence as real, yet at the same time, mediated through imagination. There is a mystical, paradoxical awareness that the divine both is and is not represented by the metaphors for the divine that the women experience and imagine.

Schneider quotes extensively from an account written by her mother, Pat Schneider, about a profound spiritual experience that she had the day after waking at night to the sound of her own laughter, so beautiful that it sounded, she said, "beautiful beyond what my body could make." She writes,

> And now, as I write, all at once there is a stillness in my mind, an absolute silence, in which I see the face of god!—I see the face of god—why not? Why not? . . . I see the face of god and there is laughter behind the eyes and behind the grin (not smile, grin) . . . What I forgot to say about the face of god was what surprised me most—not that the face was laughing—but that the face was a woman's face. And that beyond the woman's face, turned away, with just an edge of a cheekline visible, another face looked toward shadow—not threatening, not problematic—a man's face. And I know there was at least one more face—completely unseen.
>
> I have seen one of the faces of god and it is a woman's face and it is a form I can hold—no—not hold—a form to make visible to me, this: laughter. Beautiful, unspeakably beautiful, laughter.[13]

The writer describes her experience of divine presence in a series of mysteries and paradoxes. She demonstrates a paradoxical, mystical understanding of divine presence that is not conveyed in Schneider's attempted resolution of the tension among the metaphoric exemption, monotheism, and spiritual experiences. While her work is extremely helpful and provocative in laying out the many issues, Schneider's resolution lacks connection to the religious imagination of feminist spiritual practitioners.

Negative Theology and Feminist Mysticism

This same lack of awareness of paradox, imagination, and mystical process in relation to metaphors and images for the divine pervades feminist thea/ological writings. Many feminist theologians have turned to the writings of the founder of the Christian mystical tradition and Negative Theology, Pseudo-Dionysius, to support their claims that any rigid belief in one image of the divine as comprehensive and adequate is idolatry.[14] However, they mistakenly conflate the "metaphoric exemption" with Pseudo-Dionysius's understanding of the function of images of the divine in the *via negativa* (negative way).

McFague argues that metaphorical theology is "in the tradition of the *via negativa*," saying, "Finding little to say of God with certainty, it boldly makes its case hypothetically and lets it rest."[15] She argues that metaphors have the characteristic of "'is' and 'is not': an assertion is made but as a likely account rather than as a definition."[16] On the surface, this is similar to the movement of affirmation and then negation of all images for the divine found in Pseudo-Dionysius's descriptions of the use of images in referring to the divine. However, her emphasis on making a "hypothetical case" through a "likely account," as well as her assertion that no words or phrases can refer directly to God, miss the dynamic, paradoxical nature of the process that Pseudo-Dionysius advocated.

He described a process through which a person could grow closer to the divine through the use of images and names for the divine. Pseudo-Dionysius's writings embody, in both form and content, a *via negativa* that is primarily a mystical, spiritual journey of relating with images and metaphors for the divine as paradoxes. His was a journey fueled by the movement of divine love and yearning. It was not a philosophical exercise in deconstruction or social constructionism. The meaning of Negative Theology is largely lost when it is reduced to those categories by being equated with the metaphoric exemption.

Pseudo-Dionysius wrote primarily as an act of praise.[17] His writing style reflected his understanding of a mystical journey, which had divinization and union with the divine as its goal. This journey involved movement through a series of paradoxes. At the end of the first chapter of *The Divine Names*, he wrote, "As for me, I pray that God should allow me to praise in a divine way the beneficent and divine names of the unutterable and unnamable Deity."[18] In explicating the divine names, Pseudo-Dionysius saw himself as involved in a profound process of paradox. He was asking the unnamable and unutterable to help him praise its names. Within this conundrum lay the movement toward the divine.

For Pseudo-Dionysius, the process of explicating the names and symbols for the divine is initiated and given energy by the divine itself. The spiritual journey is a process guided by the powerful eros, or yearning, of

the divine for human souls to return to union with it. It is this divine yearning that is revealed in the yearning of human souls to make that return.
This yearning that moves all things toward reunion with the divine is a
passionate, ecstatic love. It is a love that breaks down boundaries, flowing
in constant motion in and through all that is, "yearning on the move . . .
traveling in an endless circle through the Good, from the Good, in the
Good and to the Good."[19]

It is within this context that Pseudo-Dionysius's understanding of
the function of images and names for the divine is best appreciated. For
Pseudo-Dionysius, symbols, images, and names for the divine fulfilled an
essential function in the spiritual path toward divinization and mystical
union with the divine. Ultimately, the divine is unrepresentable and unnamable. However, human minds work via images and symbols. Therefore, we
must begin our spiritual path toward the divine with symbols and images.
Symbols are used in order to draw our minds upward toward a more simple
contemplation of concepts. Concepts, in turn, are used to raise our minds
beyond concepts and into unknowing. It is through a process of affirmation
and then negation that symbols and concepts accomplish this motion of
raising the mind and soul.

In *The Divine Names*, Pseudo-Dionysius explained that God is within
all of creation and, therefore, that symbols for God can be drawn from any
aspect of creation. He chose to focus on those symbols that are used in the
scriptures, but in principle, symbols can be drawn from all of creation.[20]
Pseudo-Dionysius claimed that each particular symbol is used to represent
the whole of the divine rather than only a part or single attribute of the
divine, arguing that while God is oneness, "he" has processed down through
the celestial hierarchy and the earthly hierarchy into even inanimate life
forms and the earth itself, with each lower form containing less and less of
the divine light due to its progressing opacity. The light itself, although then
"clothed" in multiple forms, still remains unified and singular.[21]

Through the process of negating these many symbols and names, one
is drawn even closer to the divine mystery. Paradoxically, one holds in
awareness that the divine has every name and is at the same time Nameless.
The process of negation thus first requires the process of affirmation. It is
an exercise in moving through paradox toward a more profound awareness
of the awesome mystery of the divine. This movement through paradox
has been largely lost in the writings of feminist theologians.

In her discussion of Aquinas' use of "analogy" to describe the appropriate
function of names and images for the divine, Johnson eloquently demonstrates
her understanding of the importance of the movement from affirmation to
negation and then back to a paradoxical affirmation. She explains,

> In order to prevent affirmations about God from being inter-
> preted as direct transcriptions of reality, early Christian theology

articulated the idea that speaking about God involves a three-fold motion of affirmation, negation, and eminence. In this process, the play of the mind is supple. A word whose meaning is known and prized from human experience is first affirmed of God. The same word is then critically negated to remove any associations with creaturely modes of being. Finally, the word is predicated of God in a supereminent way that transcends all cognitive capacities . . . Every concept and symbol must go through this purifying double negation, negating the positive and then negating the negation, to assure its own legitimacy. In the process an unspeakably rich and vivifying reality is intuited while God remains incomprehensible.[22]

Drawing on Aquinas, Johnson argues that all speaking about God is required to go through this threefold analogical process to be true. She explains that there is always more in a concept used to refer to God than the "concept itself can bear." Therefore, "analogy breaks this open in an affirming movement of the human spirit that passes from light into darkness and thence into brighter darkness."[23]

The purpose of this kind of speech is to create a particular spiritual experience, a "movement of the human spirit," just as Pseudo-Dionysius describes. Johnson argues that the kind of knowing of the divine that occurs through this process is beyond rationality—yet is still a powerful kind of knowing, an intuitive "dynamic of relational knowing."[24]

This kind of knowing is demonstrated in the spiritual experiences described by Schneider, as well as those described by Theresa, Julie, Marie, and Rosalyn. It is a kind of knowing that is not fully achieved, however, through Schneider's own writing or through the writing of McFague or Johnson. In the constructive section of the book, Johnson fails to return to this paradoxical process. While she affirms female images for the divine and then repeatedly reminds the reader that the divine is nevertheless a mystery, she does not reaffirm the paradox of her She-Who-Is image through "letting-go in a transcending affirmation."

This third movement of analogy is completely lost in McFague's discussions of metaphor. She focuses almost exclusively on the movement of negation, saying repeatedly that metaphors are words used inappropriately.[25] At the same time, however, she argues that metaphors and models are the result of exercises of the imagination attempting to represent experiences of relationship with the divine.[26] Her emphasis on experiences of divine relationship might have helped her to move toward the paradoxical nature of images for the divine that is demonstrated in many spiritual experiences. However, her writing leaves the reader with a sense of metaphors and models that are separate from divine reality and solely products of human rationality. She, like Johnson, does not lead her readers through the process of yes, no, and yes again that might enable them to have a more profound, mystical knowing of the divine.

In critiquing these authors, I do not claim to write in the poetic form of mysticism that accomplishes this difficult task. However, by focusing on the stories and experiences of particular women and on the centrality of religious practices and ritual in engaging imagery for the divine, this book provides insight into the paradoxical "luminous darkness"[27] of the divine in a way that other contemporary discussions of reimaging the divine have not done.

The motion of affirmation and then negation and then paradoxical affirmation again is one of living with paradox, of learning the limits of the intellect, and of abandoning a sense of intellectual mastery and security in symbols. It is a process that frees the self to forsake the need for absolute knowledge and control. As Julie explained, "Spirituality often comes from making your head kind of take a back seat." The self is freed to interact playfully with images for the divine that do not represent the divine fully but that allow for movement toward union with the divine to occur. In this movement, the yearning love of the divine is experienced, both within our own yearning to see the divine and in the divine yearning to draw us closer to her presence.

The feminist spiritual experiences recounted by the women interviewed for this book, as well as the experiences that Schneider recounts, reveal the paradox that the divine is beyond representation yet is experienced and represented in partial ways through the women's imaginative expressions of their experiences of divine presence in the world. They appear to have taken the movement of "is/is not"[28] of McFague's metaphoric exemption to a higher meaning than she does. Feminist spiritual practitioners take her models of God as Mother, Friend, and Lover and give them flesh—flesh in the imagination. They experience these models in multiple ways yet they retain a sense that the divine is both in and beyond these images. Ultimately, they move beyond images to an awareness of immanent, intimate, divine presence.

Women in the feminist spirituality movement sense a real divine presence within creation and within images taken from creation. They sense a palpable yearning for connection with the divine. And they find profound spiritual growth when their minds are opened through interaction with new images for the divine in which they simultaneously find and do not find divine presence. Alternatively, new images emerge from experiences of divine presence that seem to defy image: "I have seen the face of god and it is a woman's face and it is a form I can hold—no—not hold—a form to make visible to me, this *laughter*. Beautiful, unspeakably beautiful, laughter"—laughter that was hers, yet beyond herself at the same time.

Pat Schneider experienced seeing the face of God, or Goddess, during a moment which she describes by saying, "All at once there is a stillness in my mind, an absolute silence, in which I have seen the face of God!" Her experience mirrors the trajectory described by Pseudo-Dionysius, except that her journey was cyclical rather than linear. Rather than reaching a state of mental stillness beyond all knowing, at the end of her spiritual journey when images of the divine cease, she saw images *after* her experience of stillness and silence—images for the divine that helped her to make visible a profound experience of divine presence.

The experiences of practitioners of feminist spirituality do not follow the neat, orderly hierarchical procession as described by Pseudo-Dionysius. Rather, the experiences are often surprising and unpredictable. Instead of a linear, hierarchical procession toward the divine on high, their experiences represent the same sort of cyclical, spiraling movement as does the yearning of the divine. Their experiences demonstrate a more congruent relationship between divine presence and an emphasis on freedom, equality, and justice for all people.

In contrast, there is a profound contradiction in Pseudo-Dionysius's writings between the fluidity and eros of divine love flowing through all of creation and his hierarchical understanding of the way men (and only men) can be led upward toward the divine by their superiors in the ecclesiastical hierarchy. His rigid, linear, hierarchical understanding of institutional control over mystical relationship with the divine stands in direct opposition to the spirituality of feminists, who often experience the presence of the divine without the mediation of religious leaders. His writings and spirituality are also profoundly misogynistic. The hierarchy of his process mirrors the misogynistic hierarchy of his all-male religious community. Feminist mysticism thus embodies a spirituality that directly challenges misogyny and hierarchy in religious experience as well as in religious institutions. The interplay of these demonstrate the need for reimagining the divine as part of breaking free from misogyny in religious and social practice—beginning with breaking free in the imagination.

Blatant misogyny and rigid social hierarchy obscure and directly contradict Pseudo-Dionysius's descriptions of flowing divine yearning. Ironically and tragically, his writings have been used for millennia as both a foundation for mystical experience and mystical reflection by Christian practitioners and scholars, and at the same time, as a justification for the all-male Catholic ecclesiastical hierarchy as divinely ordained.

Women Drawing New Images from Experience

More than fifteen hundred years after Pseudo-Dionysius is thought to have lived, women still struggle to assert their presence within male-dominated, hierarchical Christian institutions. More than forty years after its beginnings, the incorporation of feminist theology and spirituality in Christian churches is still minimal. Although more Protestant denominations now ordain women, actual liturgical and social practices have changed surprisingly little. In order to understand what is at stake for women in challenging the images of the divine (and of women) that continue to dominate Christian communities, it is helpful to look back to the beginnings of feminist theology.

Feminist theology arose originally from the cries of anguish of women in the church. Feminist thea/ologian Nelle Morton chronicled these experiences and analyzed their significance in relation to images for the divine.

Morton participated in the early Christian feminist movement of the 1960s. She experienced the power of women who were beginning to claim their full humanity and to name their experiences of the divine. Contemporary feminist theologians often quote her descriptions of early meetings of women at the beginning of the feminist movement. Women found themselves without words to describe their experiences of erasure, rejection, and oppression as women in the Christian tradition and in society as a whole. Morton described the process by which women listening to other women created a space in which they experienced "hearing into speech."[29]

Morton drew on data from regional workshops for women sponsored by the newly formed Commission on Women of the United Methodist Church in 1970 and 1971. She described a general movement of consciousness that she says was common throughout the groups and is therefore generalizable. Women would move from a state of defensiveness, not wanting to admit that they need liberation, to a sense of vague hurt and finally to a feeling of intolerable pain at the brink of despair. At this point, a new wordless consciousness would begin to emerge. She writes,

> This point, just short of despair, marks a basic aspect of the new woman consciousness, which, as already indicated, does not evidence itself easily or quickly . . . One woman referred to her moment as a "volcano erupting," another as a "dam breaking loose." Visible and audible gestures have been anything from choking, to holding the stomach "as if touching the bottom of a pit," "the very center of one's being." Pounding on the floor or table, shaking fists at the heavens, holding the sides of the chair, and shaking one's head all signified that something cataclysmic was taking place. Other times no change was visible at all. Sometimes incoherent and inarticulate sounds became audible. Once I saw a woman's throat open with a cry so great the cry could not come to sound—as in an old person who dies.[30]

It was through these explosive, excruciating moments that the women began to hear each other into speech, to name the sources of their anger, and to find new ways of speaking and of theologizing. Groups of women engaged in a "communal form of theologizing" as they listened with respect to each woman present and relied "on their own resources and on one another."

Morton argues that this process occurred because "No expertise was present to supply the proper word and no authority had been paid to keep them on track, to tell them what they think and what they see and what they hear and where they must come out."[31] Feminist theology grew from these roots. Unfortunately, too many contemporary academic feminist theologians give only lip service to "women's experience" without actually paying serious attention to the insights and experiences of particular women. Contemporary feminist authors often theologize about what is good for women and then become "authorities," "paid . . . to tell them what they think and what they see, and where they must come out." However, as Schneider's work indicates, many practitioners of feminist spirituality have taken the thea/ologies of feminist authors in unexpected and often unruly directions. They use them in their search for women-affirming and life-giving spirituality, imagery, and speech and do not seem tied to the philosophical and theological categories held so dear by many academic theologians.

Language is secondary to images. A new language, arising from women's experiences, was central to the "rising of women's consciousness," working dialectically with political actions and protests for women's rights. This dialectic between new language and political action is fueled by new images that arise out of experience. It is a cycle, moving from experience to image to language and then back to experience. Morton explains, "From a study of the women's recorded testimony it may be concluded that neither protests nor political action of the most radical sort marks the rising of woman consciousness but *the new language on the lips of those experiencing liberation.* Yet the new language both reflects and creates protests and political action."[32]

Women create new images for themselves when they go to the core of their self-images through a process of self-discovery like those described above. After the negative, false, sexist images out of which they have been living have been recognized, women can replace them with authentic images that nourish their positive self-image. Through embracing this new image, they can begin to speak with an authentic voice—the voice that had been silenced for so long. Morton explains, "Once the image is isolated, affirmed, and revered, words will come. Words may evoke images, but the image creates words—not the other way around."[33] Images function at the subconscious level and shape the way that people live with an emotional power that concepts do not convey.

This understanding of images as primary and concepts as secondary provides an inverted reflection of Pseudo-Dionysius's argument that the process of moving closer to the divine involves first affirming and negating images and then moving upward toward more simple concepts. However, Morton's descriptions of women going deep within themselves to "isolate, affirm, and revere" their positive self-image so that they can begin to speak with an authentic voice revalues images as being more powerful than concepts. Her understanding of movement toward the divine in relation with images thus involves a diving deeply into oneself as opposed to a hierarchical ascent toward a male God in heaven.

Rather than identifying the journey toward union with the divine as a journey away from images, emotions, and passions, as Pseudo-Dionysius does, Morton identifies the journey toward the divine more with the journey inward—perhaps toward the place inside oneself where the divine eros that Pseudo-Dionysius so eloquently described is moving with passionate yearning and love for union with all of creation. This journey toward the center of the self is reflected in the stories of Theresa, Julie, Rosalyn, and Marie. As they moved through false images of themselves, others, and the divine, they became more at home with the presence of the divine within themselves and within all of creation.

The relationship between concepts and images is more complex than a simple, linear relationship of one leading to the other in a neat sequence. Just as concepts arise out of images, concepts conveyed through words are also powerful in the ways that they give rise to images. Morton depicts a continual spiraling motion among words and images:

> Words do more than signify. They conjure images . . . Images refer to that entity that rises out of conscious and unconscious lives individually and in community that may shape styles of life long before conceptualization takes place. Images, therefore, are infinitely more powerful than concepts . . . Concepts can be learned, corrected . . . Concepts are linear. Images, on the other hand, can't be so controlled. They are not easy to identify or to describe. They have a life of their own. They function when persons are most unaware of their functioning.[34]

Morton's argument supports my thesis that each person needs to engage her images of the divine, of self, and of other people in ways that go beyond conceptual theorizing and argumentation. However, concepts and words need to be examined and changed when they serve to "conjure" images that function negatively.

Images must be encountered at the emotional, psychic level, both for individuals and for communities. Concepts and images continue to function at an emotional level even after individuals have repudiated them intellectually.[35] For this reason, images must be destabilized and shattered through the use of alternative iconoclastic images. Critical thinking about images can only go so far.

An image is more than a simple mental picture and is even beyond the concept of metaphor. Morton argues, "An image *is* its functioning—whether it operates consciously or deep in the unconscious; whether it operates in an individual or in a body politic."[36] Just as James Jones and Ana-Maria

Rizzuto describes images of self, other, and the divine as dynamic, active processes that both reflect and create patterns of relationship, Morton argues for an understanding of image that is a powerful, active force in social, political, and personal lives. The transformation of images of the divine and of self is therefore crucial for women. Because images of the divine are determinative of individual and social lives, old oppressive images need to be exposed, eradicated, and replaced with new, more life-giving images.

For the most part, theologians have failed to pay attention to the images that their theological concepts create, conjure, and convey. They have failed to recognize the extent to which people experience and live out of their images, not out of abstract theological concepts devoid of social content. All concepts conjure images. Morton discusses the danger of this failure:

> Following the early emphasis on iconography, images and theology have been largely separated in the public view–especially in the American scene. Images have been allowed to go underground primarily into the unconscious, into the private unconscious or into the community unconscious or both. Such a separation has injected a deep confusion not only in the religious world but also in the secular world. Theology has come to be related primarily to reason. When we speak of the theological task we refer to a certain way of thinking about ultimate values and ultimate longings, most often related to a specific historical tradition. But image, once in the subconscious, may act on its own quite apart from reason or conceptualization. This lack of understanding of the function of images has led not only to an "in" group in theological circles but also to a dangerously irresponsible use of theological knowledge and language.[37]

It was only after she retired from teaching in an academic theological setting that she recognized fully the central importance of images for theology. She writes,

> All these years, I thought I was working on theology, but in the process of preparing these essays for publication I find I have moved closer and ever closer to images and the way they function–images projected especially by theological language. Perhaps I should say "unexamined language." I think this shift has come about since my retirement from teaching in a theological school, as I have moved out of the purely academic and identified myself more closely with the common woman. Everyday women and masses of people the world around are hearing from the theologians and religious instructions that which the theologians are little aware of sending forth.[38]

This gap between academic theology and the images of the divine experienced by "the common woman" is what I hope to expose and to bridge in this book.

As theologian Thomas Thangaraj expressed, "No theologian ever said: 'God is a twelve-foot-tall white man with a beard,' but that is the image that we have. We have him in India too."[39] By continuing to refer to the divine in masculine terms (as "He" and as "God" without challenging the masculinity of that term), theologians repeatedly reinforce an image of the divine as a giant, old white man in the sky with a long, white beard. Regardless of the sophistication and complexity of their theological claims, "masses of people around the world" continue to experience the powerful functioning of this white male God image. Conversely, when feminist theologians fail to take seriously the necessity of providing alternative images (not just concepts) of the divine that people can relate to and experience as functioning in their lives and communities—or when they insist that their constructions are only conceptual metaphors—they fail to address the spiritual, emotional, and political needs of people of faith. Fortunately, women are appropriating the images proposed by feminist theologians such as Johnson and McFague and using them in their own creative ways.

New images can be experienced only after the old images have been challenged. While all the interviews for this book demonstrate that the old images are resilient, deeply rooted, and difficult to shatter, they also reveal that new images serve to gradually displace the old. Morton explains this process:

> Once old images are shattered, more positive images that allow for new forms of response to ever-changing conditions may come into play. Images have to do with the senses. They are rooted in feelings . . . Once the mind is cleared of accumulated blocks, it is free to embrace new images—positive images—in all sorts of fresh ways.[40]

The challenging of old images and embracing of new images involves the senses and the emotions rather than the intellect. This helps to explain why religious practices involving images, sounds, smell, and touch are key to the process of transformation.

Rather than understanding metaphor to be a conceptual construct, a metaphor can only be experienced as a process, a journey:

> The journey of a metaphor includes two activities. The first may be called the shattering (of an inadequate or phony image out of which one lives) or the exorcism (of what one knows one has outgrown) or the blotting out (of the image with which one comports oneself). The second is the ushering in of the new reality; the transcending to a totally new horizon or perspective that the old horizon kept hidden for so long.[41]

Morton describes one such journey that she experienced in relation to the metaphor of Goddess. She says that, being terribly afraid of heights, she hated to fly on airplanes. She explains, "Each time I boarded a plane, I reverted to a most irrational state, far from the mature faith I considered I now had. Usually I clasped my hands together and called on the powerful male deity in the sky for protection . . . I usually asked God the Father to keep the plane safe. I even made promises and confessed my wrongdoing." She would continue her pleas for safety throughout each flight and would do "much thanking" at the end of the flight. On one occasion, however, she suddenly thought, "What would happen if I invoked the Goddess? How does one call on the Goddess anyway?" She immediately experienced a profound sense of relaxation. She felt as if someone had sat down next to her, touched her arm, and told her to relax, trust, and breathe. Soon, she said, she was enjoying the flight. When she opened her eyes, wanting to thank the Goddess, she saw, "The seat was vacant. She had gone. I began to feel such power within, as if she had given me myself. She had called up my own energy. I was unafraid. Nor have I been afraid in a plane since that day."[42]

By simply invoking the metaphor of Goddess and thus raising an alternative image for prayer, Morton moved through the process of metaphor as she describes it. First, the metaphor of Goddess shattered her childhood God-image of the Father God in the sky with whom she felt she must continually plead and then thank, and second, a new reality of power, energy, relaxation, and peace was ushered in. This new perspective included both a sense of the presence of the Goddess and a profound experience of herself as full of power and energy. She also felt no guilt. She said, "The Goddess works herself out of business. She doesn't hang around to receive thanks. It appears to be thanks enough for her that another woman has come into her own."[43] The process of the metaphor of Goddess allowed Morton not only to experience a new image for the divine but also to experience herself in new ways.

The "journey of the metaphor" that Morton describes in her experience complements Pseudo-Dionysius's understanding of the movement of affirmation, negation, then paradoxical affirmation through particular images. Morton describes a process in which a new image dislodges an old image that has become reified. The old image is negated, as the new image is affirmed. However, once the new image of "Goddess" is affirmed, she "works herself out of business." Her image is also negated.

The third movement of paradoxical affirmation, in relation to both images, involved Morton's experience of divine presence and power within herself. Once she experienced the freedom to negate the reified male God-image, she became free to experience the fluid movement through images toward greater intimacy with the divine. The women whom I interviewed described a similar process. Once they began to critique the idolatry of the white, male God-image, they became free to move through multiple images—affirming, negating, and then, paradoxically, affirming them once again. Ultimately, this journey led them to experience the divine as an imminent, intimate presence beyond images yet often mediated through images.

This understanding of metaphor as process helps to explain why each individual will experience a particular metaphor in a unique manner and why a particular person will experience the same metaphor differently at different times. "A metaphor's action is never repeated in exactly the same way for all participating, nor indeed for the same person twice."[44] A person has to be willing and able to enter into the movement of the metaphor through imagination. In the psychological terms discussed in previous chapters, a person must be able to "play" with alternative images in order to experience the shattering and revelatory movements of metaphor. In addition, each person's emotional associations with the particular metaphor will determine the experience of a metaphor at a particular time.

Morton comments, "I am merely exposing the power of images. Therefore the question: What is invoked in you by Goddess? Is it dismissal? Anger? Fear? Discomfort? Then we do have some unfinished business to take care of."[45] Each person will experience a particular image or metaphor in a particular way at a particular time. Morton explains that she was ready to experience the metaphor of Goddess for the first time because of an "unconscious awareness that even though I conceptually no longer accepted a God 'out there' nor defined a 'God within' as a male, on the level of imagery the maleness was still alive and functioning in me on most unexpected occasions."[46]

The women whom I interviewed confirmed that they experienced a similar, ongoing struggle. Even as they changed their conceptual beliefs and began to experience power and freedom in new images, they still experienced their old image of a powerful, controlling, old white man in the sky to be "alive and functioning" on the level of images. They experienced an ongoing journey of encountering new images and metaphors for the divine and exploring new images of self so that gradually the old images were shattered and/or transformed and new consciousness emerged. Like Morton, they were aware that the metaphor of the omnipotent Father God was created long ago. It carried a great deal of meaning and power for the people during that time, serving as an iconoclastic shift from other religious icons. However, the image has ceased to be a metaphor and has lost its ability to be revelatory.

Alternatively, the process of encountering, invoking, and creating other metaphoric images, such as "Goddess," evokes imagination and change on both personal and political levels. Practitioners of feminist spirituality are engaging multiple images of the divine feminine with an exuberance and passion that demonstrate the enlivening and life-changing effects that Morton described.

A significant aspect of the change experienced by these women when encountering the divine feminine was a change in their experiences of themselves. Morton asserts,

> Now call on God the Mother or the Goddess. What happens? For women she appears. She says your life is the sacred gift. Pick it up. Receive it. Create it. Be responsible for it. I ask nothing in return. It is enough that you stand on your own two feet and speak your own word. Celebrate the creation that is you. Move in the new space—free. The response from women who have become aware is an overwhelming sense of acceptance and belonging and identity.[47]

Theresa, Julie, Marie, and Rosalyn all described in different ways how a female image for the divine had allowed them to embrace their experiences and their femaleness as a "sacred gift." While it was a long, ongoing, difficult process for them, they had all experienced moments of freedom, celebration, and belonging when they felt deeply that they were indeed created in the divine image and had the divine within themselves.

Central to the feminist spirituality movement is the freedom to create new images out of one's own experiences of the divine. There is not one, reified image. Instead, a "metaphorical consciousness," as described by Keller, allows for fluidity and flexibility—for movement through a mystical journey. The move toward an image of the divine as Goddess allows women to establish their authentic selfhood while at the same time encouraging them to affirm their experiences and to create new images out of their experiences. It is the freedom provided by the Goddess, who asks nothing in return, that invites women and men to continue to explore new images to express their experiences of the divine. In other words, metaphors such as "Goddess" are just images along the journey. To maintain their transformative function, the images and metaphors must remain fluid, open, changeable, leaving people free to name out of their own experiences of themselves and of the divine.

The image of Goddess, or even God the Mother, serves an iconoclastic purpose, opening up new possibilities by shattering the reified, frozen image of a white, male God. As Morton says, "God the Mother or the Goddess tends to be transparent, to make herself dispensable in such a way that in time we will be compelled to seek a totally different way of speaking of reality."[48] Therefore, while the image of Goddess may serve the purpose of breaking the mind free from "accumulated blocks" so that "it is free to embrace new images—positive images in all sorts of fresh ways," it serves this purpose in a way that challenges the patriarchal culture and restores and expresses publicly "worthy self-images for women." The old image cannot be shattered by just any image. Rather, it is shattered by a fundamental challenge to the structure of patriarchal society and religion and by a bold declaration of the divine worth of human women.

The ultimate goal is for women (and men) to be free to explore their own experiences, feelings, and senses so that they might create images that are authentic to their experiences–to move beyond all old images and oppressive language for the divine so that we might create anew. Morton asks,

> What kind of language is usable? How can we get beyond the symbols–the ancient images–back to the reality before the world was named; ahead where the reality moves before the new word is visible? . . . Once we, out of our own imaging, establish our selfhood and affirm the spiritual, which has been experienced but has not yet been named, men will be forced to deal with the patriarchal. Beyond that point we cannot now see.[49]

Morton published this essay, titled "Beloved Image," in 1977. If she were alive today, she might glimpse beyond the point of women experiencing the spiritual but not yet naming it. Many women are naming their experiences of the spiritual in diverse ways, using diverse images and multiple senses to express their experiences of the divine.

"Race" and Reimagining the Divine

As a white, middle-class feminist, I have come to the exploration of reimaging the divine from the perspective of gender first. It is only through a process of exploring what it means to be "white," and the history of the construction and enforcement of race in the United States and Europe, that I heed the call of black feminists and U.S. third-world feminists to pay attention to the dynamics of race involved in the experience of every person. Gender and race, as well as additional factors such as class and sexuality, cannot be separated within a person's experience. They profoundly impact a particular person's identity and experience. This "intersectionality"[50] must be addressed when engaging in the analysis of images.

Attention to intersectionality raises complicated questions, however. Whereas white women need the metaphor of Goddess in order to see themselves in the divine and the divine in themselves, do they need to consciously see Goddess as nonwhite in order to break down the tendency to believe that they are not "raced" and that God/dess is not "raced" in their minds and experiences? If they continue to image Goddess as white, are they reinforcing white supremacy? Or do they need to image the divine as a woman similar to themselves in order to break through their false images of themselves? How would an African American woman and a white woman experience an image of the divine as a black woman differently? Would the new image break through all old, oppressive images? Or would it reinforce some stereotypes of black women that are held by the white woman, thus disallowing the movement through the metaphor? In the interviews and discussions with the interviewees, it becomes very clear that the question of imaging the divine as gendered and raced is a complex, nuanced process, fraught with potential dangers yet also carrying powerful possibilities for transformation.

Kelly Brown Douglas addresses the intersectionality and particularity of African American women's experiences and needs in reimaging the divine. She challenges that Black theologians such as James Cone, Albert Cleage, and J. Deotis Roberts neglect to explore the impact of gender on the lives of African American women (as well as men) and therefore focused exclusively on the blackness of Christ, with no attention to the diversity of experiences within black communities.

For Cone, Christ's blackness is symbolic. It is not determined by Jesus' ethnic characteristics but is a "symbol of his existential commitments"[51] to the liberation of the oppressed. However, at the same time, Cone argues that the symbolic blackness of Christ is signified by the symbol of the black skin of black Americans because it is their black skin that bears the scars of their oppression. Therefore, Christ and God are black because they are willing to be concretely present with oppressed black people. For Cone, the person of Jesus, combined with his commitment to the liberation of the oppressed, is the key characteristic in determining the significance of Christ and God for the black community. He argues that the blackness of Christ (and God) is symbolic of Christ's solidarity with and active presence in the black community's struggle for liberation.

The symbolism of blackness represents the divine presence within the struggle for liberation against racist oppression in a white supremacist society and thus unlocks the awareness of all people that God is among the oppressed. On the other hand, whiteness is the symbol for the Antichrist. Cone says, "Whiteness symbolizes the activity of deranged men intrigued by their own image of themselves, and thus unable to see that they are what is wrong with the world."[52] People who are racially categorized as white can think, write, and act in ways that are "black"–if they are on the side of the oppressed. Cone claims, "I do not condemn all men [*sic*] who happen to look like white Americans; the condemnation comes when they act like them."[53]

Through this uncompromising iconoclastic argument, Cone successfully challenges the image of Jesus, and of God, as a white man. By calling whiteness "satanic" and blackness divine, he inverts and shatters the cultural biases in this white supremacist culture that whiteness is associated with purity, goodness, and divinity, while blackness is associated with the demonic and the unclean.

However, the maleness of God remains unquestioned and unchallenged. The evils of sexism, classism, and heterosexism remain unnamed. In addition, Douglas argues that simply calling Christ black fails to identify which aspects of blackness are affirmed by Christ. She says,

> While Black theologians attempted to affirm Blackness by identify-
> ing Christ as Black, they seemed to do so unconditionally. They did
> not sufficiently specify what it was that Christ affirmed in affirming
> Blackness. Not everything that is Black is sustaining or liberating
> for the Black community. There are aspects of Black culture and
> religion that do not necessarily foster self-esteem, nor do they
> empower Black people to fight for their freedom.

She argues that the "Blackness" of Christ must involve more than skin
color, history, or culture. Rather, it must also "include an ethical concern
and commitment to the well-being and freedom of all Black people."[54]

Reimaging Christ (and, I would add, God/Goddess) as black is essential
for freeing black people from their psychological and emotional enslavement and for empowering them to see themselves as created in the image
of the divine. One of the greatest strengths of the Black Christ is that "it
fosters a sense of self-esteem and pride in Black people as they come to
understand that who they are is not abhorred but valued by divine being.
They are able to see themselves in Christ."[55] Conversely, the "bombard-
ment of White images and symbols severely damages Black self-worth and
self-esteem." Douglas concludes that"Black worship of White images–even
Christ–is unhealthy, and reflective of Black people's psychological and
emotional enslavement to a White racist culture."[56] As J. Deotis Roberts
argues, "The most difficult task for the Black man [*sic*] is to obtain psychological freedom. If he can accept his Blackness, be proud of it and find
meaning for his life, he can know true inner freedom. This is where Jesus,
as the Black Messiah, comes in. The Black Messiah enables the Black man
[*sic*] to stand up to life."[57]

In order to overcome the problems that she saw in the Black Christ as
portrayed by the male theologians, Douglas offers new constructions for
imaging the divine as Black that allow for the affirmation of divine presence within all black people who are struggling for liberation from multiple
forms of oppression. Her womanist understanding of the blackness of Christ
comes from her analysis of the struggles of black women "within the wider
society as well as in the Black community" and through an affirmation of
black women's faith that God is with them when they fight for "survival
and freedom."[58]

Black women are–and have traditionally been–concerned not just with
survival and freedom for themselves but instead for the entire community
and whole families, men and women alike. Because of black women's holistic approach to understanding survival and liberation, Douglas argues that
womanist theology must include a "socio-political analysis of wholeness."[59]
She reasons that rather than focusing on only one form of oppression, such
as white racism, a womanist sociopolitical analysis must "confront racism,

sexism, classism, and heterosexism not only as they impinge on the Black community, but also as they are nurtured within that community."[60]

In light of this holistic analysis of the dynamics of multiple forms of oppression and of her holistic understanding of the approaches that must be taken to overcome them, Douglas offers a womanist portrayal for the Black Christ that allows for multiple images of Christ's "liberating and prophetic presence in the Black community." While she affirms the blackness of Christ, positing that "Christ has Black skin and features and is committed to the Black community's struggle for life and wholeness,"[61] and argues for the need for "Black people to be able to see themselves in the image of Christ," she does not end her discussion of imaging Christ with blackness.[62]

Instead, relying on her holistic, multidimensional method of understanding social and religious oppression, Douglas argues for a multidimensional approach to imaging Christ. She posits that Christ must be seen as a prophetic presence within the black community, as well as a sustainer and liberator, so that Christ's presence can be discerned in the prophetic actions of Black women and men who challenge both internal and external oppression.[63]

To this end, while symbols and icons are "essential tools for pointing to the reality of Christ and for helping people to see themselves in Christ and Christ in themselves," at the same time "no *one* symbol or icon for Christ can capture the presence or meaning of Christ."[64] She argues that "symbols and icons need to change as the community changes and attempts to discern Christ's involvement in their changing life situations." Therefore, womanist theology portrays "this sustaining, liberating, and prophetic Black Christ which eludes simple, static, depiction" by availing itself of "a diversity of symbols and icons."[65]

This turn toward multiple, changing images of the divine is similar to the dynamic among women in the feminist spirituality movement who are having profound spiritual experiences in relation to multiple, diverse images for the divine. However, Douglas argues that the "living Christ" should be imaged particularly through the "living symbols and icons" of contemporary and past black women (and black men) who struggle or have struggled for the wholeness of the black community.[66] Christ's presence is within everyone and is particularly discernible in the lives of people who are struggling for justice and wholeness. Therefore, the divine can be imaged in the faces of actual black people of the past and present. Douglas adds that her womanist theology of the Black Christ lifts up "the presence of the Black Christ in the faces of the poorest Black women," claiming that "these women, as an icon of Christ, are important reminders of accountability" to "the least of these."[67]

Imaging Christ in the faces of particular black women (and men) thus serves multiple purposes. It affirms the presence of Christ in black people who struggle for justice and wholeness yet it also affirms that Christ is present among the "least of these." It allows "Black women and men, girls and boys to see themselves in Christ and Christ in themselves,"[68] yet it involves an ethical obligation to recognize that Christ's presence within does not mean that Christ affirms all human actions in the black community.[69] Rather, the spirit of Christ is affirmed through the discernment of Christ's presence in women and men who embody that spirit in acts against the multiple forms of oppression and the many struggles that threaten to limit the wholeness and freedom for anyone within the black community.

By emphasizing the presence of Christ within both black women and black men, Douglas asserts that the maleness of Jesus becomes insignificant in determining the meaning of who Christ was and is. Instead, "To portray Christ in the face of Black heroines and heroes signals that it was not who Jesus was, particularly as a male, that made him Christ, but what he did. Essentially, Christ's biological characteristics have little significance in discerning Christ's sustaining, liberating, and prophetic presence."[70] At the same time, Douglas argues that it is essential that Jesus be understood as a person of African rather than European descent. In the context of struggling to overcome white racism, the biological and cultural ethnicity of Jesus remain a significant issue for her in discerning the solidarity of Jesus with contemporary oppressed black people and in debunking white supremacist images of Jesus as white.

The tension in Douglas's argument between emphasizing race or ethnicity as important in determining the meaning of Christ, and at the same time denying the importance of Christ's maleness, exemplifies the complexity of addressing gender and race in relation to reimaging the divine. Douglas sharply criticizes J. Deotis Roberts for attempting to be too universal when he claimed that Christ became incarnate as human and therefore could be imaged as any race or ethnicity. Douglas argues,

> To suggest that Christ can be any color of humanity is inconsistent with Jesus' unequivocal identification with the oppressed and nullifies Christ's Blackness . . . Because Jesus as Christ identified with all humanity, Roberts conceded that Christ could be White. To call Christ "White" in a society where to be White is to be identified with oppressors, identifies Christ as an oppressor. A White Christ undercuts Jesus' identification with the oppressed. A White Christ also nullifies Christ's affirmation of Blackness. If Christ is White, then he affirms that which "shames Black people in. their Blackness"–Whiteness.[71]

Douglas wrote exclusively for the black communities; therefore, her primary focus was on empowering black women, men, and children. However, her assertions that a white image of Christ "identifies Christ as an oppressor" and "shames Black people in their Blackness" raise the question for my research of how white people, particularly white women, can reimagine the divine in ways that affirm they are created in the divine image while at the same time avoiding images that reinforce white supremacy.

Is the solution for white people to imagine Christ and/or Goddess as a poor black woman? Or to represent Christ through images of past and present black heroines and heroes? If so, what about images of white women and men who have devoted their lives to the struggle for justice? Do they represent "Blackness" in Cone's understanding of blackness as symbolic? Douglas argues that "the male Jesus" was able to "reject the privileges of being male in a patriarchal world"[72] and should be a model for black, male theologians of how to divest themselves of their privileged male perspective. Is it possible for white people to reject the privileges of being white in a white supremacist world? If so, can people who do so adequately serve as images of Christ's presence and as models of how white people might challenge white supremacy themselves? Or is their whiteness still too closely tied to their ethnicity so that they cannot represent the Black Christ? Can white women and men image the divine as black without reinforcing stereotypes of black people that they have learned through growing up in a racist society?

Conclusion

The research for this book, as well as the authors discussed in this chapter, demonstrate the complex, paradoxical, and dare I say, mystical relationship that people have as they relate to alternative metaphors or images for the divine. Metaphor is a "journey," a "movement" that is different for each person, depending on her or his imaginative, emotional, and social realities at a particular time. The interaction with and creation of multiple, alternative images for the divine is a central dynamic of religious experience that must be taken seriously in all thea/ological reflections. When the images—whether old or new—are in human form, race and gender (as well as class, culture, sexual orientation) and the meanings that those carry for a particular person must always be considered.

It is imperative, therefore, that theologians and religious leaders remain vigilant about the images they "conjure" through their words. Do they allow for movement, play, and transformation of the status quo in individuals and in society? Or do they (often unconsciously) reinforce old, static images and unjust social relations? What conditions need to be in place in order for an image to become transformative? These questions will be explored further in the following chapter.

6

Third Story

Rosalyn

Rosalyn is a European American woman in her late thirties. She grew up in Georgia, moving to several different towns because of her father's various positions as a United Methodist minister. After several years abroad and in California, she returned home to Atlanta. She is married and has a young son. She works for an Episcopal church, helping to resettle refugees.

Imaging and Spirituality

Rosalyn has struggled throughout her life with a tension between an external, demanding, masculine image of God and an internal spirituality, manifested now in a feminine image of the divine. Her masculine image of God and her strong feeling that this God demanded something very difficult of her for her vocation came directly from her image of her father. She described her father as having a "strong personality" and explained that while she was interested in ministry from a young age, her parents discouraged her because the work of ministry was so difficult for her father. When I asked Rosalyn about her childhood image for the divine, she responded,

> Well I guess I probably had some images of God as an old, white man with a long beard, kind of like Santa Claus sitting in the clouds somewhere. But I do remember also, as a child, that Advent was always a very special time for me, and I would go into my room by myself and light a candle or the Christmas Tree–I had a little Christmas tree in my room–or sometimes I would sneak into where we had our Christmas tree to look at the lights. So lighting that candle in my room by myself, I don't know if it's really naming anything other than that I felt very special. That was a very special thing for me to do. Trying to do that in different ways.

I asked, "When you say 'to do that,' what do you mean?" She explained, "To do that; to be in my room by myself, to be alone, to turn off the lights, to light a candle. That was important somehow. That was about my spirituality somehow, but I don't really have a name or an image for that. But that was important." In discussing her childhood image for the divine, Rosalyn shifted immediately to her experience of spirituality. She felt a sense of herself as special when she had quiet, solitary moments that seemed like experiences of the holy.

In contrast, when I pushed her to describe what characteristics or experiences she had of the divine, she explained that for most of her life she had thought of and experienced God as external and demanding. She continued,

> I think as a child and probably still up until very recently. Thinking of the divine as something that's out there. That I have to guess what it wants me to do or God's will, God's calling on your life. That God had something very specific for you to do with your life and that it wasn't going to be easy. It was going to be something hard to do. And, but you had to figure out what it was and that's probably an image that's been with me from a very early age.

She struggled for years to discern what God wanted her to do with her life, often feeling frustrated and saddened by how difficult that process felt for her. Only recently had she begun to understand and to experience the divine as internal as well as external and as cooperating with her own passions and desires for her life.

Internal Feminine Divine

She explained that it was through reading feminist theologies and beginning to reimagine the divine as feminine and within herself, as well as external to herself, that she had been able to recognize that the divine is not just an external, demanding male God. She described this process of change, saying,

> I especially remember, in my twenties just really struggling with the question "What does God want me to do?" and it just always felt like God was some mystery out there. I had to guess, and struggled so hard to know what that was. I think I have evolved more to the point where God may not be just out there. That God may be in here and a part of my own wants and in cooperation with me, not against me or not me giving up of myself to follow what this outside calling was. I think that was a real source of struggle and a real source of sadness for me. Just not knowing what that was. Working to be more interior, I think that probably began to

change around the time that I began to read some of the feminist theologies. A lot of that was more interior.

Through recognizing the divine as more interior, she had also been able to name her experiences of the divine—even those of her childhood—that did not reflect the external, demanding God that she had imagined. During our second group discussion, she reflected, "Exploration of the feminine images . . . does allow more permission to perceive the experiential pieces as a valid part of the truth." Reimagining the divine as feminine as well as more interior allowed her to honor her own experiences and desires and to feel that she did not have to give up herself in order to fulfill her vocation.

Presence

She experiences God "more gently now . . . a gentle presence." She related this experience of the divine as a gentle presence within her times of quiet spirituality throughout her life. She reflected, "I think I always felt God more so in the quiet places in my life." She explained that she has always been drawn to music written in minor keys, music that she described as "slower," "more reflective," "maybe a little more brooding." She went on, "Through music, I feel God . . . I feel that presence in music more than anything else." The music helps her to connect with her sense of the holy in a way that other spiritual practices do not.

When I asked about the connection between feminine images and a sense of presence, Rosalyn responded,

> As there are other feminine images, it does seem like there's more a natural valuing of one's own experience instead of trying to constantly fit your experience into what it's supposed to be. That, as there are more of those images available, it's more of a trusting that what I feel and what I experience and what I know may be in cooperation with the Spirit, as opposed to being something other.

A plurality of feminine images allows her to value her own feminine experience. Instead of trying to fit her experience into "what it's supposed to be"—either into what an external God wants from her or into what her parents want from her—these feminine images have assisted her in honoring her own intuitive sense of the holy as being present with her, in silence or in music, making her feel special since she was a young child.

She connected the internal presence of God with her bodily experience as a woman. For her, the process of imaging the divine as internal involved "undoing" old images of the divine as only "out there," while honoring one's own "felt and known experiences" as legitimate experiences of the divine. As Nelle Morton advocates, Rosalyn is moving toward imaging and naming the divine out of her own authentic experiences. To do so, however, she has had to engage in the process of undoing the old, deeply engrained external images.

Relationships

Rosalyn explained that as a child, she was very sensitive and "did not want to hurt people's feelings." She said that she was "always making sure other people are comfortable." This sensitivity, combined with her role as a minister's daughter and her experiences of moving often, caused her to always include people who were on the outside or different in some way. This led her to her current work with refugee resettlement. On the other hand, this sensitivity and fear of hurting other peoples' feelings have made it difficult for her to challenge her father and mother on issues of theology and church practices. She finds that being in the presence of her parents is "not a safe place" for her to discuss her spirituality and feminist theology.

She experiences "hostility" from her mother, with whom she is very close, when she tries to discuss feminist theology. She had a very difficult and painful struggle with her father when she disagreed with him about the traditional marriage liturgy for her wedding. She explained that now, when she is with her parents and in their community, she has to make a great effort to be herself. She is overwhelmed by them and by their environment.

After I told her my observation about her lifelong tension between an external God, modeled on her father, and a feminine, internal experience of the divine, she said that there has been a part of her that has been true to herself and her spirituality since she was a child. She explained,

> I have to work really hard, when I move into my parents' environment, to be as much of who I am that I can be, but I guess at the same time be supportive of who they are in their environment. And sometimes those aren't always the same things. But it does feel like a tension a lot. It makes me feel hopeful that you saw something at the very beginning that was kind of mine. Because sometimes I think it can be overwhelming. My father does have a very strong personality and so I have to protect that.

Rosalyn struggles to integrate these different parts of her experience—her parents' environment of the traditional church in which she was raised and her internal sense of spirituality and of the divine, as well as her discomfort with church teachings and practices. She has begun to honor and to protect her need to have quiet time for herself in her own space.

Interestingly, she has come to realize that she is more like her mother than she had previously cared to admit. She perceives the similarities more clearly now that she herself is a mother taking care of a home. As she experiences the divine as more internal, working in cooperation with her, she also experiences God as being present in the activities that she and her mother share. She explained,

As I look at God possibly working in cooperation with me, I really do think of God's presence more, I guess as where I am, in the home, in daily activities, and those are the things that my mother did very well.

Tension with the Institutional Church

Rosalyn identified with the other women in the group when they expressed their experiences of tension with the beliefs and practices of the institutional church. While they all loved the traditional church, they were in a constant state of tension by trying to hold together their love of the church and their passion for feminist theology and spirituality.

Rosalyn described herself and her friends as having "one foot in, one foot out" in relation to the institutional church. Her description of this tension, and the discussion around that tension, echoed the voices of the women in Winter, Lummis, and Stokes's *Defecting in Place*. In her interview, she expressed that she feels "very lonely" in the institutional church (in her case, the Methodist church) but that it is not easy to leave because it is a part of her family. She described her experience of negotiating this tension of being lonely in her family, saying "I go back and forth." This language of "one foot in, one foot out," "back and forth," and the phrase "push-pull" used by Julie, reflect the active, constant state of tension in the Christian feminist spirituality movement. Each woman worked to resolve that tension in her own creative ways.

Rosalyn described how years ago, at a conference for Methodist women on the status of women in the church, she let go of the hope that she would ever feel comfortable as a woman within the church. She "gave up being able to feel comfortable . . . that I could find ways to express my faith that felt comfortable as a woman within the church." She continued to be actively involved in Methodist churches for years after that time. However, that "giving up" seems to have allowed her to let go of any expectation that she will have her needs as a woman met within the church. Instead, after that acceptance, she has sought out communities where she can comfortably express her faith and her perspective as a woman. She explained that unlike her family and the churches in which she has been a part, MMP allows her to "feel as if I have a place, a safe place to ask questions within the community of faith." She was able to express both her questions and her spirituality as a woman within this "community of faith" and to feel that she is still part of the Christian community of faith.

Rosalyn was taking responsibility for her own spiritual life. She had developed a spiritual support system that included different groups and centers that were affiliated with the church but were outside of it at the same time. She found "a lot of sustenance on the edges of the church." She said, "I find things in different places . . . little touchstones in different places–that's part of the new community–not the same church community."

She honored her newfound form of community, of MMP and of her small group meetings for worship and discernment with women friends, naming these as a new type of church community. She described these places as places where she could be more herself. Like Theresa, she had felt alone and "crazy" because of her discomfort with the institutional church. Her experiences with these groups, as well as in other conferences for Christian women, had helped her to find a new sense of community and to honor her needs, feelings, and questions.

Rosalyn was deeply committed to her Christian tradition. In planning the liturgy for this process, she emphasized including traditional elements such as the Episcopal invocation. One element of her excitement about MMP was that it has allowed her to reclaim parts of the Christian tradition and scriptures that were more affirming of her spirituality. She was passionate about remaining connected to the Christian tradition, even when she did not feel that she could meet her spiritual needs within a traditional church setting. In spite of her acceptance that the church was not likely to change soon enough for her, during a discussion of her vocation she admitted that "the reformation of the church" was her true passion.

She explained that even though the church felt like family to her while she was growing up, at the same time she felt discomfort with the liturgy from an early age. She had not been able to explain her discomfort, however. Like Theresa, she had blamed herself, thinking that there was something about her that made her feel uncomfortable. After reading her first book in feminist theology, she was finally able to name her discomfort. She explained,

> It was at that point that I really felt my uncomfortableness in the mainstream church. I always thought that it was just me . . . But after I read that book, then I began thinking that perhaps religion is, in and of itself, or religious institutions were so influenced by masculine ideals of the world that perhaps my uncomfortableness was due in a large part because I was a woman, and I was viewing the world as a woman. And so that book really sparked in me a lot, or at least named for me maybe why I was feeling uncomfortable. And that just kind of kept growing inside of me, that one could name that. Being more interested in how one, you know, what would religion in general look like if it were shaped more with a woman's reflection or woman's way of being in the world.

As this awareness and this question "kept growing inside" her, Rosalyn began increasingly to honor her own spirituality and perspectives as a woman. In doing so, she had also come to image the divine as within herself as well as within all of creation.

Spirituality and Transformation

It was through this honoring of her experiences and feelings that she had been able to move beyond her struggle of trying to "guess" the difficult job that an external God wanted her to do in the world. Instead, she now understood the work of God in her discernment of her vocation to be more internal. She saw God as working with her own desires, not demanding difficult things of her from outside of herself. Through experiences of burning out both emotionally and spiritually from trying to "do" too much in the world, Rosalyn had also come to the realization that her spirituality must involve simply "being" with God. She appreciated the emphasis in MMP of needing to both be and do. In her own spirituality, she now emphasized "resting in God, experiencing God," and not simply doing what God wanted her to do.

When I asked Rosalyn to describe her most significant spiritual experiences, she described the birth of her son. She explained that she felt the presence of the divine with her in that moment more strongly than she ever had before. She felt calm and unafraid, that she was in "partnership with something much larger" than herself.

At the same time, she felt the presence of the women of MMP there with her. She recounted a liturgy at MMP in celebration of St. Bridget's Day that she had attended while she was pregnant. She explained that St. Bridget is associated with midwifery and bringing new life. In the Irish tradition, St. Bridget is associated with the ancient Mother Goddess and her celebration incorporates elements of ancient worship of the Goddess. During the liturgy, each woman cut a piece of a cloth that had been left out overnight to be blessed by St. Bridget. Rosalyn wore the pieces of cloth when she was in labor with her son. She explained, "And it's still on my altar at home, and I just felt that somehow I had the protection of St. Bridget, of all the women at MMP. I don't know. It was an important part of that experience."

The liturgy with the women of MMP, which called for a blessing from the Mother Goddess as represented through St. Bridget, allowed Rosalyn to carry a sense of blessing and protection with her into her birthing experience. She felt protected both by St. Bridget and by the women at MMP during the birth. Her sense of divine presence during labor involved both cooperation and protection. She experienced the divine as present in her body's giving birth, as embodied in the blessing and protection given by the women in her community, and as embodied in the person of St. Bridget—as well as beyond all personal embodiments. The fluidity of her understanding of imaging the divine allowed her to move between internal and external images. Like the women in the feminist spirituality movement quoted in previous chapters, she had a mystical, paradoxical awareness of the divine as both within and beyond herself—as within and yet more than multiple images and representations. This understanding of the divine has allowed her to integrate the two aspects of her spirituality that were in tension for most of her life—the external and the internal.

7

Exploring the "Sacred Imaginary"

The Black Madonna and Her Representations

I was just thinking, is there any way to image God in new ways that isn't false in some way— . . . distancing . . . romanticizing . . . or the strong black woman . . . I mean, are you always going to be telling some sort of a lie? Or causing some sort of damage with another image?
—JULIE, DURING THE INTERVIEW DISCUSSION, MAY, 2004

When God is spoken of as personal, it necessarily sparks the imagination to picture God in human form: What kind of person is God? What does He or She look like? Complicating this question are the particular dynamics of "race," ethnicity, gender, and class within a particular context. Each person is conditioned within her or his family, community, and society to understand ethnicity, gender, and class in particular ways. In the United States, these representations are shaped by the history of slavery, colonization, and white male supremacy. The images that shape our culture and our religious expressions grow out of this history. Stereotypical images, used as tools of oppression, still circulate in our advertising, our common language, and in our religious imagery.

In Western Europe, stereotypical images of people from former colonies in Africa and Asia continue to influence the cultural landscape. When considering alternative images of the divine in contexts such as the United States and Europe, it is important to examine critically our attraction to particular images. Particularly for people of European descent, it is crucial that we question the stereotypical associations that we might hold in relation to images of people of non-European ancestry as representative of the divine.

The process of questioning images leads to critical social and theological reflection. This kind of critical reflection is essential, in concert with exploring alternative imagery of the divine in the context of worship. Otherwise, stereotypes of both race and gender might be left intact or reinforced rather than challenged through the experience of worship.

In this chapter, I examine worship of the Black Madonna in diverse cultural contexts. I chose the Black Madonna as a case study to demonstrate the complexity involved in imaging the divine in any context. Regardless of the image in question, critical reflection related to images, stereotypes, and sociohistorical context is essential in order to avoid perpetuating harmful images.

I first began to question the impact that worshiping a black, female image of the divine could have on social relationships in the United States when I read bell hooks's story of traveling in Western Europe. hooks traveled to Europe after college, full of hope that Europe would be free of the racism by which she felt stifled in the United States. Instead, she was disappointed to find racism rampant in Europe as well, in the form of a "passion for the 'primitive,' the 'exotic.'"[1] She wrote that European acquaintances repeatedly told her they could not be racist in Europe because they worshipped a Black Madonna. She described her visit to a shrine of the Black Madonna in Montserrat, Spain, in this way:

> At the shrine of the Black Madonna, I saw long lines of adoring white worshippers offering homage. They were praying, crying, longing to caress and to touch, to be blessed by this mysterious black woman saint. In their imaginations, her presence was the perfect embodiment of the miraculous. To be with her was to be in the place of ecstasy. Indeed, momentarily in this sanctuary, race, class, gender, and nationality had fallen away. In their place was a vision of hope and possibility. Yet this moment in no way altered the politics of domination outside, in that space of the real. Only in the realm of the sacred imaginary was there the possibility of transcendence. None of us could remain there.[2]

hooks's testimony raises several questions: In the context of European worship of the Black Madonna, why did the realm of the "sacred imaginary" not seem to influence the politics of the "real world"? What exactly is the relationship between sacred images, human relationships, and structures of race, gender, and class? Under what conditions can a sacred image serve the purpose of challenging racism, sexism, and classism in those who worship that image? I contend that challenging stereotypical images through critical reflection and education about the oppressive history of stereotypes can help people move toward a compassionate affirmation of shared humanity and divine presence and thus toward action for social as well as spiritual change.

I will compare some examples of worship of the Black Madonna in Western Europe, Brazil, Poland, and the United States in order to explore the answers to these questions. The same image (although the actual representations vary at different sites) can have profoundly different meanings and effects depending on particular cultural locations, as well as on the race, gender, and class of the people worshiping the Black Madonna in a specific location. A particular image for the divine can serve either to reinforce or to challenge stereotypes of race, gender, and class; in some instances, it does both.

While the focus of this chapter is on the Black Madonna, this exploration raises questions about the meanings that each person brings to any image for the divine. The challenge for religious leaders is to facilitate critical reflection about the construction of race, gender, and class in their particular context so that people might relate to images of the divine in a way that opens their minds to the full humanity of all people and facilitates intimacy with divine presence.

Western Europe

In many parts of Western Europe, the Virgin Mary is worshiped in both black and white images and statues. Interestingly, however, the Black Madonna is quite often worshiped as more powerful and more capable of performing miracles than her white counterpart. Moss and Cappannari argue, "If veneration and adoration are accorded saints and the Virgin Mary, then the only word for the degree of reverence given to this image [the Black Madonna] is that of worship. The Madonna is worshiped for her power rather than for the grace normally associated with the Virgin."[3]

This raises interesting questions about the meaning of her blackness in the imaginations of European worshipers. What power does her blackness signify? How does this power relate to Western European images and stereotypes of people of African descent as they have evolved over the centuries? Why does this venerated blackness and femaleness not translate into more social power for women of African descent in Western Europe?

While Catholic leaders have largely downplayed the significance of the blackness (or brownness, as is often the case) of Black Madonnas, arguing that they are dark because of fire damage, age, or other natural causes, scholars have recently discovered a different historical account of their origins. They have traced the origins of numerous images of the Black Madonna in Europe. All the images of the Black Madonna are considered to be "miracle workers."[4] All of them are found in regions once occupied by the Romans. They conclude that the Black Madonnas are Christian borrowings from earlier pagan depictions of Demeter, Melaina, Diana, Isis, Cybele, Artemis, or Rhea as black, the color associated with goddesses of the earth's fertility.[5]

The images of the Black Madonna in Christian churches are not merely borrowings or replicas, however. Many of the Christian sites where the Black Madonna is now worshiped were previously the actual sites of worship of the Mother Goddess. The Black Madonna worshiped in Tindari, Sicily, is in a church that was built on the site of a former temple for worship of the black earth goddess Cybele. The same is the case in Lyons, France. The image of the Black Madonna worshiped in a Christian church there, on the site of a former Cybeline temple, is assumed to be a replica of an ancient image of Cybele. Stephen Benko explains,

> The statue of Artemis is black, and so is the Virgin venerated in Notre Dame de la Confession. In Paris, a center of the worship of Isis, a black statue of Isis was actually venerated as the Virgin until the sixteenth century.[6]

In most cases, the pagan origins of the Black Madonnas have been obscured, allowing them to continue to exist without removal by the pope. Approximately four thousand statues of the Black Madonna are found throughout Europe, just as shrines to earth goddesses were great in number.

Initially the Christian church banned all images. However, it had to submit to popular wishes and traditions. Thus, when images were allowed into Christian worship,

> some very ancient images, sometimes uncouth, were miraculously discovered in unfrequented spots (woods, caves, etc.) where the pagan peasantry had hidden them. The clergy blessed these images under Christian names and often built temples for them just where they had been found. According to local legends, the images refused to stay put in the parish church. In fact, the clergy regarded them with suspicion. Pilgrimages began, distinct from the regular worship at the orthodox church. The most famous of these images were black.[7]

The ecstasy and transcendence that bell hooks observed in Montserrat seems to follow an ancient tradition of subversive pilgrimages to a very different kind of madonna.

The Black Madonna is perceived to be differently powerful because of her ancient origins as the Goddess of the Earth.[8] The explanation for her blackness usually given by Roman Catholic scholars attributes the color to "accumulated dirt and soot."[9] However, this explanation does not account for why the statues turned black even under the clothing, and not just the face and hands. The more obvious explanation is that they are black because they represent the fertile earth, "mother of us all."[10] The Black Madonnas represent the earth in the form of the mother earth goddess.

Her blackness is not so one-dimensional in meaning, however, for some of the earth goddesses, such as Isis, Artemis, and Cybele were brought to Europe from Nubian Africa. The cult of Isis was popular during the Roman Empire and worship of Isis continued in Europe well into the third century A.D. The worship of Isis spread into Europe from southern Egypt, "Nubian territory," which reached into what is known today as Sudan. The blackness of Isis, as well as of Artemis and Cybele, is probably associated with both her African origins and the blackness of the earth.[11]

This complexity causes controversy among scholars. For example, Benko takes pains to point out that statues of the Black Madonna are black in color but not in "race." He says, "In none of them with which I am familiar can Negroid features be detected; therefore, they are not black because of their race."[12] Apparently, while most Roman Catholic scholars are uncomfortable with the blackness of the statues, choosing to dismiss them as dirty, Benko felt he must qualify that they are *not* "black" in a racial sense even though they are black. This discussion demonstrates that European understandings of race impact views of the images of the Black Madonna. While Benko claims that it is not a factor, his raising of the subject indicates that he is aware that the black color of the statues is a significant factor in their meaning in Europe.

Worship of the Black Madonna in Western Europe thus continues to raise questions for Europeans about the meanings of her blackness. The historical constructions of "whiteness" and "blackness" have varied radically throughout European history, depending entirely on the political and economic interests of wealthy Western Europeans.[13] During antiquity, European attitudes toward Africa were generally positive. During the Greek and Roman empires, differences in skin color were not viewed as significant and black carried a positive meaning.[14] The blackness of the Black Madonna might be a result of the positive views of blackness that existed in Graeco-Roman times, when Mother Goddesses such as Cybele, Isis, and Artemis were originally depicted as black. During this time, there was also a great love in Europe for Egyptian and Nubian cultures. However, even at this time there was a third image of Africa–that is, a "wild, unknown Africa" that was inhabited by monstrous beings like the Cyclopes and the Amazons.[15]

During the Christian period, the association of sin with blackness and darkness caused a significant negative shift in views toward Africa and Africans. Black came to be the color of the devil and demons. However, during late medieval times Christian Ethiopia became an important ally against the Muslims. From this alliance emerged iconography that depicted black Africans in positive ways. The primary images were of the Queen of Sheba, Prester John, and Caspar the King of the Moors (a popular image of one of the three kings who visited the Christ child). The Middle Ages (the twelfth to fifteenth centuries) saw a "stylistic revaluation of black, which was no longer seen as a demonic color," and images of black saints such as Black Sara of the Gypsies were revered in the Mediterranean region.[16]

While images of Africa and Africans would begin to change drastically to justify the slave trade that began in the fifteenth century, a legacy of black saints and religious figures remained part of European culture. It is likely that Europeans who encountered images of the Black Madonna in the context of positive popular opinion of black Africa as "Europe's redeemer and help in distress"[17] would have experienced her power as related to this positive view of blackness. In addition, the cult of the Black Madonna "flowered" during the Middle Ages. Perhaps this flowering was due to the positive associations with blackness and black saints during this period of conflict.

With the beginning of the slave trade, and the colonization of North and South America and of Africa, the European notion of "savage," which had long been used to describe Europeans who lived in the wilderness, was transferred to the representation of Africans and indigenous Americans. With this designation came a double-sided stereotype—of the "noble savage," admired for innocence, virtue, and a lack of civilization and history, and of the "Wild Man," who was between beast and man. The suppression of knowledge of African history and civilization allowed Europeans to conceive of Africa as made up only of "nature." In the nineteenth century, this portrayal of Africa was used as a justification for European colonialism.[18] African "savages" were portrayed as part of the wild landscape but not rightful owners of the land. Images of European explorers venturing into vast, uninhabited—"or at least uncultivated"—jungles in Africa served to justify colonization.[19] Within this "cultural space" of precolonial and colonial Europe, how would the collective attitude toward Africa and Africans have affected the impact of worshipping the Black Madonna?

Conceivably, the association of blackness in Africa with primitive instincts, animals, and fertile landscapes served to enliven the European imagination about the Black Madonna's powers of fertility. Perhaps the Black Madonna's association with earthly power, fertility, and miracles only enhanced stereotypes about Africans as being closer to nature, without civilization, and primitive. Thus, worship of a Black Madonna could serve to reinforce stereotypes of black Africans used to justify colonialism rather than to challenge Europeans to reconsider stealing land from people who resembled their beloved Black Madonnas and then subjugating them.

Another aspect of primitivism was the European longing to return to their own "primitive," uncivilized, natural selves—to recover their instinctive, unconscious selves. Pieterse explains,

> Savagery thus acquired another meaning, as an image of the instinctive. This view was at the heart of psychoanalysis; in the works of Freud and Jung and the post-Freudians, primitives were equated with children and the mentally disturbed, in accordance with the idea that earlier stages of human consciousness were recapitulated during childhood. Thus the myth of the Wild Man, which had become a fiction, again became a myth, "a projection of repressed desires and anxieties."[20]

Apparently, a myth of a "Wild Woman" was part of this projection as well. In his 1985 book *The Cult of the Black Virgin,* Jungian scholar Ean Begg traces the pagan and pre-Christian origins of the Black Virgin (loosely, with no footnotes). His descriptions of the Black Virgin and her symbolic significance (drawing largely on his training in Jungian depth psychology) reflects much of the primitivism that Pieterse describes among nineteenth-century European attitudes toward Africans. He says, "Underneath all our conditioning, hidden in the crypt of our being, near the waters of life, the Black Virgin is enthroned with her Child, the dark latency of our own essential nature, that which we were always meant to be."[21] Begg was a well-known Jungian analyst in Europe. There is a Jung Institute of the Black Madonna in Einsiedeln, Switzerland, today, near one of her shrines. Begg's primitivist analysis of the significance of the Black Madonna demonstrates that the primitivism of nineteenth-century Europe is alive and well in the minds of some contemporary European Jungians.

Alongside primitivism, scientific racism developed in the nineteenth century. Scientists attempted to classify the anatomical differences between the "races" in order to prove the physical and cultural superiority of Europeans. With this search for significant anatomical differences, an intense focus on the sexual organs of African women developed. European stereotypes of African women (and men) as uninhibited sexually transferred, in scientific racism, to a belief that African women had sexual organs that were larger than those of European women. Saartjie Baartman, a woman from the Cape Colony, was brought to both England and France and displayed as the "Hottentot Venus" in the early 1800s. Scientists studied her and displayed her in a museum as an example of African women's sexualized nature, demonstrated in her large buttocks and in her reportedly enlarged clitoris, or "Hottentot apron."[22]

While black women were stereotyped as highly sexualized in both Europe and in the United States, the European images of black female sexuality were more complex. African female sexuality came to be seen as representative of female sexuality generally, which, in accordance with nineteenth-century medical views, was considered "pathological."[23] In addition, the sexuality of prostitutes was studied in comparison with the sexuality of black women so that they came to be associated with one another in Europe.[24]

Drawing on these popular scientific theories, European art in the late nineteenth and early twentieth centuries began to portray black women as representative of sexuality.[25] Black women were painted with increasing frequency during the early twentieth century as being representatives of exotic sexuality. Pieterse explains,

> This lyrical view of the Black Venus was not fundamentally different from the medical perspective: the black woman was sexualized and equated with the prostitute in Picasso's work as well. But the attitude toward sexuality was different—not hostile; nor was the prostitute

made a criminal. Baudelaire associated the black woman with darkness . . . but the darkness was enchanting, intriguing rather than threatening. To the extent that the African woman is represented as the "primal woman," the question of how she is valued reflects the attitude towards women and sexuality in general.[26]

In a side note about paintings of the exotic, sexualized black woman, he adds that "typically, in America there was no market for them."[27]

bell hooks experienced this particularly European form of racism when she visited Europe. She recounted her surprise at paintings of nude black females hung on the walls of her hotel.[28] The fact that there was "no market" for these paintings of sexualized, exoticized black women in the United States correlated with hooks's observation that there would be no market for a powerful Black Madonna in the United States as well. While hooks is incorrect about contemporary times, as will be discussed later in this chapter, her observation was accurate in relation to past decades. An image of a powerful black woman, whether her power was sexual or miraculous, would have been untenable in Reconstruction and Jim Crow America.

Calling the stereotype of the exotic, sexualized black woman "Black Venus" demonstrates a comfort level with images of black goddesses in Europe that was not evident in U.S. history. Nevertheless, this history in Europe did not challenge stereotypes of black women as oversexed and exotic. The devotion and passion that Europeans had in worshipping the Black Madonna were genuine and profound, and still are. However, it is probable that the image of the Black Madonna as having extraordinary power in relation to fertility and miracles was and still is mutually reinforcing of stereotypes of black women as primitive and highly sexual. Ironically, although the Black Madonna is also called the "Black Virgin," her relationship with fertility and her connection with the power of the earth could easily connect in the subconscious minds of worshippers with their stereotypes of the black woman as highly sexualized and closer to the earth.

Critical reflection about divine images in Western European contexts must include, therefore, education in the history of stereotypical images of Africa and Africans in the context of colonization, colonialism, and slavery. While these surely vary by country, similar themes affect the imaginations of Western European worshippers as they encounter the Black Madonna and other black saints. Ideally, this kind of critical reflection would allow worshippers to move through the process of negating stereotypical representations of people of African descent as well as of the divine images that are represented as black, and then affirming the divine in all people—not as romanticized, exoticized "other" but as an imminent, mysterious presence of liberating love.

Brazil: "Mother to All"

In Brazil, the relationship of worshippers to the Black Madonna is quite different from the dominant perceptions in Europe. While she is also understood in Brazil to be "Mother to All," who performs great miracles, she is especially known for performing miracles for people who are poor and, in previous generations, for slaves. She represents divine love and power in solidarity with those who are oppressed.

Legend tells that two poor fishermen who could not catch any fish found a two-foot statue of the Black Madonna in 1717 in the Paraiba River in Brazil. As soon as they raised the statue out of the river in their net, they caught many fish. The statue was passed from house to house and many miracles occurred. One miracle is recounted of a slave who was shackled in chains stopping to pray at the doorway of the then small shrine of the Madonna. When he knelt, his chains broke apart. His master immediately freed him, on the command of the Madonna. While this event did not lead to the ending of slavery, the sharing of the story led to the Black Madonna's image as symbol of liberation for the poor and enslaved.[29] She became so popular that she was declared the patron of all Brazil.

Today, Brazil's national shrine of *Aparecida* (the name given to the Black Madonna) is larger than St. Peter's Cathedral in Rome. Author China Galland attended a service with seventy thousand worshippers in the shrine. Banners hung in the shrine that said, "Aparecida, Mother of the Excluded of Brazil." The Archbishop in Brazil, Dom Aloysius Lorscheider, told Galland "that all who have been marginalized by conventional society are upheld and revered in the figure of this Virgin—the poor, the broken, and the dark. She is their champion. She is black because she is the Mother of All."[30] As in Europe, the Black Madonna represents a primal mother in Brazil. However, in Brazil her maternal care leads to her identification with those who are marginalized by structures of oppression. Devotion to her has led to a national valorization in postcolonial times of those who suffer from poverty, racism, and oppression. She is embraced as a symbol of solidarity and hope for those who suffer for economic and political reasons.

Throughout the eighteenth, nineteenth, and twentieth centuries, Mary has been "the great companion and mother" of many popular struggles in Latin America. Many peasant movements for liberation in countries such as Brazil, Bolivia, Peru, and El Salvador have been motivated by "the people's love of the Virgin fighting with them for liberation."[31] However, most of these images of the Virgin are not black. Some, like Our Lady of Guadalupe in Mexico, are depicted as brown, like the indigenous people of Latin America.

Significantly, in Brazil, with its large African population, the statue of the Madonna that became *Aparecida* had turned black in the river before the fishermen found her. Gebara and Bingemer argue that "the enslaved blacks of Brazil read the signs of Mary . . . to indicate her disapproval of slavery in Brazil. Henceforth, the black Virgin, who appears to the poor, has become a part of the inalienable heritage of the oppressed and marginalized black people of Brazil."[32] The Black Madonna in Brazil is thought to represent one of the Orishas that were brought to Brazil from Africa, are now worshipped in the Afro-Brazilian religion known as Candomble, and are easily disguised as Catholic saints.[33] The Black Madonna thus reminds Afro-Brazilians of their African heritage while inspiring their struggles against oppression.

The meaning of the Madonna for women in Brazil is complex, however. Galland recounted that immediately following a celebration of the Feast of the *Aparecida,* the Mother of the Excluded, the priests were exhorting people, particularly women, to "be more like Mary . . . be obedient, reasonable, serene. Above all obedient." In this context, the priests tried to domesticate the powerful image of the Black Madonna, using the traditional image of Mary "meek and mild" to control parishioners and caution against the empowerment that the *Aparecida* represented.[34] The powerful Goddess represented by the Black Madonna is easily obscured by religious leaders' use of Mary to symbolize patriarchal Christian norms of how women should behave. Her symbolism for the liberation of women from sexist oppression is therefore ambiguous, even when she symbolizes liberation from poverty, oppression, and racism. Critical reflection about worship of the Black Madonna, therefore, needs to include reflection about gender roles and the ways that representations of Mary have been used to reinforce oppressive roles for women.

This type of critical reflection occurred during the interviews for this book. During our second group discussion, Theresa explained her experiences of Mary while growing up in Colombia. Mary, whether black, brown, or white, represented simply a mediator, a woman who would understand her pain and speak to Jesus on her behalf but not a powerful woman in her own right. Mary might "help you with your pain. But not because she's going to be able to make any decision and solve your problem."[35] Significantly, she described Mary with the exact terms that she used to describe her own mother's role in the context of her patriarchal family. To her, Mary was "like a good mom, but with no power."[36]

Theresa's reflections demonstrated that a critical examination of the worship of divine images necessarily involves deeply personal as well as sociocultural and historical analyses. While Colombia's history and culture are obviously very different from Brazil's, the efforts of the priests to assert the Black Madonna's obedience, reasonableness, and serenity demonstrate that the male hierarchy of the Catholic Church tries to limit the power of Mary, and thus of women.

Throughout Latin America, Mary is therefore an ambiguous, multivalent image. On the one hand, she is the radically loving, empowering

Mother of All, representing movements for liberation throughout the region. On the other hand, she has traditionally been represented as obedient and meek, and less powerful than the male Christ and God.

Poland: "Queen of the Workers"

Lest the distinction between Europe and Brazil be drawn too neatly, it is important to note that in Poland, where members of the Solidarity movement struggled against the authoritarian government, the Black Madonna of Czestochowa was worshipped as being on the side of the Solidarity movement. As in Latin America, this Madonna is seen to represent divine love as siding with liberation from oppression. During the 1980s, many people throughout Poland carried illegal Solidarity banners during the annual pilgrimages to the Black Madonna of Czestochowa of about one million people. The marches were not stopped by the government because they were simply too large to control. This freedom to go on pilgrimage to see the Black Madonna who blessed the Solidarity movement was an essential part of the struggle for freedom in Poland. The movement's leader, Lech Walesa, worshiped her. When he won the Nobel Peace Prize, he dedicated it to the Black Madonna of Czestochawa.[37] In 1988, Polish cleric Monsignor Jankowsky explained, "You want to know about the Madonna and Solidarity. She is our patron. She is the Queen of the Workers. This is a very special relationship, very important. The workers believe that she will take care of them in every situation. She is the hope of the Solidarity movement."[38]

For over 350 years, the Black Madonna of Czestochowa has represented liberation from oppressive rule to the Polish people. She was named "Queen of Poland" by King John Casimir in 1656 A.D., after one hundred monks at the Monastery of Jasna Gora (where her icon is housed) and 250 soldiers miraculously defeated 8,500 Swedish soldiers.[39] This defeat marked the end of Swedish rule in Poland. The Madonna is also credited with securing the independence of Poland from the Bolshevik army in 1920. Poland achieved independence after 125 years of having been partitioned between Prussia, Austria, and Russia. The defense of Warsaw, called by the Polish the "Miracle of Vistula," resulted in the reestablishment of Poland as a sovereign country.[40] The Madonna of Czestochawa has thus been seen as the protector of the nation of Poland for centuries.

In renaming the "Queen of Poland" as the "Queen of the Workers," the Solidarity movement claimed that their spirit is the true spirit of Poland. During martial law, "a copy of the icon of the Black Madonna circulated through villages . . . but it sparked so much resistance that authorities placed the painting under house arrest."[41] Just as in Brazil, the circulation from house to house of an image of the Black Madonna sparked resistance and a movement for freedom.

While Polish people have been influenced over the centuries by the stereotypes about blackness and Africa that were generated in Western

Europe during colonialism and the slave-trade, in this Eastern European country the Black Madonna has nevertheless taken on a similar role to that in Brazil, where she more closely resembles the Brazilian people of African descent. While she, like the Black Madonnas of Western Europe, is associated with miracles, her significance does not rest primarily in her connection to fertility. Rather, she has come to represent the spirit of freedom and solidarity that is most cherished by the Polish people. Love for her and hope in her inspired the nonviolent movement of millions of Polish workers for freedom from totalitarianism.

In spite of the overwhelming love in Poland for this Black Madonna, however, there is still controversy over calling her "black." The negative meanings associated with blackness in Western Europe are also found in Poland. Galland recounts conversations with two Polish art historians who disputed the name "Black Madonna" for the Madonna of Czestochawa. One art historian told her that "some art historians objected to the Madonna being called the Black Madonna, *Czarna* Madonna." He explained that while she was dark, she was dark brown rather than black. While he conceded that she appears black in black-and-white representations, "not everyone approved of this term 'Black Madonna.'"

A second scholar told Galland that the expression "Black Madonna" is inaccurate for the Madonna of Czestochawa. He explained that it is a recent term, "possibly sparked by the popularity of a song written by a nun in the sixties." He reflected that perhaps the term "Black Madonna" became popular as a "linguistic way to oppose the authorities." However, black "represents something negative in European culture" and was "not used in painting icons." This scholar went on to argue instead that the Madonna is actually "cosmic red," a red derived from the "painter's intuition that as these figures descended from above the earth, they would have to burn through the atmosphere."[42]

This art historian did not explain how Byzantine artists of the early centuries of Christianity—when the original painting of the icon of this Madonna is thought to have been painted—would have known about objects burning red when they enter the atmosphere. He also did not explain how the nun's song about the Madonna as black and the use of the name "Black Madonna" would serve to oppose the totalitarian authorities and to inspire the solidarity movement in its resistance. It seems that blackness does not simply "represent something negative" in Polish culture. Instead, calling the Madonna "black" carries a different, subversive, and inspiring meaning. Because she wrote the song in the 1960s during the time of the civil rights and Black Power movements in the United States, perhaps the Polish nun identified the struggle of the Polish workers with the struggle of black Americans for freedom. Perhaps this Polish nun was influenced by American Black Theology and, by symbolizing the Madonna as black, was claiming that the Madonna is on the side of the oppressed workers in Poland.

In this context, diverse cultural threads come together to influence the meaning of the image of the Black Madonna in Poland. Critical reflection about worship of this Madonna thus involves a complicated historical, cultural, and sociological analysis of the unique context of Poland as it has interacted with many cultures throughout its long history, as well as of gender, ethnic, and class dynamics in contemporary Poland.

United States

While worship of the Black Madonna is well-established in Poland, Brazil, and Western Europe, such images are relatively new in popular awareness in the United States.[43] Since the 1950s, the Black Madonna has been revered in the Pan-African Orthodox Church—with local congregations called "Shrines of the Black Madonna" now in Detroit, Atlanta, and Houston. In recent years, many European American women have been drawn to images of the divine as feminine. Women involved in both the Christian and non-Christian feminist spirituality movements have incorporated diverse images of and meanings for the Black Madonna in their worship practices, seeing her as representative of the Mother Goddess as well as the Mother of God.

Because the research for this book took place in the Southeastern United States within the context of the Christian feminist spirituality movement, the treatment of the cultural context for worship of the Black Madonna in the United States will be more substantial than other sections. The reflections thus far about Western Europe, Brazil, and Poland may serve as helpful comparisons and contrasts while engaging an imaginative exploration of the raced and gendered context of the United States as it relates to the worship of a black, female image for the divine.

In the early 1990s, bell hooks argued that a Black Madonna could never be worshipped in the United States because "there is no cultural space within the United States that would allow white folks to deify black femaleness . . . Racism and sexism combine to make it impossible for white folks, and some black folks, to imagine a black Madonna, since such figures are representations of purity and innocence."[44] While hooks was incorrect in claiming that Black Madonnas primarily represent "purity and innocence," she was correct that worship of the Black Madonna has been sparse in the United States until recently.

However, interest in the Black Madonna has been growing over the past fifty years, raising many significant questions. What new cultural spaces have emerged in U.S. culture to allow the worship of a Black Madonna? How might African American women and men relate to such images? What does a Black Madonna symbolize in African American communities? What issues of gender would this raise in African American communities? What stereotypes of blackness, and of black women in particular, might be part of the European American subconscious in relating to those images? What is the relationship between sacred images, human relationships, and structures of race, gender, and class in the United States? Under what conditions can a sacred image serve the purpose of challenging internalized racism, sexism, and classism in those who worship that image of the divine?

Shrines of the Black Madonna

The Pan-African Orthodox Church was founded in Detroit, Michigan, in the 1950s and was originally called the Black Christian Nationalist Movement. The movement has grown to include three Shrines of the Black Madonna—in Detroit, Atlanta, and Houston.[45] Founder Jaramogi Abebe Agyeman argued that the African American church should build a Black Nation within the United States, strengthening Black pride, Black unity, Black power, and Black consciousness so that African Americans might obtain self-determination.[46] The church teaches Black Theology, with an emphasis on the fact that Christ was a Black Messiah and that God is the liberator of black people. A booklet that describes the theology of the shrine does not mention the significance of the Black Madonna.[47] Similarly, Marsha Foster Boyd does not mention the meaning of the Black Madonna in her doctoral dissertation about the shrine in Atlanta. A bishop at the Atlanta shrine explained to me that the Black Madonna represents the mother of the Black Messiah.[48]

The Black Madonna is therefore a symbol of Black Nationalism and Black Liberation in the United States. As in Brazil, her significance comes from her resemblance to the people who worship at the shrine and their revaluation and affirmation of blackness in the U.S. context. It is interesting that she was chosen as the symbol of the community even though her significance is rarely discussed in the literature or in worship.[49] Perhaps the term "Black Madonna" was chosen in order to indicate solidarity with international worship of a black figure. However, the lack of emphasis on the Black Madonna in the worship and literature of the shrines indicates a patriarchal avoidance of the female image, instead emphasizing the male image of the Black Christ.[50]

Even in this community that is dedicated to the empowerment of black people through their identification with the Black Christ, the power represented by the divine feminine image of the Black Madonna is denied. Black women in these communities are therefore denied access to an image that could serve more directly as a symbol of their power, liberation, and identification with the divine. To be fair, this reflects the Mariology (or lack thereof) of most Protestant churches. However, in this community, founded on the need for reimaging the divine and named after the Black Madonna herself, the omission of her presence and significance is striking. Interestingly, a national study done in 1991 found that "African Americans, as well as Asian Americans, are more likely to endorse a Mother image of

God than those of Anglo-European origins, in part because in these cultural groups 'mothers' are respected as powerful figures."[51] This suggests that emphasis on a Black Madonna as representing Mother God would resonate within these communities. Critical reflection in this community would require examining gender roles and relationships within African American culture, and churches in particular, as well as theological and personal reflection about why emphasis on the Black Madonna as the divine feminine has been avoided.

Feminist Spirituality and the Black Madonna

In contrast, in the (largely white) feminist spirituality movement in the United States, the Black Madonna has been embraced over the past several decades as a symbol of the divine feminine. In her, this rapidly growing movement finds the ancient goddesses that she came to represent in Europe and in Latin America. In her representation of the Goddess, she is a source of empowerment for practitioners of feminist spirituality.[52] While this is a positive development in relation to the Black Madonna, the cultural heritage of white supremacy in the United States leads me to question what "cultural space" the Black Madonna might occupy in the minds of European American feminist women. As in Western Europe, do stereotypes of black women in the minds of European Americans serve to render this black, female image of the divine powerful only in "the realm of the transcendent" but powerless to challenge sociopolitical realities of racism and sexism?

While African American feminists have been reclaiming African religious traditions that included worship of a Mother Goddess, European American feminists have also been looking to traditional African religions, seeing Africa as "the cradle of humanity, and thus the source of the earliest goddess-worship humanity has known." In addition, the symbolism of darkness for the goddess serves the interest of spiritual feminists in subverting traditional patriarchal symbol systems. Eller argues,

> Liturgically, spiritual feminists often talk about "going into the dark," "going underground," "entering the night," as a point of contrast to the New Age or Eastern call for "enlightenment." Adopting African religions and black goddesses is another way of reversing traditional symbol structures, siding with the oppressed and making them the real heroines of spiritual feminist culture.[53]

The work of European American spiritual feminist China Galland reflects this when she says, "The association of the word 'darkness' with something negative, with evil, is precisely the problem I am naming. That kind of association is one of the cornerstones of racism. Racism is evil, not darkness. There is a redeeming darkness that I seek."[54] This acknowledgement among European American spiritual feminists that racism is one of the evils that they seek to eradicate, even in relation to how they imagine the divine, is an important development in European American culture.

In spite of these positive steps in relation to denouncing racism and siding with oppressed people, the heritage of primitivism and the romanticization of African American women still lingers. In the paragraph after she speaks of seeking redeeming darkness, Galland demonstrates that she has been deeply influenced by Jungian thought:

> Seeing the Madonna of Einsiedeln proved to me that the longing for darkness is a deeply felt human need that cuts across, goes beyond, and at the same time includes issues of ethnicity. This is a multivalent darkness. This is the darkness of ancient wisdom, of people of color, of space, of the womb, of the earth, of the unknown, of sorrow, of the imagination, of death . . . of the body, of the shadow of the Most High.[55]

In this statement, she reinscribes "people of color" as being closer to the earth, to the body, to shadows. At the same time, she romanticizes them as related to the unknown, to ancient wisdom, and to the imagination. While she is trying to revalue darkness and to counter racism, unfortunately her inclusion of the "darkness" of the ethnicity of people of color in this list with other images of darkness serves to reinforce stereotypes and to separate white people as categorically different from people of color. This romanticization of people of color as closer to the earth is just one of several stereotypes of black women in the United States that could significantly impact worship of the Black Madonna by European American practitioners and thus decrease the potential for transformation that she might represent.

The Earth Mother and the Mammy Tradition

The veneration of a black woman by European American spiritual feminists as the primal/original mother of humanity is also problematic in relation to imaging the divine as a Black Madonna. Charles Johnson explains that the black female body has been spiritualized through her depiction as the "original body of humankind." He says, "The Ur-mother profile is a mythology that obscures and one-dimensionalizes our possibilities for experiencing each black person as individual, historical, and so unique."[56] In the context of the United States, there is also the danger that the image of the black mother (or Black Madonna) reinscribes the Black Mammy image within the subconscious minds of European Americans. As in Europe, the association of the Black Madonna with a primary stereotype for black women would decrease the ability for the worship of the Black Madonna to challenge structures of racism.

Historically, white Americans have often claimed to love their "Black Mammy" yet this love has not caused them to challenge slavery or racial oppression in general. Albert Murray imagines confronting William Faulkner after he has lovingly eulogized his black mammy, saying,

> Damn, man, if the mammyness of blackness or the blackness of mammyness was so magnificent and of such crucial significance as you now claim, how come you let other white folks disrespect and segregate her like that? How come you didn't put yourself out a little bit more to please her? How can fellows like you be so enthusiastic about her and yet so ambivalent and hesitant about her brothers and sisters?[57]

The danger is that as European Americans reclaim the Black Madonna as an image of a sacred, primal mother, this romantic portrayal will not challenge racist attitudes that the black mammy is somehow different from other black people. Neither will it challenge the racist consciousness that allows for white people to love a black woman as mammy with a childish, selfish love that does not allow them to see her needs and her full humanity.

While Murray criticizes Faulkner for not trying hard enough to "please" his black mammy, a recent development for European American feminists reads as a paralyzing need to please African American women. Ann Ducille quotes white feminist Jane Gallop, who "confesses that African American women have become for her what French men used to be: the people she feels inadequate in relation to and tries hardest to please in her writing. This fear of black feminists 'is not just idiosyncratic,' Gallop believes, not just hers alone, but a shared anxiety among white women academics." Ducille describes Gallop "like the white child who insults its mammy one moment and demands a hug from her the next."[58] Similarly, womanist theologian Katie Cannon says, "White women in particular are always looking for blessings of assurance from women of color."[59] From these examples, it is clear there is a pervasive cultural dynamic within the United States for European American women to seek "blessings of assurance" or approval from African American women, perhaps out of fear of their own weakness or guilt over their own racism.

What, then, are the psychological dynamics in a European American woman's mind when she encounters an image of the Black Madonna and seeks her blessings? Johnson argues that contemporary black women in America have succeeded in representing themselves as primarily "spiritual," rather than primarily physical, like the stereotypes of black men.[60] However, stereotypes of black women as highly sexual and primarily physical still abound in U.S. culture, deriving from the legacy of slavery, where white men needed to justify their access to the bodies of slave women. Nevertheless, the portrayal of African American women as highly spiritual might also play into the European American subconscious in the sense of looking for spiritual nurturance and absolution from African American women. In the United States, then, the Black Madonna might stand in for both of these stereotypes of black women. On the one hand, she is the primal Earth Mother connected with fertility and sexuality. On the other, she is the spiritual nurturer who gives endless care and blessings to a troubled "white" soul.

Stereotypes from Slavery

In addition to the stereotypes of Earth Mother and mammy, a third stereotype for black women in the United States—that of the "strong black woman" and derived from black women's experiences during slavery—could be reinforced through the worship of a Black Madonna. Delores Williams explains that the primary "surrogacy roles" of African American women during slavery still shape the realities of many women today and have resulted in the primary stereotypes of black women in the larger culture. Williams names these stereotypes as the Mammy, the Superwoman, and the Jezebel. Williams explains that during slavery, surrogacy roles were forced on black women, and after slavery, social pressures continued to cause many black women to fill some surrogacy roles:

> Coerced surrogacy, belonging to the antebellum period, was a condition in which people and systems more powerful than black people forced black women to function in roles that ordinarily would have been filled by someone else. For example, black female slaves were forced to substitute for the slave-owner's wife in nurturing roles involving white children. Black women were forced to take the place of men in work roles that, according to the larger society's understanding of male and female roles, belonged to men.[61]

Coerced surrogacy in the area of sexuality, in which slave women were forced to "stand in place of white women and provide sexual pleasure for white male slave owners," was the most threatening to slave women's self-esteem.[62] The stereotype of black women that resulted from their inability to escape sexual violation by white slave owners was as the oversexed "Jezebel."[63]

All three of these stereotypes of black women, based on their forced roles during slavery, are still alive in U.S. culture. Williams explained,

> From the mammy tradition has emerged the image of black women as perpetual mother figures—religious, fat, a-sexual, loving children better than themselves, self-sacrificing, giving up self-concern for group advancement . . . The antebellum tradition of masculinizing black women by means of their work has given rise to the idea that black women are not feminine and do not desire to be so.[64]

Furthermore, she argues, the masculinization of female slaves was justified by the slaveholders' attitudes that "blacks could stand any kind of labor, could not be overworked and were 'comparatively insensitive to the sufferings that would be unbearable to whites.'" This has led to the stereotype of black women as "superwomen" with significantly greater physical strength and capacity to bear pain than white women.[65] This stereotype of the superwoman or "strong black woman" has caused many black women to be isolated in their vulnerability and pain. Because they are expected to be strong, the larger culture does not provide them with proper resources and opportunities to be vulnerable and to receive much-needed support to overcome the many wounds from racist and sexist oppression as well as from other life struggles.[66]

For European Americans, worship of a Black Madonna might serve to worsen rather than challenge these stereotypes. An image of a woman who is unconditionally loving and giving (like mammy) and, at the same time, strong and powerful beyond the expectations of strength and power for white women, might serve to reinforce stereotypes of mammy and superwoman, rather than to allow an awareness of the sacred humanity of black women—in vulnerability, in refusal to sacrifice themselves and their well-being for others, and in the complexity of their full humanity. Conversely, for women at the Shrine of the Black Madonna, the relegation of the Black Madonna to the one-dimensional role of mother of the Black Christ denies them the opportunity to see themselves in a powerful and loving female image for the divine. The ability to see themselves in the divine might allow them to recognize the divinity within themselves and in the women they love, thus helping them to struggle against sexism and to heal their vulnerable, wounded places.

In addition to the images of the strong black woman and the self-sacrificing mother, the stereotype of black women as oversexed also results in the denial of the vulnerability, full humanity, and legal protections for black women. Williams explains that the stereotype of black women as "loose, over-sexed, erotic, readily responsive to the sexual advances of men, especially white men" is derived from the slave owners who blamed slave women for their own victimization. Thus, responsibility for the rape of slave women was placed on the women themselves. They were labeled as "'immoral' slave women—black females whose 'passionate' nature was supposed to have stemmed from their African heritage."[67] bell hooks argues,

> this kind of white, antebellum image-making about black women's sexuality has contributed greatly to the process of devaluing black womanhood that continues to this day . . . [T]he rape of slave women led to the devaluation of black womanhood in the American psyche. This devaluation is reflected in images of black women on television as "fallen" woman, the whore, the slut, the prostitute.[68]

Research into the rates of convictions and sentencing for rape in the United States supports hooks's claims. In her analysis of a 1990 study about rape convictions in Dallas, Texas, Kimberlé Williams Crenshaw demonstrated that stereotypes of black women, Hispanic women, black men, and white women continue to influence attitudes about rape. Racist attitudes continue to be reflected in legal decisions, so that white women are valued more highly than women of color. The average sentence for raping a white woman was ten years, the average sentence for raping a Hispanic woman was five years, and the average sentence for raping a black woman was only two years. The longest sentences were for black men convicted of raping white women. These statistics demonstrate that women's bodies and lives are valued differently in this white supremacist society, depending on their race. In addition, racial stereotypes such as the image of black women and men as highly sexed contribute to the belief that the rape of a black woman is not really rape.[69]

In reimagining the divine as a Black Madonna, therefore, Americans must be careful to interrogate critically the stereotypes and emotional associations that they may be bringing to the imaging process. In order to avoid perpetuating harmful stereotypes, European Americans must learn the history of stereotypical images and the horror they have justified and perpetuated. They need to be challenged to engage multiple images that provide insights into the full humanity of and the divine presence within people of all ethnicities.

Ethnographic Exploration

The following ethnographic research discussion helps to illuminate how stereotypes can surface in surprising ways despite our best intentions. Although the three European American women that I interviewed had all been involved in antiracism work from a very young age, the stereotypes of the strong black woman and of the black woman as an Earth Mother figure emerged when we discussed imaging the divine as a black woman. These images are still very present among white Americans. During our second group discussion, I said,

> So I just wanted to ask you all to think about—if the white, male God-image that we talked about—the cranky, white, Santa Claus, on a throne—is replaced with an image, for example, of a Black female Goddess, as opposed to a white Goddess, or a white female image, what difference does that make? Does that make any difference? [Long pause] If you've had that experience, or if you can sort of imagine how that would be different, how you might relate to that image differently, or . . .

I asked about a "Black Goddess" image rather than the Black Madonna because I did not know if they were all familiar with the Black Madonna. However, the following discussion and analysis are relevant for the Black

Madonna as representative of a Black Goddess. Marie responded to my question:

> *Marie*: I remember one time a presenter came to MMP and did a program for us where she projected images on a slide projector up on the wall. And a lot of them were goddesses from other cultures, like from India.
>
> It was interesting how, there was one picture of a large, Black woman who had on a sleeveless dress, and a bra strap or a slip strap was hanging down here, and she's kind of leaning out a window, looking at something, you know, and I just thought, "Now that is a very interesting image of God." You know, that particular, the mother, that kind of earth mother that is often in black culture, taking care of generations of children, providing the stability. And it really, it worked for me in a whole different kind of way.
>
> And then right after that was a picture of a thin, white woman, very middle-class, and let me tell you, there was *nothing* that happened for me. It was so close to an image of who I was, that I couldn't conjure up that as being a worthy God-image. It was sort of startling to me, to realize how much I did not think of myself as capable of being a God-image.
>
> *Julie*: But that was something that you'd worked on early on.
>
> *Marie*: Yeah. I mean I've been at it for years. [Laughter] Actually, you know the work that I'd done when I described God as a young mother, which is what I was. And this was when I was at MMP, this other image of a white woman, middle-class, so I must have been at least ten years into the exercise of trying to reimagine God, but then, suddenly it flashes up there. It was like, "That's not my image of God. I can go with Shiva, and I can go with all these other images, but not one of myself." It was revelatory.
>
> *Rosalyn*: I think that corresponds to what Julie was saying earlier about the need to constantly bring up those things over and over again. It's not just that you think of one. It really does take a reconditioning, over and over and over again, to counter other conditioning.
>
> I haven't done a lot of extensive work like Marie, but the first thing that popped into my mind when you were talking about that particular image was something political–it was like a power shift of looking at the divine as the cranky old white Santa Claus. And the black woman made me think of a redefinition of what power is.

Because, my immediate impression was, this first image, kind of all-powerful, controlling, and the other image is not powerful, but maybe powerful in a different way, but powerless. I always translate strictly from kind of political and social. That, next to, in this country, Native American women, black women are some of the most oppressed individuals in this country.

Julie: It really connected with me, that in some ways it's easier to imagine an older black woman as God. That the power . . . or I think about the strong singing voice . . . and like the power of being able to, the strength in being able to endure and continue to nurture. And then I thought about a young black woman, and I thought, still it seems like a powerful figure.

I have this vision of young black women as . . . even though oppressed in our society, there's just that, I imagine a strength there. And then when you were talking about imagining God as yourself, then that was totally new to me. It seems really foreign. It seems like there's *no* power there. [Laughter]

After a brief conversation about whether all people have a difficult time seeing themselves as worthy images of the divine, or whether old, white men might be conditioned to see themselves in the image of God, Theresa interjected, "Now, will a black woman identify herself the same way that we are talking about?"

I explained that the stereotype of the "strong black woman" can be damaging and that African American women in a course that I had taught recently had struggled to see themselves as being in the divine image, just as the white women did. Julie was disturbed by this conversation. She said, "I was just thinking, is there any way to image God in new ways that aren't false in some way, that distancing, that romanticizing of the woman with the hair, or the strong black woman, is there a way to do that that's not . . . I mean, are you always going to be telling some sort of a lie? Or causing some sort of damage with another image?"

This discussion illuminated that even though these women were very aware of issues of racial injustice, the cultural stereotypes of black women as "earth mother" and as stronger than white women still shaped their way of seeing black women. While they all struggled to see themselves as worthy and powerful enough to be equated with an image for the divine, the distance between themselves and the experiences of black women allowed them to romanticize and to see images of black woman, old and young, as powerful and as mother figures—worthy images for the divine. Thus, for these women, an image of the Black Madonna might serve to reinforce their images of black women as powerful and mothering without enabling them to recognize the power within themselves. Julie experienced herself as having "no power," even while she saw black women as being powerful in the face of their oppression.

Interestingly, Theresa, the only woman of color in the group, was the one to raise the question of whether a black woman might see herself in the same way that black women were being imagined by the white women in the group. In her individual interview, she described how she experienced racism after coming to the United States. She said she realized "that being Latina here meant something, in that you were not very good either . . . that I have kind of less value in this society. Similar to blacks." Perhaps her experiences of struggling against both racism and sexism in the United States enabled her to perceive the romanticizing and stereotyping of black women that occurred in the conversation. Her question allowed us to explore the ways that stereotypes can shape our images of the divine and the way that we relate to those images—thus inhibiting our relationships with the divine and with other people. Even when we think an image is positive, its connection with stereotypes of race and gender can contribute to the reinforcement of, rather than the challenging to, oppression.

Julie's question—"Is there any way to image God in new ways that aren't false in some way . . . I mean, are you always going to be telling some sort of a lie? Or causing some sort of damage with another image?"—goes to the heart of this book. The discussion demonstrates the need for critical reflection about our images of the divine and how we relate to personal images as both gendered and raced. Marie and Julie both identified this as the central part of their learning during the research process, choosing quotes from this conversation to include as readings in the liturgy that we created at the culmination of the research process.

Rosalyn's insight that a shift to a black, female image of the divine would involve a political "power shift," as well as a "redefinition of what power is," helped to explain why all the women in the group struggled to see themselves as worthy images of the divine. After struggling for years to see the divine image as feminine, all the women admitted that it was still very difficult. For Theresa, it was "almost impossible." This is because she experienced women as powerless. For all the women, the association of the divine with power—and of power with the political, social, power of dominance and control exerted by men (and particularly white men in this culture)—made it extremely difficult for them to associate the divine with a female image.

A stereotypical image of black women as stronger than white women allowed for a black, female image to be more tenable than a white, female image for two of the women. Rosalyn's statement that black women are, in political and social terms, "not powerful, but maybe powerful in a different way, but powerless" raises the contradiction between the stereotype of the strong, black woman and the social reality of oppression and lack of power faced by black women in the United States. The "powerful in a different way" that she suggested implies a definition of power as internal spiritual power rather than external social power.

In this sense, she and the other European American women in the group may have recognized a spiritual strength in some African American women—an embrace of divine presence within themselves and their lives—that they thus far had not been able to embrace within themselves. However, the danger of the stereotype of the strong, black woman requires that European American women embrace this divine power and presence within themselves rather than simply projecting it onto others. Only then will they be able to engage in the paradoxical movement of affirmation, negation, and transcendent affirmation of images that look like themselves as well as those of different ethnicities.

Stories of Resistance

The question remains: is it possible for an image of the divine to challenge political and social power relations? Or will it remain relegated to the realm of the transcendent? Since the white, male God-image is associated largely with omnipotence, control, and "power over," can a reimaging of the divine as a black female image like the Black Madonna lead to an increase in social and political power, as well as spiritual power, for black women? In Brazil and in Poland, the Black Madonna serves to empower those who struggle against oppression. It is not just due to her black, female image, however. The stories and histories of her resistance to slavery and fascism accompany the images and these give her meaning and power. Thus, while the ruler image of God is a white, male image, the black female image serves in both contexts as an image of resistance to that rule. This kind of story is needed in the United States in order to make the Black Madonna (or any female image) representative of "a power shift"—the power of resistance and social change.

Black Female Images of Resistance

Several contemporary authors provide stories of black female images for the divine that embody this reimagined divine power. Theologian Kelly Brown Douglas and novelist Sue Monk Kidd each bring together the political and psychospiritual aspects of imaging the divine as black and female within the United States. Both offer stories of black female images for the divine that represent unconditional love and resistance to oppression. Rather than images without stories, which can easily allow European Americans to project stereotypical meanings onto them, the images they offer derive their power from their attached stories of resistance to racism, sexism, and other forms of oppression.

It is precisely the kind of "power shift" that we spoke of during the research discussions—that of shifting to the power of love, solidarity, and resistance rather than dominating power and control over—that Douglas aims to achieve when she argues that the divine should be imaged in the form of "living symbols and icons" of contemporary and past black women (and black men) who struggle or have struggled for the wholeness of the black community.[70] Douglas assigns special value to those people in the Black community who have worked for justice and wholeness, arguing that to see Christ in the faces of those people would enable black people to see Christ's presence both with and within themselves, particularly when they struggled for justice and wholeness.

While Douglas focuses on the Black Christ, expanding on and responding to Black Theology, which does the same, it is conceivable that she might find the presence of the Black Madonna in those who struggle for wholeness as well. By naming the divine presence as resident within struggles for justice and wholeness, she brings together the political and the personal, psychological aspects of reimagining the divine. Through her argument that the divine is particularly present and active within people who resist oppression in all forms, she affirms that imaging the divine might serve simultaneously to challenge sociopolitical structures of oppression and to inspire mystical awareness of the divine as immanent within all people.

Douglas insists, however, that imaging Christ (or God) as white is unacceptable in the context of the United States because it reinforces white supremacy. This raises interesting questions in light of this research. If all people, not just black people, were to image Christ (and God or Goddess) in the images of the poorest black women and in the images of black women and men who struggle for justice, how could stereotyping and romanticizing be avoided? And if white women should not see themselves in the image of the divine because of the danger of reinforcing white supremacy, how can they move beyond their deep sense that they are not worthy images of the divine and that they are not powerful? If the divine is present within everyone, should we not aim toward a multiplicity of images—images that allow for vulnerability and frailty, love and power—demonstrating the full humanity of all people and challenging stereotypes while pointing toward the divine?

This discussion of worship of the Black Madonna demonstrates that images for the divine in human form raise significant dilemmas in a raced and gendered culture. When European Americans reimage the divine as a black woman, stereotypes and systems of oppression are not necessarily challenged. However, imaging Christ in the face of a particular black woman who has struggled for justice and wholeness might serve to educate and inspire European Americans. This image of Christ would help to shift power away from white, male dominance in the American consciousness and to raise awareness about struggles for justice and wholeness within the black community.

Nevertheless, the danger of reinscribing the stereotype of the strong black woman, for example, would still be present unless the particular woman's vulnerability, as well as her strength, is included in the imaging process. For this reason, we must remain critically reflective about the images we use, whatever the ethnicity and meanings we ascribe to them. We must also allow for multiplicity in imaging so that all people might see themselves (and all other people and aspects of creation) as worthy of being in the image of the divine and might therefore be less likely to romanticize or submit to others as more worthy. The challenge, then, is to provide a divine image that inspires resistance to oppression yet that also allows for a paradoxical, mystical awareness that the divine is both within, yet more than, any particular image.

In *The Secret Life of Bees*, European American spiritual feminist and devotional writer Sue Monk Kidd offers a representation of the Black Madonna in the United States that holds in tension a thea/ology that the divine is within everyone regardless of race or gender with the fact that the image and history are profoundly rooted in the history of the oppression of black Americans. She weaves together the personal, political, and paradoxical nature of imaging the divine in a story of a community of black women who worship the Black Madonna. This is not the Black Madonna of Europe or Brazil, however. She has her own story. Kidd blends the stories of the Black Madonna in Poland and Brazil to create a myth about a statue of the Black Madonna that had been circulated during slavery and after. She is called "our Lady of Chains."

In the novel, set in the 1950s in South Carolina, a fourteen-year-old white girl named Lily runs away from her abusive father with Rosaleen, the black woman who has been her surrogate mother for ten years. Rosaleen is in danger of being lynched because she spat on white men who were challenging her when she went to register to vote. The fugitives go to the home of three sisters, August, May, and June, who are the proprietors of "Black Madonna Honey." Unbeknownst to Lily, the sisters take them in because Lily looks just like her mother, who died when Lily was only four years old and whom August took care of when she was a child.

The novel is a story of Lily finding a mother in the Black Madonna, the Black Madonna in herself, and mothers among this group of African American women. Surprisingly, however, Kidd manages to avoid stereotyping the women as mammy figures. They are each complex, full characters. While Rosaleen and August have both served in a mammy role, they are not defined by that role. June is openly angry and hostile toward Lily because of her frustration that her sister worked as a nanny during her younger years. Rosaleen is far from self-sacrificing, risking her life for her dignity. August is well-educated and professional, organizing a large business of beekeeping and honey production. Her sensitive sister May suffers from mental and emotional illness caused by the racist traumas she has experienced in her life.

Unfortunately, in the context of the United States, the fascination of millions of readers with the Black Madonna and with the romanticized, idyllic community of black women can serve to reinforce stereotypes of black women without challenging white readers to interrogate the history critically.[71] While the characters are complex as individuals, they still serve the purpose of saving the white girl, thus fulfilling surrogate roles in the plot and reinforcing stereotypical fantasies of white readers or viewers. As Veronica Bedford argues, "The fascination with the novel and film is filled with imagery of surrogacy that is celebrated and not critiqued from a historical reality . . . There is no critical questioning of how [Lily's] intrusion, in search of her mother figure, has disrupted the lives of others."[72]

Within this disturbing dynamic of surrogacy lies a story of the Black Madonna herself. Her story holds the transformative potential of the book. August, the leader in this family of women, tells the story of "Our Lady of Chains" during the weekly worship service of the "Daughters of Mary," a small group of women and one man, held in the sisters' living room. The three-foot-tall statue of Our Lady holds a prominent position in the living room. August recounts how a slave named Obadiah found a black, wooden figure of a woman washed up on the shore of the river. Her fist was raised. He did not recognize who she was but he remembered "how they'd asked the Lord to send them rescue. To send them consolation. To send them freedom."[73]

Obadiah brought the statue with him to the praise house the following Sunday. The oldest slave, a woman named Pearl, proclaimed that the statue was Mary, the mother of Jesus. The people felt that Mary knew their suffering. The novel depicts a liturgy that concludes by each person going forward and placing their hand on the heart of Our Lady of Chains.

Weeks later, in private, August explains to Lily that the spirit of Mary is everywhere, within all people and within all of creation, but sometimes becomes concentrated in certain places like the statue of Our Lady of Chains.[74] This panentheistic Mariology, in relation to the very particular image of the Black Madonna, allows for her to be both in a particular image and more than that image. The "spirit of Mary" is represented through the story and the statue of Our Lady of Chains, demonstrating divine love and opposition to oppression. At the same time, this spirit is understood as being present in all of creation.

August explains later that Mary is within Lily's own heart, not a being external to her. She places Lily's hand over her own heart and tells her that the Lady of Chains was the inner voice who led her to say "I will not bow down" to her father's maltreatment.[75]

In this story, Kidd represents the Black Madonna as mother and helper of African American slaves. The Black Mary serves as a symbol of divine suffering with the oppressed. At the same time, she also represents the power and love within each person that allows them to claim their full, wonderful humanity and to resist anyone who would diminish it. She is represented as black and feminine, but at the same time is understood to be present in all of creation and in the hearts of all people.

Kidd's imagination of the Black Madonna was shaped both by her experiences as a white, Southern woman and by her involvement in the feminist spirituality movement. In *The Dance of the Dissident Daughter*, she recounts her journey from being a Baptist devotional writer, through a painful exploration of the history of sexism in Christianity and in her own life, and finally to her embrace of the divine feminine in herself and in all of creation. Like the feminist spirituality practitioners discussed in earlier chapters, her spirituality and thea/ology allow for a mystical awareness of the divine as present in both the particular and the universal. She explained in this book that her connection to the divine feminine inspired her to begin to write fiction.

In her foreword to the devotional book *Prayers and Seven Contemplations of the Sacred Mother*, written by Mary Kingsley, Kidd describes her process of embracing the Black Madonna:

> In the midst of my journey to find a feminine dimension of the Divine, Mary came to me in a dream. She appeared to me as a weeping black woman, sitting on a porch of a quarantined slum. She wore an African headdress. A red one. And despite her sadness, she looked like she could straighten you out if necessary. As I passed her by, I recognized her true identity and cried out to her: "I will come back for you." This is how I discovered that Mary was living impoverished and quarantined within my own soul. As it turned out, I did go back for Mary . . . I began to meditate on her, and it was not long before she had taken up residence not only in my heart, but within my creative life as well.[76]

Kidd wrote in her fiction of the Black Madonna living in every person's heart because of Kidd's experiences of her within her own heart. The fact that Mary first appeared to her in a dream as a weeping black woman, wearing a red African headdress but looking like "she could straighten you out if necessary," demonstrates that black women figured in her white, Southern, female imagination as women who were oppressed and weeping yet were also self-protective and proud of their heritage.

Her image of a black woman as poor, living in a "quarantined slum," inarguably can be seen as stereotypical image of black women as symbols of oppression, and Kidd's mission to "come back for her" can be seen as a white woman offering patronizing assistance to a poor, black woman. However, the dream carries more complexity as well. In her imagination, the oppression of black women symbolized the suppression and segregation of the divine feminine in herself and in the larger culture. Through her exploration of the divine feminine and her reclamation of Mary within herself, she claimed the Black Madonna as symbolizing the divine spirit of love, power, and opposition to oppression within black women, within herself, and within all of creation.

Conclusion

The realm of the sacred imaginary holds immense power, yet so do cultural legacies of racism and sexism. In this chapter, the worship of the Black Madonna serves as a lens through which we might peek into the imaginations of people engaging her image in Western Europe, Poland, Brazil, and the United States. The history of a Black Madonna within a particular cultural context, the cultural legacies of the people who worship her there, the structures of oppression in relation to "race" and sex in that culture, and the social power or powerlessness of the worshipers all determine the significance that she might hold in a particular setting and for a particular person. This exploration has allowed us to theorize about the ways that imagination of the divine (regardless of the image) is deeply impacted by the representations of race and gender that are active in a particular culture.

In order for people to experience transformation in relation to their imaging of the divine, it is crucial to engage them in a process of critical reflection about representations of race and gender so that they might avoid valorizing stereotypes in their imagination of the holy. In addition, they need to engage multiple divine images in the context of worship. These images should be presented in the form of narrative or poetry, whether during preaching or in other sections of liturgy. Narratives and poetry can allow the paradoxical, mystical nature of the divine to be upheld and can portray a complex, nuanced divine image that embodies divine love and resistance to oppression of all kinds.

Challenging images through critical reflection and education about the history and context of stereotypes can help people to move toward compassionate affirmation of a shared humanity, toward a more full understanding of divine presence in all people, and thus toward action for social as well as spiritual change. The challenges for religious leaders are twofold: to facilitate critical reflection about the construction of race and gender in their particular contexts and to provide effective narrative or poetic images for the divine in the context of worship. Both of these practices can facilitate relationship with the divine by helping people recognize the full, complex humanity of all people, the divine presence within all people, and the divine at work within all struggles for justice and wholeness. Specific practices for transformation in religious communities will be discussed in the following chapter.

8

Fourth Story

Marie

Marie is a European American woman in her fifties. She is married, an ordained Episcopal priest, and the mother of two young adult daughters. She grew up moving often—between countries as well as cities—because of her father's job as an Episcopal priest. She became a priest in the mid 1980s, when there were very few women priests, so she had never known a woman priest before. She has worked in various forms of teaching throughout her career. She founded MMP in 1993 with the support of a small group of women interested in studying feminist theology.

Imaging and Relationships

Marie was certain that her childhood image of God came directly from her father. When I asked her to describe her childhood image, she said, "God was a man. Jesus was his boy. Daddy was his . . . It was kind of a straight line. God, Jesus, Ray. Might have been God, Ray, Jesus." While she incorporated her father into her image of God, she also included traditional imagery, saying that she had pictured God as "an older white man—of course he had a beard . . . he had a big throne." Marie's experience exemplifies how children blend traditional religious imagery with representations of people close to them into their image for the divine. She explained that her emotional associations with God were identical with those she felt in relation to her father. She described both her father and God as loving yet also disciplinarian. In our group discussion, she explained,

> I am very aware that, emotionally, I experienced my father as God, and of course part of that, he was up front on Sunday mornings, talking about God, and literally being God's conduit for the congregation. So I mainly had positive feelings about God as somebody

who was fair, and loving and warm and affectionate, but also a disciplinarian. All that I've just said is exactly what my father was.

She also grew up with a strong understanding of God as a God of justice. Her father not only taught this message in his ministry but also embodied it through his work in the civil rights movement, in Latin America, and in other ministries.

Marie did not refer explicitly to her mother or to their relationship when describing her image of the divine or when describing the most important and influential relationships in her life. When I asked her to name and describe those relationships, she responded, "Clearly my parents," but then went on to talk exclusively about her father. When I returned to the subject of her mother and asked "How would you describe your mom?" she provided a brief description of her mother as a person but did not provide any information about their relationship. She described her mother as "gracious, a good hostess, dressed well" and "pretty."

She went on to explain that her mother had grown up in an orphanage. Her father died when she was two and her mother had a nervous breakdown and was institutionalized. Marie's mother pursued an education and became a director of religious education and social worker in Panama, where she met Marie's father. She had "tremendous compassion for the poor because she herself had been poor." Marie explained that her mother "settled into the role of rector's wife" once she was married. She took great care in making their home beautiful.

Marie was not able to fully appreciate her mother's role until much later in life. She explained,

> For a long time because of my coming of age during the feminist movement, I didn't appreciate the things my mother had accomplished in her years of homemaking. But now that I am a homemaker for all these many years, I know what it takes to organize a home and to keep it running smoothly. And I do appreciate what she did and how lovely she made her home and she was so self-taught in all of these things. That makes it even more important to me that she was able to channel that.

After saying these words of appreciation about her mother, she immediately changed the subject to talk about another woman, Dorothy, who had been very influential in her life. She avoided speaking directly about any aspect of her relationship with her mother. While she was perhaps uncomfortable sharing intimate details about their difficult relationship in the interview setting, her continued avoidance of the topic suggested an absence of emotional connectedness between them.

The lack of empathy with her mother was revealed in a story about their relationship that she shared during our first group discussion. She described her mother's harsh reaction when Marie told her that she wanted to become an Episcopal priest. Her mother told her, "You don't deserve to be a priest." Marie explained that she did not understand until years later, during psychotherapy, that her mother was probably terrified of her becoming a priest because it would put too much strain on her family. Having supported her own husband in his priesthood, she understood the life of a priest to be one of long hours and difficult work that took you away from your family and forced you to move often. Because of her own pain and fear, her mother was unable to support Marie in her vocation as a priest.

The fact that Marie avoids talking about her mother and their relationship demonstrates that it is a painful topic for her and that it was a relationship that lacked the emotional intimacy that she needed from her mother. In Kohut's terms, she experienced both empathy from and idealization of her father. She did not idealize her mother and her role as rector's wife and housewife, however, and she did not experience adequate empathy and attachment with her mother. Her description of her mother was thus almost completely void of emotional content.

However, her image of the divine as feminine includes aspects that she might have derived from her mother, particularly her emphasis on God as a "God of beauty" and on Mother God as interested in the beautiful details in the world, like butterflies and babies' eyelashes. When I mentioned this, she responded with surprise and then agreement. Even though she had been involved in reimagining the divine as feminine for many years and had dedicated her full-time ministry to providing a safe place for other women to do the same, she had never thought that any aspect of her image of God as mother had come from her experience of her own mother. She had only imagined God as mother in terms of her own experiences as a mother.

When she acknowledged that some of her imaging of the divine feminine as loving beautiful details might have come from her associations with her mother, she immediately went on to add that she had probably internalized her mother's physical care of her when she was a child. This was one aspect of her care in which her father did not participate. While the "mother-love" that she speaks of certainly included more than just physical care, her emphasis on the physical intimacy with her mother, in contrast to her emotional, spiritual, and intellectual closeness with her father, demonstrated that this care of her when she was a small child was the most significant form of intimacy that she experienced with her mother.

Self-Image and the Divine Feminine

Marie challenged her male image of God when she was in seminary. She explained that before seminary, "There was no reason for it to change. Nobody ever said anything different. I went to church on Sunday. We sang all of those hymns and we read all that scripture. And I heard all those sermons. And I never once heard a feminine pronoun in anything."

Growing up, she did not have any access to female images of God. She was comfortable with her male image of God, modeled after her loving father, and did not challenge it. However, during her first semester of seminary, she was required to use gender-inclusive language or to alternate male and female pronouns when speaking of the divine in all of her papers. She described the process of engaging female pronouns for God as revelatory. Simply changing the language caused her to begin to challenge her image of God as well. She recounted,

> When you start using different pronouns for God it begins to change your images of God. And I used to really practice envisioning God as female. I used to try see God as mother and to understand that as mother she would do the things that I would do with my children. I would love to look at them, enchanted with them as babies. And I begin to shift images of God from this powerful male god who made the mountains, like a kind of masculine imagery, to some real female imagery, seeing God interested in making babies' eyelashes. And making the wings on butterflies and the petals on roses, you know.

Her children were young when she was in seminary and began this process of reimagining. Instead of imagining God as similar to her own mother, she imagined a feminine God-image as being more like herself. She explained that by imagining God as a young, white woman in her thirties, as she was at the time, she was able to imagine God as more like herself and, conversely, herself as more in the image of God. In our second discussion, she recounted,

> When I was first doing some reimagining of God when I was in seminary, I reimagined God as a young, white woman in her thirties, which is what I was, and it made a tremendous difference. Because I imagined that that God would be interested in the same kind of things that I would be interested in—would be interested in nurturing children, would be interested in me, would be interested in gardening, flowers, and that kind of creation—as opposed to the male images of God creating the mountains and the heavens, and also, it made a difference to me in thinking about the Abraham and Isaac story because I could never imagine a female God who would think that they needed to sacrifice their child. That just doesn't compute if you change the imagery. I think the male God, Abraham, and Isaac all go together, but if you take it and change one piece of that, it doesn't work as well.

The image of the male God as demanding Abraham's sacrifice of Isaac had been a significant and frightening story for her. When she first thought about becoming a priest, she was terrified. Her immediate thought was,

"My goodness, does that mean that God has called me? And if I don't respond to this call, will he do something like he did to Abraham and ask me to sacrifice my children?"

Reimagining the divine as female, and as a young mother like herself, freed her from this terrifying image of God. She was also able to imagine a new kind of intimacy with the divine. This God would be interested in her and her passions and concerns. This female God would also, in her mind, be incapable of sacrificing a child. This image of God allowed her to relate more intimately with the loving, creative nature of God by valuing her own experiences of love and creation.

Through reimaging the divine as a mother in her prayer life, and not just as an intellectual exercise, she was able to experience this new intimacy with the divine. She said that the male God on the throne (even though modeled after her loving, affectionate father) was still "distant and difficult to approach." She imagined Mother God's love for her like her love for her own children and was able to experience that love in a new way.

At the same time, it allowed her to honor herself—her role as cocreator with God and as an embodiment of divine love for her children. She explained,

> Then, I remember in my prayer life, trying to think about the things that I would think about as a mother of a child. And to try to understand God's love for me as I love and was intimate with my children—you know everything about your little baby. When they've got a dirty diaper, when they need to eat, it's an amazingly intimate relationship when you have a young child. And there had never been any images, for me, of my relationship to God that would have that kind of intimacy. Because God was distant and had a throne and was difficult to approach . . . Never changing diapers, that's right, and never cleaned up anybody's throw-up.
>
> And so, to somehow value my relationship with my children and to use the parent-child language that is readily available between Jesus and God as father and son, I began to see this as mother and daughter. That just opened up a whole new identification of myself—of *myself*—as God-person. Because I was representing God to my child. I was the one that was taking care . . . I gave my child life; I took care of my child; I fed my child with my own body. But also, some kind of understanding of how I might relate to God and God might relate to me, if God were mother instead of father.

While it was obviously very significant that she began this imagining of God as mother during her experience as a mother of young children, the complete absence of any mention of her own mother when imagining "how God might relate to me if God were mother instead of father" is striking.

Beauty and Presence

Marie's reimagining of the divine as feminine has allowed her to appreciate new aspects of the divine that she had not associated with her masculine image. Marie recognized that her image of God as Father was closely connected not only with her relationship with her father but also with the theology he taught. She was "raised on a God of justice" but now also appreciates a God of beauty.

It has only been in the past ten to twenty years that she has allowed herself to appreciate God in beauty without feeling self-indulgent or guilty. She grew up believing that beauty, even natural beauty, was not "worthy of attributing to God." Since she had emphasized her mother's role of making their home beautiful, it is clear that her belief that beauty was not worthy of attributing to God contributed to her devaluing of her mother's passion and work for the family's well-being. This added to her inability to include aspects of her mother in her image of God. By beginning the journey of reimaging the divine as feminine, she opened up new possibilities for the nature of God and for her experience of the divine. She became aware of a divine presence in nature and in creative expression.

It is through this awareness of the divine in creation, as well as in herself, that Marie has come to a spirituality of presence. After years of trying to reimage the divine as feminine in her prayer life and in her ministry, she has now moved to a place where she does not try to imagine the divine. She acknowledges that she has reached the limits of her imagination—that the divine is so much more than can be imagined. In her mystical journey, she has moved through multiple images and come to a place beyond images. Instead, like Rosalyn, she simply experiences the divine as presence.

She explained, "Now in my own prayer life, I just don't imagine God anymore. God is just presence. And the other thing that has happened for me is that God is no longer located externally alone, but internally." She explained that she struggles with thinking of God as internal to her because "If I am a manifestation of God; we're all in trouble." However, she affirmed her panentheistic belief that God is within herself, all people, and all of creation. She explained, "So I have come to believe in an indwelling God in all of us and in all of creation . . . I guess that's all; God now is just presence."

Through her journey, she has come to the awareness that ultimately, the divine is beyond her intellectual or imaginative capacities. She has reached the paradoxical moment of negation yet also of the superaffirmation described in negative theology. It is precisely at the moment that she recognizes the limits of her knowledge and of her imagination that she is profoundly aware of divine presence.

The Long, Difficult Process of Reimagining

In spite of this intimate, mystical relationship with the divine, Marie admitted that it is an ongoing struggle for her to reimagine the divine. As with the other women described, it is a long, difficult process for Marie to shake her deep, emotional connectedness to her childhood image and her related belief that she is not worthy to be an image for God. For many years, she worked diligently to change her image of God. She found the process difficult and frustrating. She found that she needed to "tear down" her old imagery before she could be free to explore new images.

She explained, "I spent a lot of time with images of God where I just felt totally frustrated. I couldn't move from one to the other. It was . . . there was this sort of just tearing down of imagery of God." For her, reimaging God is an ongoing job because the language in the church reinforces the traditional white male image as well as the emotional male image from childhood. "You just have to work so hard on those [new] images, when every week in worship there's nothing to affirm them."

In spite of working on these issues for twenty years, she finds that the journey is cyclical. On some days she finds herself back at the place where she began.

As discussed in the previous chapter, in our second group discussion, she recounted a day several years ago, during a workshop at MMP, when the presenter was showing slides of different feminine images for the divine. Marie was moved by an image of a large, black woman as well as by images of goddesses from other cultures. However, when an image of a middle-aged, middle-class white woman flashed on the screen, she explained, "There was *nothing* that happened for me. It was so close to an image of who I was that I couldn't conjure up that as being a worthy God-image. It was sort of startling to me to realize how much I did not think of myself as capable of being a God-image."

When Julie recalled that Marie had worked on imagining God as being like herself when she first began her process of reimagining, Marie replied, with laughter, "Yeah. I mean I've been at it for years." She explained that while the early work she had done in reimagining the divine as feminine was during the time when she was a young mother like herself, this image of a woman so much like herself today did not resonate with her as a worthy image for the divine. She shared, "I must have been at least ten years into the exercise of trying to reimagine God, but then, suddenly it flashes up there, it was like, 'That's not my image of God. I can go with Shiva, and I can go with all these other images, but not one of myself.' It was revelatory."

The intensity of her struggle to see herself, as well as other women, as beloved of God and created in the image of God was revealed when I asked Marie to describe a significant spiritual or religious experience. The first that came to mind was a moment in which she realized that God loves variety—particularly in the shapes and sizes of women. She described attending an exercise class at the university in which a number of the women were not "lithe and beautiful and young" like their instructor. Afterward, walking out of the class, she recounted,

> And I mean it just hit me like a ton of bricks. God loves all those women. God made all those women in all those different shapes and sizes because that is what God loves. God is crazy about variety. And some sort of self-acceptance and understanding diversity as being beloved of God instead of the mass media, you've got to look like this. And if you depart from being 5'8 and 120 pounds, and twenty years old, you're not worth a damn. So that was a big moment of spiritual insight.

She experienced a sense of self-acceptance through seeing herself as beloved by God. At the same time, she recognized the beauty of the many people around her. This has contributed to her awareness of divine presence within all of creation and indwelling all people. In turn, her openness to multiple images for the divine allows her to celebrate this presence.

As in negative theology, for Marie, images for the divine can be taken from any aspect of creation, even perhaps a "city dump," because the divine is present in everything. At the same time, she has a profound awe and awareness of the fact that the divine is much greater than creation and greater than she can imagine as well. Her journey through reimagining the divine has freed her to appreciate the diversity of creation, the multiplicity of images for the divine, and the beauty and divinity indwelling her female self.

This journey has allowed her, through continued struggle, to move beyond one static male image of God. She now experiences the divine as presence and does not try to image. However, her embracing of feminine images and images from nature has allowed her to experience that presence and to appreciate different aspects of the divine. She continues to move in a cyclical, dialectical motion, touching now and then—through activities such as this research process and other programs at MMP—on reimaging the divine and recognizing where the old image is still holding sway and where she still struggles to affirm her own worthiness as created in the divine image. She then moves back to her experiential knowledge that the divine is also simply present, beyond her imagination.

9

Practices for Transformation

The process of transforming images and relationships is long and difficult. It requires emotional and spiritual transformation. Images of the divine, the self, and others cannot be changed simply through cognitive, intellectual discourse. A person's conceptual understanding of the divine, "the God of the theologians," is often in tension with the images of the divine that she may have created through her emotional experiences. Therefore, leaders must give significant attention to the complexity of the relationship between conceptual theologies, cultural images, and personal, internalized images. They need to engage people at a level where they can do the work of soul-searching and self-scrutiny in relation to their emotional and conceptual images of the divine. At the same time, they need to create spaces for people to progress through affirmation, negation, and then "transcendent affirmation" of their images as they move through this paradoxical, mystical process. Because of their holistic approach to faith formation through multiple religious practices, religious communities are ideal places in which people might engage in this transformative process.

People cannot be forced to engage in this difficult work of transformation. They are profoundly attached to their images of the divine, themselves, and others. Rizzuto warns that it is dangerous to try to force someone to alter her image of the divine. Rather, change can occur through experiences of alternative images during liturgy combined with opportunities for discussion without judgment where people can explore their images of the divine and what alternatives or additions there might be to those images. As Julie explained, her experiences of rituals at MMP helped her to do the "slow, slow work" of transforming her image of God. She had tried to change her image through intellectual work alone and found it ineffective. As the findings of this research reveal, the relationship between experiences of divine images in liturgy and experiences of the divine itself is a relationship of journey through paradox. Julie was excited not only about experiencing a feminine image of God but also because the experience of opening to new images of God allowed her to be more receptive to the "real and living God" who is beyond any "narrow image" yet whose presence is conveyed through images.

Because each person needs to be engaged at all levels in order to experience this type of transformation, multiple practices must be incorporated into the life of a community simultaneously. In this chapter, I outline complementary practices in religious education, pastoral care and counseling, worship, and preaching that can be used in religious communities to help members examine and transform their images of the divine. This discussion of practices is by no means exhaustive. However, the purpose of this chapter is to provide a research-based roadmap to guide religious leaders and practitioners in addressing the issue of imaging the divine. The practices that I describe can be used as guidelines, a general framework for addressing issues in religious communities. I encourage creativity and innovation in the actual implementation.

Play

Within the context of a nonjudgmental loving community, religious practices allow people the opportunity to "play" imaginatively with their divine images. The experience of "playing" with images is impossible without a foundation of safe relationship. Play can happen only within the emotional, imaginative, and psychic space created in the context of relationship. Playing occurs in the area of experience where the "dichotomy of objectivity and subjectivity" is transcended and where both internal and external realities contribute to the creative transformation.[1]

The spirituality of the feminist spirituality movement demonstrates a mentality of "play" in relation to religious symbols and divine images. As discussed in previous chapters, women in the feminist spirituality movement experience divine images as profoundly real, even while they recognize the role of their imaginations—whether in dreams, visualizations, or interactions with images during worship. They are flexible in relation to images and names for the divine, preferring multiple names and images. They are comfortable transcending claims to "objectivity," and they maintain that their experiences of divine presence transcend isolated, individual subjectivity. Their subjective encounters with the divine are seen as experiences of relationship—with the divine being present within other people, in creation, and within themselves.

The freedom to play with multiple images for the divine in religious practices allows women to experience transformation in their images of the divine, of themselves, and of others. This emotional, spiritual transformation enables them to embrace greater intimacy with the divine, enhanced self-esteem, and improved relationships with others. This process of playing with paradox in relation to images enables them to name and move through false images of themselves, other people, and the divine, and then to move closer to an affirmation of divine presence within themselves, within other people, and within all of creation.

Religious institutions should provide opportunities for adults and children alike to play, to engage with a variety of religious symbols. James Jones argues, "Reimmersion in the primary process through moments of rapture and ecstasy are necessary times of psychic refreshment and rejuvenation and are the source of creativity, sanity, and a full human life."[2] The "ecstasy and rapture" that Jones describes are associated with the psychological state of the transitional space, or playing.

Resistance

Often, religious institutions do not offer opportunities for such refreshment and rejuvenation. As the stories of the interviewees demonstrate, women often experience frustration and stagnation in church. They find themselves trying to translate what is said in church into a different language so that they might relate to the divine differently. Too often, they feel that their time in church reinforces their childhood image of the white, male, ruler God that they have been painstakingly trying to dethrone with other, more life-giving images. They critique the churches that they have attended for being "too much in the head"—too focused on following a written order of service and not allowing times of silence or times in which to engage the imagination.

If a person is not given the opportunity to play with alternative symbols and images within the worship context, she may remain stuck with a God-representation that is detrimental to her spiritual and psychological well-being. Opportunities to play, to experience ecstasy and rapture in relation to the symbolic world, can allow people the freedom to recreate their representations of the divine, and, correspondingly, their self-representations and their relationships. It is crucial, therefore, for churches to provide a multitude of images of the divine in preaching, worship, and other ritual and educational forums. Churches need to engage the divine with what Keller calls a "metaphorical consciousness"[3] so that one particular metaphor or representation is not reified to the point of the exclusion of other images.

Maintaining this type of playful, fluid consciousness in relation to images for the divine is a difficult task for a number of reasons. Theresa's story demonstrates her struggle with feeling "frozen" and unable to play. Religious leaders need to be sensitive to those people who, like Theresa, are uncomfortable entering into a realm of play. Whether it is because of painful formative relationships or because of a culturally ingrained fear of losing power or control, many people will be wary of worshiping in a context that incorporates elements of play and embodies a metaphorical consciousness about the divine. In addition, challenging the whiteness and maleness of the divine is likely to trigger many white people's shame and pain about their socialization into whiteness, as well as resistance from both men and women out of fear of challenging a male image to whom they have related for their entire lives.

In spite of the difficulties that many people may experience with playing, the church should not sacrifice the elements of play and metaphorical consciousness in order to make people more comfortable. Rather, there should also be opportunities within a supportive context for discussions of conceptual theology, construction of race and gender, and personal reflection on internalized representations of self, others, and the divine. Leaders should make it very clear that they are not trying to take away old images or to deny the value of those images. Rather, they should clarify that a multiplicity of images is more true to the fullness of the divine and more useful for the spiritual development of practitioners. We now turn to particular practices that can help in this process.

Religious Education

Religious educators need to provide a supportive, nonjudgmental educational setting in which people can explore the often emotionally difficult components of their images for the divine, self, and others. Educators are faced with the challenge of creating authentic community across lines of difference in the educational setting so that people might honestly examine their images without fear of judgment, ridicule, or condemnation. Only in this kind of supportive, unconditionally accepting community can transformation occur. In this section, I offer an eight-week curriculum that can be used in religious education settings. It is based on the interview format for this research but is modified to be more practically useful within a religious community. In addition, I offer other creative practices that can be used to stimulate reflection about images of the divine, self, and other people.

Curriculum

Because the religious education curriculum that follows involves extensive personal sharing, these issues can be addressed most effectively in a small group setting with one person as the facilitator of the group. A small group format allows for the maximum personal sharing for each person involved within an allotted time and can allow the group to build a sense of trust more quickly if everyone shares openly. Within the same congregation, several small group classes could engage the curriculum simultaneously. It could also be used effectively in school or community settings. The curriculum could be prodictive for youth as well as for adults.

This curriculum should be modified to fit a particular community. Questions could be added or the order in which the topics are addressed could be changed. However, it is important that all the topics are included in the process. It is inadequate to consider any aspect of imaging the divine without considering the others as well. Significant relationships, self-image, understandings of race and gender, and cultural teachings about and images of the divine are all interwoven into a person's divine image. To consider one aspect without the others is to miss this complexity and interconnectedness. Religious education is the ideal context in which to help people engage with these complex issues on the intellectual, emotional, and spiritual levels.

An essential part of this process is the in-depth analysis of the connections between a person's divine image, self-image, formative relationships, and understandings and images of gender and race. This type of analysis is best done through reading a person's story rather than during the flow of a discussion. The process of reading the interview transcripts for this research revealed many more insights and connections than were first apparent during the interviews themselves. However, an educational process does not allow for the taping and transcribing of discussions. Therefore, I suggest that each person share his or her responses to the primary interview questions during group discussions and then write those responses, along with any further reflections on that week's topic, in a journal that will be kept for the duration of the class.

Format

Liturgy

Each class session begins with a time of liturgy that relates to the divine through many names and images. These liturgical experiences create a space of safety and of freedom to play. The liturgies can include creative exercises such as guided meditations, inviting participants to draw their images, or centering prayer. The leader might choose to ask participants to rotate leadership of these short, five- to ten-minute exercises. This allows each person to insert her or his creative vision into the class.

Sharing Circle

After an introduction of the class during the first session by the facilitator, the first five sessions involve the facilitator's asking the questions listed below and allowing each person to share her or his response without feedback or response. The sharing goes around the circle, with each person allotted equal attention and time. At the end of the class, the facilitator opens up the discussion for general reflections and responses. However, people should be able to speak freely during the sharing times, without interruption. In addition, the facilitator can invite the class to brainstorm discussion guidelines to which they are willing to covenant. These should include an agreement to confidentiality.

The sessions should proceed as follows.

Session 1: Images of the Divine

Questions: How did you picture the divine when you were a child? What did you imagine God to be like? How has your image of the divine changed over time?

Session 2: Relationships

Questions: What have been the most important and influential relationships in your life? How would you describe these people? How would you describe your relationships with them? How have the relationships changed over time?

Session 3: Childhood/Gender

Questions: How would you describe yourself as a child? When you were growing up, how did you feel about being a girl (or boy)? What was that experience like for you? How did you feel about becoming a woman (or man)? What were your feelings about boys and men (or girls and women)? How did your understanding and experience of sexual orientation affect your gender identity?

Session 4: Race/Ethnicity

Questions: Do you remember when you first understood that you were part of a particular ethnic or racial group? How did you feel about being part of that group? What feelings or questions did you have about people from different racial or ethnic groups? How did your understandings of economic "class" affect your views and experiences of "race"?

Session 5: Spiritual/Religious Experiences and Practices

Questions: Take a moment and remember a significant spiritual experience. Can you describe it for us? How did you feel? How did you experience the divine? What is the significance of the experience for you? What spiritual or religious practices have been important for you? Why?

Session 6: Guided Discussion—Critical Reflection about Race, Gender, and Imaging

In the sixth session, the facilitator takes a more active role in the discussion. In this discussion, she or he introduces concepts about the construction of race and gender and the dangers of reinforcing stereotypes through divine images. An effective entry into this discussion is to show the class traditional images of God and Christ—such as Michelangelo's painting of the Creation of Man on the ceiling of the Sistine Chapel or an image of a blonde-haired, blue-eyed Jesus—and to ask the class members to reflect on how the image would affect them if the image were of a different ethnicity and/or gender. For example, the facilitator could ask, What would it be like to pray to an Asian female image for the Creator God? An African female image? A Black Christ?

Discussing these questions will probably elicit a wide range of responses, depending on the ethnicity of the people in the group as well as their willingness to imagine different images for God and Christ. During this discussion, the facilitator can raise the question of how the reliance on solely a white, male image reinforces racism, neocolonialism, and sexism. In addition, she or he should help people interrogate whether their responses to images reinforce stereotypes. The facilitator could draw upon examples in popular fiction, such as *The Shack*, in order to demonstrate the danger of stereotypes. While the information provided in this book is primarily about the construction of "whiteness" and about stereotypes about black women, the facilitator should educate herself or himself about racial, gender, and class stereotypes about women and men of Asian and Hispanic descent, African American men, and diverse Asian, African, and Hispanic cultures so that she is prepared to address those in the discussion as well.

Journal Sharing

After the first six weeks, each person is asked to share her or his journal with another trusted group member. Two group members read each other's journals for themes. The reader should ask himself whether he sees any parallels between the person's image of God and her descriptions of her significant relationships. He should examine whether her descriptions of her experiences of the divine correlate with her image of God or whether her spiritual experiences reveal an experience of the divine that challenges her internalized God-image. He should ask how her childhood understandings of and feelings about gender and race are reflected in her divine image, self-image, and relationships with others. During the seventh session, each group member shares reflections with the person she or he analyzed, offering insights about connections noticed between the person's imaging of the divine and her formative relationships, spirituality, and understandings of gender and race.

Session 7: Journal Analysis Discussions

In the seventh session, participants meet in pairs to discuss their analyses of each other's journals. Each class member is given time to respond to the analysis of her journal, sharing whether it rings true, as well as any other insights that are sparked by the analysis. After the pairs have shared, the facilitator should invite the group back together for a larger discussion of the themes, insights, and questions raised by the experience of writing, sharing, and analyzing the journals.

Session 8: Liturgy Creation

The class members work together to devise a liturgy that reflects the themes of their discussions. The liturgy process allows for a creative integration of all that has been shared and realized. The liturgy encourages class members to begin to experiment with new images for the divine in a communal worship experience based on the insights raised by the class. This provides an opportunity for participants to experience the divine in a new way and to feel the support of their religious community as they do so.

Planning of the liturgy can be done in many ways. The facilitator can ask participants how they would like to proceed. They can discuss whether they want to focus on a particular theme and choose a different part for each person to play. They might also choose to each contribute a poem, prayer, song, dance, or ritual that reflects their personal learning during the process and then work together to weave these into a coherent whole.

Session 9: Group Liturgy

People should hold the liturgy at a time conducive to attendance from the larger church. Before the liturgy, the facilitator or one of the participants should welcome everyone and provide a brief description of the process that has led to this point. Afterward, they might choose to invite visitors to stay and engage in reflection and discussion about their experience of the liturgy.

The sharing of the liturgy reinforces the commitment of the entire church to address these issues in worship. In addition, elements of the liturgy (prayers, songs, stories, symbols, and so on) can be incorporated into the regular worship services of the church throughout the year. This type of communal engagement allows the participants to share their insights and growth with the larger community while also demonstrating the support of the leadership to this work.

Session 10: Reflection

The group should meet one final time to discuss their experiences of the liturgy and the process as a whole. They might also discuss how they would like to proceed after the formal process is over so that they can continue their work of transformation in community.

Popular Fiction and Religious Education

The novels *The Shack*, *The Da Vinci Code*, and *The Secret Life of Bees* have been so wildly popular that churches across many denominations have responded with adult education classes devoted to engaging the questions and images they raise. These novels can be an effective way to discuss the issues raised in this book. However, if this approach is taken it is essential that all aspects of the process are involved. In particular, it is crucial that the participants be asked to question the gender and racial stereotypes being evoked in the images and story presented and the implications for readers of different backgrounds.[4]

For example, in William P. Young's *The Shack*, the protagonist, a European American man named "Mac," encounters God as an African American woman named "Papa," while he envisions the Holy Spirit as an Asian woman.[5] Several stereotypes are resonant with these images–the "strong black woman," the mammy image, the stereotype of Asian women as ethereal and meek and somehow less strong and assertive than African or European women. If this novel is used in a religious education context in order to spur conversation about reimagining the divine, it is essential that critical reflection about the dangers of these images be undertaken.

The use of fiction as an entrée into the topic can be helpful in that readers can take a step back from their own experiences and imagination and enter into the imagination of an author.[6] Participants might be more willing to join the class if they know they will discuss these novels. On the other hand, the effort of exploring the imagination of the author and the characters can sometimes deflect from real conflicts within the class. For example, I have found that responses to *The Secret Life of Bees* vary widely depending on the cultural location of the readers. European American women longing for an idyllic interracial community tend to find the book uplifting and inspiring while the African American students in my class were disturbed by the surrogate roles of black characters and the lack of realism in depicting black–white relationships in 1950s South Carolina. The discussion of the book thus ran directly into deeply held frustrations and tensions within the class.

This kind of tension can be fruitful if the facilitator can steer the conversation productively into an exchange about the history of stereotypes, racism in the United States, and imagination of the divine. However, because the novels often touch such intimate, vulnerable places in readers, it becomes difficult to shift to a critical discussion without first addressing those emotional resonances. This type of vulnerable discussion is difficult when mistrust and frustration about racial tension are also high. In a community where these tensions run deep, I recommend addressing these issues directly through the curriculum and then returning to fiction as a follow-up. This way, participants are more prepared both intellectually and emotionally when they begin to discuss the novels. In addition, a greater trust has been established within the group after the completion of the curriculum. The discussion of the novels can serve as a way for the group to continue their work together.

Worship

Another crucial practice for engaging divine images is to allow people to play with alternative images in the context of worship. People need to encounter alternative images in worship in order to shift their old images at the emotional and spiritual level. If the images are challenged only conceptually, the emotional image remains untouched. As discussed previously, it is crucial that multiple images for the divine be incorporated in worship. The language and imagery used in prayer, liturgy, and music to depict the divine should reflect multiple perspectives. This freedom and fluidity with language and imagery allows people the opportunity to imagine and to relate to the divine differently within the sacred context of worship.

In addition to simply incorporating alternative language for the divine during worship, those images should be explicated in the form of narrative or poetry, whether during preaching or in other sections of liturgy. Narratives and poetry can allow the paradoxical, mystical nature of the divine to be upheld and can portray a complex, nuanced divine image that embodies divine love and resistance to oppression of all kinds.

While new images for the divine can spark the imaginations of congregants, allowing them to relate to the divine in new ways, the danger still exists that they might project stereotypes onto the new image, thus impeding their relationship with the divine.

Narratives or poetry that affirm the paradox that divine love and power are within all people and all of creation, yet also more than any images taken from creation can convey, support the self-love of all people in the congregation. They challenge them to see the divine within all others and all of creation. In addition, narratives that bring to light the vulnerability as well as the strength of divine love may challenge inhuman stereotypes of people (such as the "strong black woman" stereotype or the heroic ideal for white men) while also allowing people who experience vulnerability and oppression to recognize themselves in the divine image more easily.

While these narratives should include stories from Christian scriptures, the relative paucity of explicitly feminine and gender neutral images for the divine in the Bible, particularly those that are often avoided because they challenge traditional images, necessitates finding or creating additional stories or poems to include within the context of worship. As Christine Smith explains, feminist preaching and liturgy should involve naming God in creative ways including poetry, image, dance, and song, drawing from women's experiences of the divine as well as from the biblical tradition.[7]

When incorporating alternative imagery and language for the divine in the context of worship, it is inadequate to simply change to "inclusive language" because even the word "God" is a male term.[8] Simply changing male pronouns such as "He" to "God" will not serve to transform a person's internalized image of God as male. A lifetime of hearing "God" as referring to only a male God will not be undone simply by changing pronouns to be gender-neutral. Transformation is a long, slow process that requires repeated experiences of alternative images in the context of worship.

Therefore, rather than inclusive language, multiple images (including female, male, and nongendered language and imagery such as Spirit or imagery from nature) can serve to transform people's previously held images and to create an enlivening, freeing worship experience. In the current religious climate, it will take a concerted effort to find or create and incorporate hymns, prayers, readings, and rituals that do not reinforce the traditional image of a dominating male God. However, it is crucial to make this effort. Relying solely on traditional hymns and prayers simply because they are more easily available would be a grave disservice to the congregation. While there is a place for these resources, they need to be used in the context of a congregation that is equally committed to other language and imagery for the divine in worship.

In order to foster this type of congregation, the educational work of preaching and religious education is essential. People resist change, particularly in worship. In her research among United Church of Christ congregations in western Massachusetts, half of which had female senior pastors, Alison Stokes reports that 83 percent said that they were not comfortable with female language and imagery for God within the context of worship. Interestingly, however, 63 percent said that they were "better able to think of the Divine in female terms *as long as they are thinking abstractly.*"[9] Worship is not simply an intellectual exploration into theology. Worship engages people at their most vulnerable, intimate level. It is the time when they come to relate to the divine as well as with the gathered community. For this reason, people build up emotional associations with traditional language and imagery for God. For many, it carries great meaning and numerous memories of profound spiritual experiences.

However, the refusal to include alternative language and imagery for the divine in worship alienates and causes great conflict for many people who are longing for their worship experiences to include female language and imagery as well as nongendered imagery from nature. In order to avoid losing those people and to provide greater spiritual growth for other congregants through engaging multiple images, it is crucial that the traditional images be balanced with alternative imagery and language. Religious leaders are responsible for conveying the complex reasons that multiple images for the divine must be engaged through preaching, education, and counseling.

Preaching

Preachers can engage congregations on both the cognitive and emotional levels by addressing directly in sermons the issue of reimaging the divine. Preaching can be a time for educating the community about the issues raised in this book. Simply addressing these issues from the pulpit signals the congregation that they are in a "safe space"—a space where it is safe to question and to play. In the preaching context, the minister can model the use of multiple images for the divine in the sermon. The inclusion of multiple images during the sermon, including feminine language and imagery from nature, allows congregants to engage imaginatively with new models. As discussed above, narratives or poetry that portray a complex, nuanced divine image are most effective. As they listen to a sermon, people are generally at their most open and receptive, ready to hear a new, good word about how the Spirit is working in their lives. This openness blossoms in a congregation within which the minister has worked with members to nurture a context of loving, trusting, just relationships. If a congregation is highly conflicted, some members will probably sit in hostile judgment on any sermon, particularly one that challenges the status quo.

The preacher might mitigate any hostility or resistance, however, by addressing the issues around imaging the divine directly in sermons, offering pastoral and therapeutic reasons for the importance of exploring personal images and incorporating multiple images in worship. Examples such as the stories provided in this book serve as particularly effective tools for engaging people at an emotional, empathic level. In addition, the preaching event is an opportunity to educate the congregation about feminist biblical and theological research (such as Elizabeth Johnson's *She Who Is*, Elisabeth Schüssler Fiorenza's *In Memory of Her*, and Elaine Pagels' *The Gnostic Gospels*) that demonstrates the historical tradition of feminine imagery and language for the divine (such as Sophia) within the Christian tradition as well as the ways most feminine language and imagery has been suppressed through almost all of Christian history.

Pastoral Care and Counseling

Pastoral care and counseling are also helpful practices for transformation in relation to divine images, self-image, and relationships with others. James Jones described how clinical counseling could be an effective practice for people to work through their representations and internalize new patterns of relationship, and thus new representations, through transference with the counselor. In addition, imaging the divine can be engaged effectively in group counseling contexts. The educational process described above can be used effectively as a form of group pastoral counseling led by a pastor, a lay caregiver, or a clinical pastoral counselor.

It is crucial that pastors or pastoral counselors address issues related to imaging the divine directly during individual counseling. As the research for this book demonstrates, peoples' images of the divine are profoundly connected with their formative relationships and with their images of themselves. In order for a person to experience healing in her relationship with the divine as well as healing of her relationships with others and of her self-image, she needs to become aware of the ways that her relationship with the divine is patterned after her significant human relationships. The caregiver must pay close attention to any parallels between a person's relationship with the divine and his patterns of relationship with others. At an appropriate time, the caregiver should raise these insights with the client or congregant, seeking her responses.

In looking for parallels in a person's image for the divine, formative relationships, and self-image, it will be helpful for the caregiver to ask the questions that James Jones raises in relation to each client. He asks three central questions about the affective bond with the sacred. First, he asks, "How does a person's relationship with the divine disclose primary patterns of transference in her life?"[10] Second, he asks, "What inner relational patterns go into our devotional exercises, meditational disciplines, philosophical theologies?"[11] The third central question is "What is the connection between the coming of a new sense of self and the development of a new image of God?" He argues that the answering of these questions involves "tracing a person's sense of self and transferential patterns and seeing how these changes are mirrored in relation to God."[12] As each person talks about her significant relationships or as she talks about her relationship with God, the pastoral caregiver should be asking these questions.

Put simply, she should be asking whether there are similar patterns in a person's relationship with God and in her important relationships. Does she use similar language to describe God as she uses to describe an important person in her life? Does she have similar struggles in relating with God as she has in her human relationships, including with the counselor? While one should not try to force a person to change her image of God, the caregiver can help her to gain awareness of the way her image of and relationship with God are deeply shaped by formative relationships and connected with her sense of self. As Jones' case study of his client named Phil demonstrated, simply naming these connections can create an opportunity for transformation.

The pastoral caregiver should also help each person to think critically about gender and race in relation to the larger society, as well as other issues that may arise such as sexual orientation, physical ability, and economic status. Pastoral counselor Christie Cozad Neuger argues that people struggling with depression, particularly women, are greatly helped by developing critical awareness about issues of gender and race.[13] They are able to recognize that their problems are part of a larger social system and not simply a fault of their own. Through developing strategies of resistance to sexism and racism, they experience a sense of personal empowerment that helps to lift the depression. Similarly, psychotherapist Mary Pipher argues that the teenage girls whom she sees in counseling are better able to develop and maintain a positive self-image when they are guided during counseling in critical reflection about the construction of gender.[14]

By helping each person to understand the historical, political, and social dynamics at work in the construction of gender and race and the ways that these constructions affect her self-image, divine image, and relationships, the caregiver or counselor can empower the client to claim her sense of agency in resisting racism, sexism, and similar issues. Just as the caregiver should ask questions about connections between the client's formative relationships and her divine image, she should also look for connections between the person's understanding of gender, race, sexuality, class, her self-image, and her divine image. As the discussion of whiteness in the first chapter revealed, the person may have significant shame and pain in relation to her identity. Therefore, it is crucial that these issues be addressed in concert with the focus on familial relationships and relationship with the divine. This in-depth approach allows the person to address the emotional, spiritual, and political connections between these various issues. In Morton's terms, this work can help people isolate the "false images" out of which they have been living their lives so that they can create new images, resonant with their authentic selfhood, out of which they can live in a new way.

Conclusion

It is my hope that this discussion of religious practices for engaging divine images will spark the imaginations of religious leaders and practitioners alike to explore ways in which they might most effectively engage imaging the divine in their communities. I hope that this discussion of practices, along with the information, stories, and analyses provided in previous chapters, offers substantial motivation and practical help for communities struggling (or longing to even begin the conversation) to address these issues effectively. As the stories of the women I interviewed demonstrate, the struggle is urgent and profoundly worthwhile.

While these practices are essential for the transformation of adults and youth, they are also crucial for the formation of children. Engagement with multiple images for the divine, combined with stories of divine love, justice, power, and peace, will be foundational for the formation of a new generation—a generation of women and men who can engage the world faithfully in all of its rich complexity, unfettered by the burden of forced conformity to one idolatrous image.

The closing prayer for the liturgy created during this research, written and led by Julie, beautifully reflects the spiritual journeys of the women:

> In our desire to know you and be true to you, we seek your face. Sometimes we get stuck with one name, one image. We find ourselves closed off and resistant to the many ways you might be revealed to us. We ask you now to open us to images of you that will enlighten, renew, and challenge. Instead of diminishing our experience of you, we trust that we will be enriched by finding a face that is a partial reflection of the One who includes us all . . . Keep our minds open and our hearts wild, so that we will never be enslaved to one image, but free to look for you in all of creation. Amen.

Julie's prayer demonstrates the spiritual process of many women involved in the Christian feminist spirituality movement. As they engage in the difficult work of challenging their deeply engrained divine image from childhood, they discover a freedom to experience the divine within themselves and within all of creation. They then image the divine from those new experiences, beginning a spiraling cycle of image–experience of presence–and image that embodies the paradoxical, mystical process of moving through images. The "wildness" and freedom of this movement can seem threatening to institutional Christianity. However, the passionate spirituality of the women involved and the pain of the tension with their beloved tradition call for churches to learn from their experiences and to incorporate these insights into their practices. Rather than threatening the tradition, this process will enliven it, allowing others to experience the love and power of the divine within themselves and all of creation.

Notes

Introduction

1. Roberta Bondi, *Memories of God: Theological Reflections of a Life* (Nashville: Abingdon Press, 1995), 108.

2. Discussion with Mary Elizabeth Moore in July, 2003.

3. Pseudo-Dionysius, *Pseudo-Dionysius: The Complete Works* (New York: Paulist Press, 1987), 56.

4. I am indebted to my colleague, Jennifer Watts, for her understanding of the mystery of every person.

5. My understanding of internal images as creations arising from multiple sensual and emotional experiences and memories is drawn from Ana-Maria Rizzuto's *The Birth of the Living God: A Psychoanalytic Study* (Chicago: University of Chicago Press, 1979), 54–55.

6. Rizzuto theorizes that the God-image can be created out of characteristics of the "wished-for parent" as well as characteristics of an actual parent; see *Birth of the Living God*, 44.

7. I put the word race in quotations to denote that race is a social construct rather than a biological reality. Therefore, the fluctuating, varied meanings of the word "race" are entirely a creation of our collective and individual imaginations. However, the social realities of racial categorization and oppression are all too real. This is what Patricia Williams refers to as the "paradox of race."

8. See Cynthia Eller, *Living in the Lap of the Goddess: The Feminist Spirituality Movement in America* (Boston: Beacon, 1993) for more information about the feminist spirituality movement and the women who leave both Christian and Jewish communities in order to embrace the divine feminine.

9. Leonard W. Moss and Stephen C. Cappannari, "In Quest of the Black Virgin: She Is Black Because She Is Black," in *Mother Worship*, ed. James J. Preston (Chapel Hill, N.C.: University of North Carolina Press), 65.

10. Ibid., 63.

11. Ibid.

12. Jan Nederveen Pieterse, *White on Black: Images of Africa and Blacks in Western Popular Culture* (New Haven, Conn.: Yale University Press, 1992), 37.

13. These stereotypes in Western Europe are discussed at length by Jan Pieterse in *White on Black*, 30–37, 181–82.

14. China Galland, *Longing for Darkness: Tara and the Black Madonna* (New York: Penguin Books, 1990).

15. Eller, *Living in the Lap of the Goddess*, 7.

16. Ibid., 31.

17. Elizabeth A. Johnson, *She Who Is: The Mystery of God in Feminist Discourse* (New York: Crossroad, 1992), 64.

18. The use of the concept of "play" is from Rizzuto, *Birth of the Living God*, 81–82.

19. David Tracy, *The Analogical Imagination: Christian Theology and the Culture of Pluralism* (London: SCM Press, 1981), 71.

20. Ibid., 70.

21. Years after coining using this term, I discovered that Beverly Lanzetta has also recently used the term "feminist mysticism" in her book *Radical Wisdom* (Minneapolis: Fortress Press, 2005). Our approaches are very different yet complementary.

22. This concept of affirmation, negation, and transcendent affirmation is taken from Elizabeth Johnson's discussion of Thomas Aquinas in *She Who Is*, 113.

23. These include Carol Lee Flinders, *At the Root of this Longing: Reconciling a Spiritual Hunger and a Feminist Thirst* (New York: HarperOne, 1999); China Galland, *Longing for Darkness* and *The Bond Between Women: A Journey to Fierce Compassion* (New York: Riverhead Books, 1998); Sue Monk Kidd, *The Dance of the Dissident Daughter: A Woman's Journey from the*

Christian Tradition to the Sacred Feminine (New York: HarperOne, 2006); and Patricia Lynn Reilly, *A God Who Looks Like Me: Discovering a Woman-Affirming Spirituality* (New York: Ballantine Books, 1995).

24. Eller, *Living in the Lap of the Goddess,* 33.

25. James W. Jones, *Religion and Psychology in Transition: Psychoanalysis, Feminism and Theology* (New Haven, Conn.: Yale University Press, 1996), 51–52.

26. "Reciprocal ethnography" is a method developed by Elaine Lawless in her work *Holy Women, Wholly Women: Sharing Ministries through Life Stories and Reciprocal Ethnography* (Eugene, Oreg.: Wipf & Stock Publishers, 2010). I have adapted her method for this book's research.

Chapter 1: Psychology and Imaging the Divine

1. Ana-Maria Rizzuto, *The Birth of the Living God* (Chicago: University of Chicago Press, 1979), 44.

2. Ibid., 55.

3. Ibid., 78.

4. Ibid., 79.

5. Ibid., 81.

6. Ibid., 82.

7. Ibid., 90.

8. Ibid., 134.

9. Ibid., 164–65.

10. James W. Jones, *Contemporary Psychoanalysis and Religion: Transference and Transcendence* (New Haven, Conn.: Yale University Press, 1991), 62.

11. Ibid., 64.

12. Ibid.

13. Ibid.

14. Ibid.

15. Ibid., 44.

16. Ibid., 44–45.

17. Ibid., 66.

18. Ibid., 73.

19. Ibid.

20. James W. Jones, *Religion and Psychology in Transition: Psychoanalysis, Feminism and Theology* (New Haven, Conn.: Yale University Press, 1996*),* 37.

21. Heinz Kohut, *The Analysis of the Self: A Systematic Approach to the Psychoanalytic Treatment of Narcissistic Personality Disorders* (New York: International Universities Press, 1971), 171.

22. Heinz Kohut, "Religion, Ethics, Values," in *Self Psychology and the Humanities: Reflections on a New Psychoanalytic Approach,* ed. Charles Strozier (New York: W. W. Norton, 1985), 261–62.

23. Charles Strozier, *Heinz Kohut: The Making of a Psychoanalyst* (New York: Farrar, Straus, and Giroux, 2001), 329.

24. Ibid., 332.

25. Rizzuto, *Birth of the Living God,* 142–43.

26. Ibid., 143.

27. Jones, *Religion and Psychology in Transition,* 51–52.

28. Ibid., 52.

29. This is not to stereotype women and mothers as necessarily more nurturing than men. Rather, it is to demonstrate how larger cultural and religious norms coincided with the father's image to such a significant degree that both Daniel and Phil were unable to incorporate any aspect of their mothers into their image of God.

30. Ibid., 55–56.

31. Catherine Keller, *From a Broken Web: Separation, Sexism, and Self* (London: Beacon Press, 1988), 38–39 and 44.

32. Ibid., 38.

33. Virginia Woolf, *A Room of One's Own* (New York: Harcourt Brace, Jovanovich, 1963), 35, quoted in Keller, *From a Broken Web,* 44–45.

34. Keller, *From a Broken Web,* 91.

35. Ibid., 223.

36. My conversations with Dr. Thomas Thangaraj and with theology students from South Korea, as well as with African American students, confirm this.

37. Traci West used this term in her talk, "What Difference do Women Leaders Make?: Confronting Racism and Heterosexism in the Church," at Emory University, Atlanta, GA, on October 22, 2003. West used this term when describing heterosexuals' insistence on speaking often of their spouses.

38. William P. Young, *The Shack* (Newbury Park, Calif.: Windblown Media, 2008), 84; 91–105.

39. See Maria Lugones, "Hablando Cara a Cara/Speaking Face to Face: An Exploration of Ethnocentric Racism"; Chela Sandoval, "Feminism and Racism: Report from the 1981 Women's Studies Association Conference"; and Lynet Uttal, "Inclusion Without Influence: The Continuing Tokenism of Women of Color," all in *Making Face, Making Soul/Haciendo Caras: Creative and Critical Perspectives by Women of Color*, ed. Gloria Anzaldua (San Francisco: Aunt Lute Books, 1990). See also Delores Williams, *Sisters in the Wilderness: The Challenge of Womanist God-Talk* (Maryknoll, N.Y.: Orbis Books, 1993), chap. 4.

40. Thandeka, *Learning to Be White: Money, Race, and God in America* (New York: Continuum, 1999), 1–2.

41. Ibid., 103.

42. Daniel Stern, *The Interpersonal World of the Infant* (New York: Basic Books, 1985), 69.

43. Thandeka, *Learning to Be White*, 104.

44. Ibid., 106.

45. Ibid.

46. Ibid., 127.

47. Alice Miller, *For Your Own Good: Hidden Cruelty in Child-Rearing and the Roots of Violence*, trans. Hildegarde and Hunter Hannum, 3rd ed. (New York: Noonday Press, 1990), 90.

48. Ibid., 91.

49. Ibid.

50. Andrew Hacker, *Two Nations: Black and White, Separate, Hostile, and Unequal* (New York: Charles Scribner's Sons, 1992), 63.

51. Michael Omi and Howard Wanant, *Racial Formation in the United States* (London: Routledge, 1994).

52. Abby Ferber, *White Man Falling: Race, Gender, and White Supremacy* (Lanham, Md.: Rowman and Littlefield, 1999), 28.

53. Ibid., 29.

54. Thandeka, *Learning to Be White*, 42–43.

55. Ferber, *White Man Falling*, 35.

56. Ibid., 30.

57. Socialization into "white" womanhood obviously varies widely based on economic class, region, ethnicity, age, and other factors. Feminist movements have made strides in changing what is expected of European American girls in terms of control over their sexuality, expectations of assertiveness, and access to education and various careers. However, a metanarrative of needing a man, combined with conflicting messages of the objectification of women and violence against women, continued inequalities in pay, and assertiveness in the workplace justify continued examination of these dynamics of the construction of womanhood, in this case, in the way that "whiteness" serves to define femininity.

58. Ibid., 41.

59. Toni Morrison uncovers this construction of white American masculinity in *Playing in the Dark: Whiteness and the Literary Imagination* (New York: Vintage Books, 1992).

60. Ibid., 38–39.

61. Ibid., 44.

62. Ibid., 45.

63. Ibid.

64. Ferber, *White Man Falling*, 22, 145.

65. I am grateful to Candler School of Theology student Craig Tichelkamp for challenging me to consider "gender-bending" as part of the process of challenging images of the divine.

66. Presentation by Patricia Lynn Reilly at Claremont School of Theology, 1999.

67. Jones, *Religion and Psychology in Transition*, 44.

Chapter 2: First Story

1. Ana-Maria Rizzuto, *The Birth of the Living God* (Chicago: University of Chicago Press, 1979), 48.
2. Ibid, 81.
3. James W. Jones, *Religion and Psychology in Transition: Psychoanalysis, Feminism and Theology* (New Haven, Conn.: Yale University Press, 1996), 129.
4. Rizzuto, *Birth of the Living God,* 82.
5. James W. Jones, *Contemporary Psychoanalysis and Religion: Transference and Transcendence* (New Haven, Conn.: Yale University Press, 1991), 66.
6. Roberta Bondi, *Memories of God: Theological Reflections of a Life* (Nashville: Abingdon Press, 1995), 108.

Chapter 3: Christian Feminist Spirituality

1. Lila Abu-Lughod, *Writing Women's Worlds: Bedouin Stories* (Berkeley and Los Angeles: University of California Press, 2008), 8–9.
2. The predominance of European American, educated women in feminist spirituality groups, both Christian and post-Christian, is documented by Cynthia Eller in *Living in the Lap of the Goddess: The Feminist Spirituality Movement in America* (Boston: Beacon Press, 1993), and by Miriam Therese Winter, Adair Lummis, and Allison Stokes in *Defecting in Place: Women Claiming Responsibility for Their Own Spiritual Lives* (New York: Crossroad, 1994).
3. Eller, *Living in the Lap of the Goddess,* ix.
4. Ibid., 18.
5. As a result of their extensive mailings, Winter, Lummis, and Stokes solicited responses from a diverse group of women from across the United States, as well as from 112 men. The women ranged in age from 30 to over 70, with the majority between the ages of 35 and 55. One-third of the sample was Roman Catholic, which was intentional on the part of the researchers. Half were Protestant, with four out of five belonging to traditional "oldline" denominations such as Episcopal, Lutheran, Methodist, United Church of Christ, and Disciples of Christ. The remainder of the Protestant women came from a variety of denominations. As in Eller's study of the feminist spirituality movement, most women in the sample were highly educated, and were European American. Of the 3,746 women, 49 were Asian American, 63 were African American, and 173 were Hispanic/Latina. Eighty of the women identified as lesbian. Nineteen percent of the women who responded were ordained ministers, and 13 percent were Roman Catholic sisters with religious vows. This 32 percent of the sample has a large investment in, and a potentially profound impact on, changing the church to be more compatible with their feminist values.
6. Winter, Lummis, and Stokes, *Defecting in Place,* 6.
7. Ibid., 7.
8. The authors explained that only 14 percent of all the groups surveyed were associated with a particular congregation, while 41 percent were associated with a particular denomination or religious order. Forty-five percent of the feminist spirituality groups were ecumenical, like MMP, with women participants from a variety of denominations.
9. Ibid., 151.
10. Ibid., 150.
11. Ibid., 34.
12. Ibid., 45.
13. Ibid., 47.
14. Ibid., 188–89.
15. Ibid., 190.
16. Ibid., 159.
17. Ibid., 167.
18. Ibid.,162.
19. Ibid., 177–78.
20. Ibid., 177.
21. Ibid., 182.
22. Ibid., 178.
23. Ibid., 179–80.

24. Ibid., 178.

25. Ibid., 160.

26. Ibid., 161.

27. For examples of such movements, see Vandana Shiva, ed., *Close to Home: Women Connect Ecology, Health, and Development Worldwide* (Philadelphia, Penn.: New Society Publishers, 1994); Chung Hyun Kyung, *Struggle to be the Sun Again: Introducing Asian Women's Theology* (Maryknoll, N.Y.: Orbis, 1990); and Rosemary Radford Ruether, ed., *Mujeres Sanando la Tierra: Ecología, Feminismo, y Religión: Según Mujeres del Tercer Mundo* (Santiago, Chile: Sello Azul, 1999.)

28. This approach to ethnography was inspired by the work of Elaine Lawless, who created a process of reciprocal ethnography to address the danger of imposing her interpretations on the lives of the people whom she interviewed. In her research, Lawless interviewed a group of Protestant women ministers individually about their lives and ministries. She also participated in their regular meetings. She brought her interpretations of their stories, as well as the transcripts of the interviews, to the women as a group, and she included transcriptions of excerpts of their group dialogues about all of the material in the book. While she said that, as a scholar, she had an obligation to share the patterns and themes that she observed through a process that she called "over-reading" the women's stories, she also allowed her interpretations to be challenged by the women's diverse perspectives. In engaging in the process of reciprocal ethnography, she argued that she was explicitly paying attention to the ethical and political implications of her research and writing. She urged that all ethnographers must do the same, because all choices in research and writing involve ethics and power dynamics. See Lawless, *Holy Women, Wholly Women: Sharing Ministries through Life Stories and Reciprocal Ethnography* (Eugene, Oreg.: Wipf & Stock Publishers, 2010).

29. Ibid., 127–28.

30. Ibid., 55.

Chapter 5: Inclusive Language Is Not Enough

1. Alice Walker, *The Color Purple* (New York: Simon and Schuster, 1982), 176–77.

2. Ibid., 178.

3. Ibid., 179.

4. Since my original writing of this text, Beverly Lanzetta has published her book entitled *Radical Wisdom: A Feminist Mystical Theology* (Minneapolis: Fortress Press, 2005). However, her discussion and understanding of feminist mysticism differs from mine in significant ways.

5. In using the term "feminist," Schneider acknowledged that the term has come to be associated with exclusively white women's interests. However, she stated, "The term 'feminist' continues to seem to be the one more appropriately generalized than other, more culturally specific identifiers such as womanist, mujerista, queer, or white feminist. It continues to represent basic concerns with sexism and culture that are shared and argued over among women and men who are also black, white, Hispanic, Asian, African, Native American, straight, lesbian, Jewish, Christian, pagan, and so on . . . I have not yet come upon a better term than 'feminism' for the general task that I am attempting here. I look forward, however, to the time when it may be eclipsed by another, less burdened term" Laurel C. Schneider, *Re-Imagining the Divine: Confronting the Backlash Against Feminist Theology* (Cleveland: Pilgrim Press, 1993), 7–8. Schneider referred to the writings of white feminist, womanist, mujerista, and Asian feminist authors in her work. Therefore, the use of the term "feminist" in discussing her work should be taken to include all of these perspectives.

6. Ibid., 8.

7. Ibid., 119.

8. Ibid., 160.

9. Ibid., 169–72.

10. Ibid., 175.

11. Ibid., 87.

12. Ibid., 108.

13. Ibid., 117–18.

14. Ibid., 142.

15. Sallie McFague, *Models of God: Theology for an Ecological, Nuclear Age* (Philadelphia: Fortress Press) 40.

16. Ibid., 33.

17. I am grateful to Dr. Mark Jordan for his teaching in his 2002 doctoral seminar on Negative Theology in Emory University's Graduate Division of Religion about the activities of praise and negation in Pseudo-Dionysius and for his insistence that the form of writing is as important as content.

18. Pseudo-Dionysius, *Pseudo-Dionysius: The Complete Works* (New York: Paulist Press, 1987), 58.

19. Ibid., 83.

20. Ibid., 56.

21. Ibid., 66.

22. Elizabeth Johnson, *She Who Is: The Mystery of God in Feminist Theological Discourse* (New York: Crossroad, 1992), 113.

23. Ibid., 115.

24. Ibid., 114.

25. McFague, *Models of God,* 33.

26. Ibid., 39.

27. *The Luminous Darkness: A Personal Interpretation of the Anatomy of Segregation and the Ground of Hope* (Richmond, Ind.: Friends United Press, 1989) is the title of a book by mystic thea/ologian Howard Thurman.

28. McFague, *Models of God,* 23.

29. Ibid., 54.

30. Ibid., 14–15.

31. Ibid., 18.

32. Ibid., 18–19.

33. Ibid., 136.

34. Ibid., 20–21.

35. Ibid., 46.

36. Ibid., 131.

37. Ibid., xxii.

38. Ibid., xxi.

39. Thomas Thangaraj expressed this insight at the Fall Retreat for the Program for Women in Theology and Ministry, Candler School of Theology, Emory University, Atlanta, Georgia, in September, 2003.

40. Nelle Morton, *The Journey Is Home* (Boston: Beacon Press, 1986), xxii.

41. Ibid., 152.

42. Ibid., 157–58.

43. Ibid.

44. Ibid., 154.

45. Ibid., 151.

46. Ibid., 155.

47. Ibid., 143.

48. Ibid., 144.

49. Ibid., 145–46.

50. Kimberlé Williams Crenshaw wrote the essay titled "Mapping the Margins: Intersectionality, Identity Politics and Violence against women of Color" in *Critical Race Theory,* edited by Kimberlé Crenshaw, et. al. (New York: New Press, 1996). Crenshaw explained that feminist discourse has relied on the experiences of white, middle-class women, while antiracist discourse has been primarily focused on the experiences of black men. The association of gender with white women and of race with black men causes many problems for women of color, particularly in the legal system, where these discourses are played out in determining decisions about justice. Crenshaw said that the experiences of women of color have been relegated to an unmarked domain and that she wanted to mark it. She named the position of women of color through the use of a term she coined: "intersectionality." Intersectionality describes the ways that aspects of a person's identity and social location cannot be separated out from one another. Instead, they intersect in a whole.

While Crenshaw focused on the experiences of women of color, the principle of intersectionality applies to all people, so that a white man and a white woman have intersectional identities as well. Just as white feminists have failed to examine the ways in which their particular experiences are affected by race, and have therefore been blind to the experiences of women of color, male Black theologians have focused exclusively on race, neglecting to see the gendered nature of their own experience and thus failing to recognize the particularity of Black women's experiences.

51. Kelly Brown Douglas, *The Black Christ* (Maryknoll, N.Y.: Orbis Books, 1992), 58.

52. James Cone, *A Black Theology of Liberation* (Maryknoll, N.Y.: Orbis Books, 1986), 29.

53. Ibid., 28.

54. Douglas, *The Black Christ,* 84–85.

55. Ibid., 84.

56. Ibid., 47.

57. J. Deotis Roberts, "Black Theology and the Theological Revolution," *Journal of Religious Thought* 28 (Spring–Summer 1972): 16, quoted in Kelly Brown Douglas, *The Black Christ,* 61.

58. Douglas, *The Black Christ,* 97.

59. Ibid., 98.

60. Ibid., 99.

61. Douglas argued that Cone does not emphasize the blackness of the historical Jesus adequately. She affirmed the efforts of Albert Cleage to prove that Jesus was actually African and argued that his efforts have successfully challenged Western religious scholarship and provided a means for African Americans to have increased self-respect. (See Douglas, *The Black Christ,* 80).

62. Ibid., 107.

63. Ibid., 107.

64. Ibid., 107–8.

65. Ibid., 108.

66. Ibid., 108.

67. Ibid., 108–9.

68. Ibid., 116.

69. Ibid., 110.

70. Ibid., 108.

71. Ibid., 81.

72. Ibid., 91.

Chapter 7: Exploring the "Sacred Imaginary"

1. bell hooks, "Power to the Pussy," in *Outlaw Culture: Resisting Representations* (New York: Routledge, 1994), 10.

2. Ibid.

3. Leonard W. Moss and Stephen C. Cappannari, "In Quest of the Black Virgin: She Is Black Because She Is Black," in *Mother Worship: Theme and Variations,* ed. James J. Preston (Chapel Hill, N.C.: University of North Carolina Press, 1982), 63.

4. Ibid., 56.

5. Ibid., 65.

6. Stephen Benko, *The Virgin Goddess: Studies in The Pagan and Christian Roots of Mariology* (Leiden, The Netherlands: Brill, 1993), 214.

7. Emile Saillens, "Letters from the Mailbag" (Paris: *New York Herald Tribune,* 1958), 4, quoted in Moss and Cappannari, "Quest of the Black Virgin," 68.

8. Benko, *The Virgin Goddess,* 213.

9. Ibid.

10. Ibid., 215.

11. Martin Bernal, *Black Athena: The Afroasiatic Roots of Classical Civilization,* vol. 1 (New Brunswick, N.J.: Rutgers University Press, 1987), 2.

12. Ibid., 213.

13. Jan Nederveen Pieterse, *White on Black: Images of Africa and Blacks in Western Popular Culture* (New Haven, Conn.: Yale University Press, 1992), 31.

14. Ibid., 23.

15. Ibid., 24.

16. Ibid., 25–27.

17. Ibid., 29.

18. Ibid., 30–37.

19. Ibid., 35.

20. Ibid., 37.

21. Ean Begg, *The Cult of the Black Virgin* (New York: Routledge, 1985), 144.

22. Pieterse, *White on Black*, 181.

23. Ibid.

24. Ibid.

25. Ibid., 182.

26. Ibid., 183.

27. Ibid.

28. hooks, "Power to the Pussy," 10.

29. China Galland, *The Bond Between Women: A Journey to Fierce Compassion* (New York: Riverhead Books, 1998), 182–83.

30. Ibid., 185.

31. Ivone Gebara and Maria Clara Bingemer, "Mary," in *Systematic Theology: Perspectives from Liberation Theology*, ed. Jon Sobrino and Ignacio Ellacuria (Maryknoll, N.Y.: Orbis Books, 1993), 175.

32. Ibid., 176.

33. Galland, *Bond Between Women*, 240.

34. Ibid., 190.

35. Group Interview 2, May 6, 2004, Atlanta, Georgia.

36. Individual Interview with Theresa, January 29, 2004, Atlanta, Georgia.

37. China Galland, *Longing for Darkness: Tara and the Black Madonna* (New York: Penguin Books, 1990), 280–81.

38. Ibid., 280.

39. Moss and Cappannari, "In Quest of the Black Virgin," 57.

40. Galland, *Longing for Darkness*, 191.

41. Ibid., 286.

42. Galland, *Longing for Darkness*, 288–89.

43. Worship of the Black Madonna in the United States before this time is not well documented. However, immigrant groups such as the Sicilians carried their worship of Black Madonnas with them to the United States. See Lucia Chiavola Birnbaum's account of her Sicilian American women relatives and their "subversive memory" of the Black Madonna in *Dark Mothers: African Origins and Godmothers* (Lincoln, Nebr.: Authors' Choice Press, 2001). In addition, *scholars of religion* sometimes classify Our Lady of Guadalupe, patron saint of Mexico, as a *"Black Madonna,"* although she is thought to resemble the indigenous peasants of Mexico to whom she first appeared. Mexican American immigrants have worshiped her in the United States as well. See Malgorzata Oleszkiewicz-Peralba, *The Black Madonna in Latin America and Europe: Tradition and Transformation* (Albuquerque: University of New Mexico Press, 2007.)

44. hooks, "Power to the Pussy," 19.

45. Marsha Foster Boyd, *Self-Help in the Shrine of the Black Madonna #9 in Atlanta, Georgia: A Study of A Congregation and Its Leadership* (Ph.D. diss., Graduate Theological Union, Berkeley, Calif., 1996).

46. Ibid., 20.

47. Shrine of the Black Madonna, *The Theology of KUA*.

48. Interview with Bishop Ayanna Abi-Kyles, June, 2001, Atlanta, Georgia.

49. Ibid.

50. Ibid.

51. Miriam Therese Winter, Adair Lummis, and Allison Stokes, *Defecting in Place: Women Claiming Responsibility for Their Own Spiritual Lives* (New York: Crossroad, 1994), 178–79, drawing from a revised paper for the Association for the Sociology of Religion meeting in August, 1991, by Elaina Kyrouz, titled "Of God and Gender: The Influences of Familial, Religious,

Political, Educational, and Subcultural Socialization and Experience on the Adoption of Maternal Images of God."

52. Cynthia Eller, *Living in the Lap of the Goddess: The Feminist Spirituality Movement in America* (Boston: Beacon Press, 1993), 7.

53. Ibid., 73.

54. Galland, *Longing for Darkness,* 172.

55. Ibid., 153.

56. Charles Johnson, "Phenomenology of the Black Male Body," in *Michigan Quarterly Review* 32, no. 4 (1993), 612.

57. Albert Murray, *South to a Very Old Place* (New York: McGraw-Hill, 1971), 53. I am grateful to Kimberly Wallace-Sanders for this reference.

58. Ann Ducille, "The Occult of True Black Womanhood," in *Female Subjects in Black and White: Race, Psychoanalysis, Feminism,* ed. Elizabeth Abel, Barbara Christian, and Helene Moglen (Berkeley: University of California Press, 1997), 36.

59. Katie Cannon and Carter Heyward, "Can We Be Different but Not Alienated? An Exchange of Letters," in *God's Fierce Whimsy: Christian Feminism and Theological Education,* ed. Katie Cannon, Carter Heyward, and the Mudflower Collective (New York: Pilgrim Press, 1985), 38.

60. Johnson, "Phenomenology of the Black Male Body," 612.

61. Delores Williams, *Sisters in the Wilderness: The Challenge of Womanist God-talk* (Maryknoll, N.Y.: Orbis, 1993), 60–61.

62. Ibid., 67.

63. Ibid., 70–71.

64. Ibid., 70.

65. Ibid.

66. I am grateful to students in the course I taught at the Candler School of Theology, "Issues for Women and Theology in the Christian Tradition," for sharing their struggles to overcome the stereotype of the strong black woman in order to acknowledge their own woundedness and to find help and healing.

67. Williams, *Sisters in the Wilderness,* 70.

68. Ibid., 71.

69. Kimberlé Williams Crenshaw, "Mapping the Margins: Intersectionality, Identity Politics, and Violence Against Women of Color," in *The Public Nature of Private Violence,* ed. Martha Albertson Fineman and Rixanne Mykitiuk (New York: Routledge, 1994), 368; http://www.wcsap.org/Events/Workshop07/mapping-margins.pdf.

70. Brown-Douglas, *The Black Christ,* 108.

71. Interestingly, the 2008 film version of *The Secret Life of Bees* was directed by African American director Gina Prince-Blythewood. She changed the portrayal of the sisters and their relationship with Lily significantly in order to portray a more distant, less romanticized relationship, and changed the story of Lily's relationship with Zach to include Zach's imprisonment and potential lynching for dating Lily.

72. Veronica Bedford, "A Different Approach to God," final seminar paper for course at Candler School of Theology, 2009, 5.

73. Sue Monk Kidd, *The Secret Life of Bees* (Middlesex, England: Viking Penguin, 2002), 164.

74. Ibid., 141.

75. Ibid., 288–89.

76. Sue Monk Kidd, foreword to Mary Kingsley, *Prayers and Seven Contemplations of the Sacred Mother* (Boulder, Colo.: Woven Word Press, 2004), vii–viii.

Chapter 9: Practices for Transformation

1. James W. Jones, *Contemporary Psychoanalysis and Religion: Transference and Transcendence* (New Haven, Conn.: Yale University Press, 1991), 129.

2. Ibid., 135.

3. Catherine Keller, *From a Broken Web: Separation, Sexism, and Self* (London: Beacon Press, 1988), 223.

4. For more on *The Da Vinci Code* and *The Secret Life of Bees*, see my chapter "Re-mythologizing the Divine Feminine in *The Da Vinci Code* and *The Secret Life of Bees*," in *Religion and Popular Culture in America*, ed. Bruce Forbes and Jeffrey Mahan, 2d ed. (Berkeley and Los Angeles: University of California Press, 2005).

5. William P. Young, *The Shack* (Newbury Park, Calif.: Windblown Media, 2008), 82–89.

6. For more on the effectiveness of fiction in religious education, see the writings of Carol Lakey Hess, including her forthcoming work, *Fiction as Soul-Truth: The Value of Fiction for Theology and Education.*

7. Christine Smith, *Weaving the Sermon: Preaching in a Feminist Perspective* (Louisville, Ky.: Westminster/John Knox Press, 1989), 75–76.

8. See Marjorie Procter-Smith, *In Her Own Rite: Constructing Feminist Liturgical Tradition* (Nashville: Abingdon, 1990), 63–84, for her helpful discussion of "emancipatory language" in worship.

9. Allison Stokes, *Women Pastors: The Berkshire Clergywomen* (New York: Crossroad, 1996), 132.

10. Jones, *Contemporary Psychoanalysis and Religion*, 65.

11. Ibid.

12. Ibid., 66.

13. Christie Cozad Neuger, Annual Women's Forum, Candler School of Theology, Emory University, Atlanta, Ga., November, 2004.

14. Mary Pipher, *Reviving Ophelia: Saving the Selves of Adolescent Girls* (New York: G. P. Putnam's Sons, 1994), 44.

Index